The Christian at Prayer

medieval & renaissance texts & studies

Volume 44

Master Peter the Chanter with Master Alain de Lille.
British Library, Additional Manuscript, no. 19767

The Christian at Prayer

An Illustrated Prayer Manual

Attributed to

Peter the Chanter (d. 1197)

by

RICHARD C. TREXLER

medieval & renaissance texts & studies
Binghamton, New York
1987

Library of Congress Cataloging-in-Publication Data

Trexler, Richard C., 1932–
  The Christian at prayer.

  (Medieval & Renaissance texts & studies ; v. 44)
  1. Petrus, Cantor, ca. 1130–1197. De penitentia. 2. Petrus,
Cantor, ca. 1130–1197. De oratione. 3. Prayer—History of
doctrines—Middle Ages, 600–1500. 4. Posture in worship—
History of doctrines—Middle Ages, 600–1500. I. Petrus, Cantor,
ca. 1130–1197. II. Title. III. Petrus, Cantor, ca. 1130–1197. De
penitentia. 1987. IV. Petrus, Cantor, ca. 1130–1197. De
oratione. 1987. V. Series.
BX1749.P363T74   1987   248.3'2   87–1591
ISBN 0-86698-027-X (alk. paper)

This book is set in Baskerville typeface
smythe-sewn and printed on
acid-free paper to library specifications
It will not fade, tear or crumble.

Printed in the United States of America

For the *other* Mary and Joe, friends.

Contents

Acknowledgments

Like any scholarly effort, this work required the help of many friends, colleagues, and institutions. My debt is greater than usual, however, because I lacked expertise in studying a twelfth-century scholar, a complex manuscript tradition behind one of that scholar's inedited works, and a corpus of medieval illustrations this work inspired.

Since it is evident that any errors are an author's own, I have always resisted that bit of scholarly rhetoric. Here I cannot. Having worked through these texts of Peter the Chanter, I hope I now have the expertise, but it is still I who speak when I fail.

Saul Levin and Daniel Williman deserve special thanks for sharing their many skills with me. John Baldwin encouraged me when I started studying Peter, and provided an invaluable critique as an outside reader. Jean-Claude Schmitt, whose own forthcoming book on medieval theories of gesture is eagerly awaited, provided me with much intellectual stimulation and camaraderie. Though several art historians looked at the pictures with me, it was Penelope Mayo who set me straight at the beginning and taught me the ground rules. Susan M. Dupont discussed certain manuscripts with me, and it was she along with Julian Plante of the Monastic Film Project and Gary Cohen who furnished me with microfilm and some of the pictures. Carol W. Doherty introduced me to computer editing. Bernice J. Trexler read the whole work in draft. Finally, Paul Meyvaert helped by identifying certain patristic texts for me.

I reserve a special note of thanks for one group of colleagues. I finished all but the final draft of this work in the academic year 1984–85 with the help of a fellowship of the John Simon Guggenheim Memorial Foundation and through a resident fellowship at the Center for Advanced Study in the Visual Arts (National Gallery of Art, Washington, D.C.). With gusto and great intelligence, my colleagues at the Center helped me see. I appreciate their companionship and participation.

Preface

The following pages make available for the first time a work of Peter the Chanter, and perhaps of his circle, that is as unknown as it is unique. The *De penitentia et partibus eius* contains one book that is titled *De oratione et speciebus illius*. In it, the author describes seven postures for praying. Uniquely, he also calls for pictures of these modes of prayer. Eight copies of this work have been found that have pictures of these body postures.

In this volume, I try to familiarize readers with the *De penitentia* as a whole and, in more detail, with the verbal and pictorial texts of the *De oratione*. These texts are important as documents of behavioral history; therefore, I have analyzed the words and pictures about behavior in Part I. So central are the pictures to the analysis that the illustrations are not arranged by manuscript, but are grouped together by each mode of prayer.

After this interpretation of the reverential behavior recommended by Peter, the work turns in Part II to a study of the manuscripts. The goal is to determine the structure of the whole *De penitentia* and, more precisely, that of the one book *De oratione*, as they are revealed in the several manuscripts.

The work culminates in Part III with an edition of the book *De oratione et speciebus illius*, as it is found in the Klosterneuburg manuscript. Eight other manuscripts have been collated against that text. As is explained more fully in the introduction to the edition, this is not a critical edition. Our collation aimed only at establishing some basic familial relations between the texts.

Abbreviations

A   Altzella ms.

Bible   Cited as is customary, with Vulgate citations being converted to modern usage: Vulgate 3 and 4 K = 1 and 2 K; Paralip. = Chron; Thren. = Lament.; Apoc. = Rev.

Gratian   The decretals are cited as usual: d(istinction), C(ause), c (hapter), q(uestion), etc.

CCSL   *Corpus Christianorum. Series Latina* (Turnhout, 1953–).

CSEL   *Corpus Scriptorum Ecclesiasticorum Latinorum* (Vienna, 1866–).

DVV   *De vitiis et virtutibus* (= *Verbum abbreviatum*; PL, 2O5).

K   Klosterneuburg ms.

O   Ottobeuren ms.

M   Munich ms.

Pa   Padua ms.

Pe   Pegau ms.

PL   *Patrologiae cursus . . . patrum . . . latinorum . . . .* (Turnhout, 1844–91).

Pr   Prague ms.

V   Venice ms.

W   Walther, Hans, *Proverbia sententiaeque Latinitatis Medii Aevi*, 6 vols. (Göttingen, 1963–).

Z   Zwettl ms.

Introduction

Peter the Chanter was the leading Parisian intellectual of the last quarter of the twelfth century. Born probably in the second quarter of the twelfth century, he came to Paris some time in the early 1170s, and became chanter of its cathedral in 1183. He was a leading light in the life of the city and its schools as well as an important judge delegate for the papacy. At least once and perhaps twice during his life, Peter travelled to Rome. It was on the eve of his departure for the Eternal City in late 1196 or early 1197 that he was elected dean of Reims after having long held a prebend in that cathedral. Death at Longpont near Soissons on September 25, 1197 prevented his investiture in that office.[1]

Peter left behind a large number of students who spread his name and theology. He was evidently a good and popular teacher, a man of some daring in his theological stances, but above all an orthodox innovator who had a seminal role in elaborating the theological foundations of scholasticism at a crucial point in the early life of that intellectual system. A portrait of Peter in a manuscript containing one of his works gives us an idea of what at least one contemporary thought he should look like (see frontispiece).[2]

It is Peter's writings, propagated by his students and by later scholars, that have assured his name in history. Certainly his most monumental work, compiled at least in part by his students, is his summa on the sacraments, critically edited by Dugauquier in the 1950s and 1960s and containing, among much else, the substance of what was Peter's outstanding contribution to medieval thought, an advanced eucharistic theology.[3]

Much more widely known is a work commonly called the *Verbum abbreviatum* after its opening words. The long version of this work is rarely consulted by moderns and seems to have been almost as seldom used by Peter's immediate successors. Indeed, only three complete texts of this long version seem to be extant, all of French origins (Arras, Paris, Vatican), and the whole of it has never been published.[4] The short version of the

Verbum abbreviatum achieved an immediate popularity, on the other hand, and still remains the most accessible of Peter's writings. The extent of its popularity shortly after the Chanter's death is demonstrated by the numerous early manuscripts found throughout Western Europe, mostly in France and England. It has only been edited once, at Mons by Georges Galopin in 1639, but that edition was then incorporated into Migne's Patrology in 1855, insuring its ready consultation by students interested in the master's theology.[5]

Today's historian is fortunate to have a census of the manuscripts of the works of Peter the Chanter in John Baldwin's excellent study of the master and his age.[6] I came to this work through my own specialty of formal behavior in the late Florentine Middle Ages and Renaissance. Included among the photographs of my *Public Life in Renaissance Florence* are illustrations of seven prayer modes that I had examined at the State Archives of Venice after first encountering them in Molmenti's *Storia di Venezia*.[7] These early illuminations illustrate the prayer modes that are described in the Latin text of the Venetian codex. The Archive attributed this *Opus penitentiale*, which began with the Pauline words *Verbum abbreviatum* (Rom. 9.28), to Peter of Poitiers and, knowing nothing of the matter, I erroneously repeated that attribution in my book.

Later I decided to follow up this lead into the problem of devotional behavior. What could be more significant and exciting than to trace a tradition of medieval manuscripts that not only wrote down how to pray, but drew pictures of how to do so? An instruction manual in words was as unknown as was one with pictures for this early date. It seemed that no one had imagined that words and pictures might have been combined in a medieval "how to pray" book.

I soon determined that Peter of Poitiers and Peter the Chanter were commonly confused, and it was that link which brought me to Baldwin's work and to his invaluable census of the manuscripts of the short version of the so-called *Verbum abbreviatum*. Baldwin thought that Peter had only written one work that began with the words *Verbum abbreviatum*: in his view, the long version of ca. 1191/92 had been reduced perhaps by Peter himself to a short form first mentioned in 1199, and that short form had later been subject to various transformations by other scholars. Among the later transformations of the short version that he developed from his study of the manuscripts, Baldwin noted what he called "reorganized abridgements" of the work that had illustrations of various physical postures for prayer. He carefully stated that the eight manuscripts in this category he had identified needed further study.[8] Here was the illustrated prayer manual tradition I had sought.

The Galopin/Migne *Verbum abbreviatum* which Baldwin analyzed in his text says little of a substantial nature about how to pray, so Baldwin's idea that the picture-manuscripts were only a transformed version of the Migne text was improbable on its face. A simple comparison of the explicits strengthened that impression. While the picture-manuscripts begin with the same words *Verbum abbreviatum*, they all end with the quite distinct explicit *premium perfectorum*, one not found in the Migne text. In Part II of this work I will show that this instruction manual is indeed separate from and probably later than the long and short version of the *other Verbum abbreviatum*.

The conventional identification of the long familiar work by its first words is what has led to the confusion. In reality Peter the Chanter started two separate works by saying that he would analyze the Bible or Christ's brief words (*verbum abbreviatum*). In the *Verbum* written about 1191 or 1192 the author developed Christ's brief words on the virtues and vices; in the later work he in fact calls the earlier *Verbum* by the conventional title *De vitiis et virtutibus*,[9] so we shall refer hereafter to the Migne edition of this work as "DVV." Then in this later work, written after 1192, the Chanter elaborated on Christ's brief words about penance, and he meant this work to be called *De penitentia et partibus eius*. Although he sometimes used text from previous work, the overall result was indubitably an original effort. In Peter's scheme, prayer was one of the categories of penance. The book within his *De penitentia* (as I shall henceforth abbreviate the correct title *De penitentia et partibus eius*) that deals with prayer is titled *De oratione et speciebus illius* and contains the instruction manual for prayer in words and pictures. It is this book, plus a short section on prayer from elsewhere in the work, that is published here for the first time.

Peter the Chanter proves to be not only a moral theologian of stamp, but an early behavioral scientist of some importance. Indeed the one roughly contemporary image of Peter, referred to above, comes from a manuscript of his behavioristic *De penitentia* and not from one of his better known works. Our understanding of twelfth-century culture will not remain unaffected by the discovery and analysis of this *De penitentia*. The age of Peter the Chanter has been known since Lynn White's *Medieval Technology and Social Change* as a period of intense technological speculation and experimentation that produced treatises on plowing and warring.[10] It also produced a technical treatise on prayer postures, to be followed a century later by a Dominican prayer manual of similar character.[11] It is this technological aspect of Peter's book on prayer that draws our immediate attention.

Part I of the study contains my analysis of the textual and illustrated contents of Peter's book on prayer. I begin, therefore, by assuming that almost all the text to be analyzed did exist by the second quarter of the thirteenth century and thus represents the thinking of that age about body prayer, whatever the ultimate decision on questions of authorship and text attributions may be in part II. When particular texts of analytical import occur only in certain manuscripts or versions, readers will be alerted to that fact. All references within the following study are to the lines in this edition or, for texts other than the *De oratione*, to the manuscripts themselves.

Part II deals first with the manuscript tradition of the *De penitentia* as a whole, and then studies in greater detail the texts of the *De oratione*. I will argue that Peter the Chanter did write the *De penitentia*, but that it can be dangerous to assign particular statements to him. First, just as does the well-known *Verbum Abbreviatum*, the present work exists in long and short versions. I will argue that Peter authored most of both versions, although, I shall show; he had written the *De oratione* itself as part of a different work before he decided to write a work on penance and fit his prayer manual into it. Thus my study of the entire *De penitentia* shows how the author constructed the work. Then, largely through a study of the manuscripts' external elements, it constructs their genealogy based on comparisons of the eight parchment and one paper texts. With much greater detail and attention to internal text matters, our study of the *De oratione* and its pictures then confirms and enriches that genealogy. The prayer book, including its illustrations, has been collated in Part III of the present edition.[12]

For ease of reference, the following tables show the results of the pending genealogical effort. In the genealogical table, the four manuscripts descending on the right are those with the short version, while the five descending on the left are those of the long version:

Genealogy Table

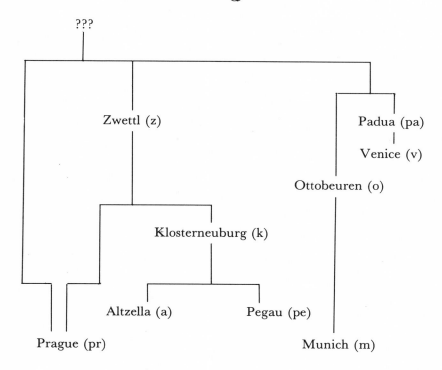

Chronology Table

	text	*pictures*
v	1220	1220, after text
pa	1220	1 and 2: after text; 3–7: 1375 +
o	1246	1246, during writing
m	1400	———
z	1240	1240, after text
k	1250	1325
pe	1275 +	1275 + , after text
a	1260 +	1260 + , after text
pr	1400	1400, after text.

Part One
The Study

HOW TO PRAY

Chapter One

Peter's Words

Peter the Chanter's introduction to his book on prayer outlines the first
third of its contents (276–80). He has just finished a treatise on penance
and on fasting, he says. Of the three parts of penance, Peter continues,
he has dealt elsewhere with fasting and alms. Now it is the turn of prayer
(272–76).

He says he will define prayer, and then does so in the rubric "On
Prayer" ("De oratione"; 324–28). This is the only rubric in the book whose
text the Chanter got mostly from his earlier *On the Vices and Virtues* (*De vitiis
et virtutibus*).[13] Next, the Chanter says that he will distinguish the species
of prayer, and then does so (395–98) by distinguishing vocal from real
prayer. Vocal prayer is the subject of the book of the *De penitentia* edited
here; real prayer is the concern of the following book in the same work.
Next Peter announces he will show the differences between the various modes
of praying, and he admirably fulfills this task in the first third of the book
on prayer.

Finally in his introduction Peter says he will state what prayers are
necessary to every activity (*omni negotio*; 279). This goal is less admirably
fulfilled. In fact, the only systematic exposition of the use of prayer in a
specific activity is done after the short version of the book has ended (2110
ff.). There, in the long version, the author takes the supplicant through
a church and prescribes his behavior at each step. Thus the introduction
does not outline the remaining two-thirds of the book. While full of information on and categories relevant to the modes of prayer, its contents cannot be easily outlined.[14]

My study will not follow Peter through his text; the author's order can
be followed in the edition itself. Nor is my purpose to study the contribution his work makes to the liturgy. Rather, I aim to analyze the Chanter's
concept of prayer by situating it within the social and spiritual universe
he posits. That conception must be reconstructed from the whole book on

prayer, and from references to corporal and vocal prayer in the other books of the treatise.

Peter the Chanter assumes that prayer occurs in certain contexts, and my study begins with an outline of these contexts. Since the nature of prayer is central to the author's concerns, it is also necessary to analyze his understanding of prayer. One of the characteristics of prayer of which the Chanter is keenly aware is that a supplicant figures and signs in shaping and then showing his body. This phenomenon, Peter thinks, is related to the "painting" an author does. The present study, therefore, will examine Peter's comprehension of the rhetorics of writing and showing, that is, of the normative and symbolic relations of the author with his supplicant, viewer, or reader. Once the ideas of Peter the Chanter on these subjects have been studied, I shall turn to the drawings and illuminations that make these manuscripts so unusual. At that point, I will study the supplicants' postures in a full *social* context. The supplicants whom we see in the plates of this volume are, following the author and the supplicants whom Peter describes, the last of the representative agents in these manuscripts.

The Contexts of Prayer

> — The Philosopher (Seneca) says that words that
> are transposed signify the same thing. Never-
> theless, when praying with words, order is to
> be observed (1725–26).

As was fashionable in his time, Peter the Chanter divides humanity into three "diversities" or "genuses" (2011–65): *oratores*, or those who pray; *bellatores* or fighting knights; and those who work (*operarii*): peasants, poor, and manual laborers. Merchants are not mentioned in this context. These genuses are respectively the eyes, hands, and feet of the ideal social body (2548–50). The long version adds that Jerome had adapted only a bipartite division: that between the clergy and the laity (2016–24).

Peter defines the first task of the genus (not "ordo") of warriors as fighting the enemies of the church so that they abandon error. Workers, on the other hand, only perform rather than having a duty or task: almost rectors of the world in Peter's view (2059), they provide all "our" sustenance, that is, that of the warriors and supplicants. In the context of defining the workers in terms of what they do for both other genuses, Peter also defines a second task of the warriors, one they share fully with the *oratores* or supplicants:

both have the duty to protect and defend the workers. Both fail miserably at this task. The knights have become looters, but the clergy, too, violently rob the workers through exactions. As we know from the work of Georges Duby, such sympathy toward the poor and antagonism to the warriors were common in the late twelfth century.[15]

Despite these rubrics on a tripartite division of society, however, the book of prayer as a whole reveals that Peter actually operated more with Jerome's traditional bipartite division of the social body, which is rooted in a distinction between the literate and illiterate. As we shall see, Peter assumed that reading ability bestowed a distinct intellectual character that separated the literate from the "idiots." Yet how and why does Peter link this ability to read with the praying function? Uncertainty on this score is one of the central characteristics of the book. Although he addresses the clergy, and their right prayer is uppermost in Peter's mind, he definitely states that the prayers he recommends are for everyone (eg. 1539), and in the long version, at least, insists that it attempts to reach out to both sexes, every age, and every status and profession (8–10, 64–67).

Thus Peter does not deny that illiterates pray. For example, while he nowhere characterizes the knights as a reading class any more than he does the workers, whom he always assumes to be illiterate, the Chanter sees it as the duty not only of the *oratores* but of the warriors to intercede and pray for the workers (2061–62). The illustrations that distinguish this work were implicitly meant for illiterates as well as literates.

Yet at a more fundamental level, the Chanter believes though he never explicitly states that only the clergy can pray effectively. In what follows, I will outline Peter's idea that to pray effectively one must read, and to read is to understand. Those who understand in the bipartite division of society are defined, therefore, as those who act by praying in the tripartite. This position effectively links an intellective to a behavioral division of society.

One learns to read in school. A social institution and not a Platonic idea generates the genuses of society. Our work contains different opinions on the value of the trivium and quadrivium, but it is unvaried in praising the schools for teaching reading.[16] Reading in turn is the key to *dogmata* or *doctrina*, by which the author means as much the norms of that pious behavior which marks off its initiates from others in society as it means "doctrine" in the modern sense. One appreciative reader of the Chanter's treatise praised its exposition of this "sacra dogmata morum" (o: 216r) and, as we will see later, Peter himself justifies one of his modes of prayer by citing the behavior of the French scholars before he refers to any biblical authority (725–30).

Thus the author sees the schools as the primary context where people learn to pray meaningfully.[17] They are "schools of the arts *and of virtues*" (726). In Peter's view, inculcating such virtues is the central task of the *magistri et doctores* of the schools (k: 30rb), of which he was one of the most illustrious.

The medieval schools required students to demonstrate their skill in public as well as reading. Indeed, Peter often equates reading with public utterances, just as, following Cassiodorus, he defines *oratio* or prayer as something uttered, an "oris ratio" or reason of the mouth (326).[18] Schools are presumably also the source of one's ability to remember, and Peter will repeatedly emphasize that verbalizations of prayer which cannot be remembered are ineffective. Thus in the author's mind, reading and praying are intimately linked to intellective faculties. While Peter will spend long paragraphs warning his readers that prayerful acts without intent are meaningless, intent for this author is basically an intellective quality. Although the references are few, the schools are for Peter the social context from which springs effective action.

Peter wants to distinguish those who can read from the remainder of society, but he is determined to avoid a similar division between the world of prayer and that of work. After the social genera and the schools, work is the third social nexus in which he places his supplicants. Doubtless he wants no confusion. Right at the start he makes short shrift of the Benedictine notion that work is prayer, by "getting down to specifics" (383–85), and he later says that because verbal prayer is so much worthier than any mechanical activity, there is no direct comparison between the two (1344–47). Yet in two ways he modifies his stand. First, he describes the corporal works of mercy, or simply "work" or "works," as "real prayer." Second, in a striking phrase, Peter insists to his reader (*lector*) that a supplicant is an artisan:

> The materials of prayer are letters and syllables, dictions and prayers.
> The *orator* is an artisan, for whom knowledge is necessary. It teaches
> him to pray in one of the seven modes that will be stated (300–2).

Thus the shaping and showing of the body that are at the core of this book on prayer are heralded at the beginning by the idea that the supplicant is the artisan of these seven body postures. Given Peter's emphasis on intellect and the words which express it, we can see that an emphasis on the body as an effective transformer of material and spiritual environments could only be justified by viewing the supplicant as a worker. The mechanics of prayer — its technology — are central in this work as they were in the schools, despite Peter's conventional denunciation of mechanics.[19]

With this concept of body work in place, we may quickly review other contexts in which Peter places his supplicants. As we have seen, the author divided prayer into vocal — that is, the words and accompanying body modes discussed here — and real prayer, or the corporal works of mercy, which Peter thought of here as synonymous with alms-giving and charity. In true medieval fashion, he associated mercy with daytime activity and vocal prayer with dusk and night (1566–71, 1662–64). Because it was not enough to know how to pray, he characterized the science of these body modes as the theory of prayer, despite its eminently practical nature, and the works of mercy as practice (776–802). Again, despite the corporeal emphasis of the whole book, Peter thought that mercy belonged to the active life and verbal prayer to the contemplative (1701–4).

Peter makes these distinctions without much elaboration, almost as if the penchants of the age required them. But one final contextualization he makes is important, and that is the distinction between public and private. The tension between the two spheres is evident. The emphasis on intent leads the author to stress privacy, and indeed Peter associates prayer itself with the contemplative life (1702–4). Yet the point of Peter's book on prayer is to authenticate his prayer modes, and all the biblical events he cites to this end are public rather than private in character. The effectiveness of solitary prayer can not be authenticated unless someone has witnessed the prayer, that is, unless it is not truly solitary.

Certainly Peter wanted his own prayerful work read in the cell, but it had to be validated in the public schools. The rhetoric of the writer Peter the Chanter was not intended only for the private sphere. Without images for all to see and hear, no authentication, no rhetoric of showing or writing was possible.[20] Thus the author could no more categorically assign prayer to either the public or the private realm than he could dismiss the artisanal nature of prayerful body shaping. The division of public and private will remain the most ambivalent category of prayer in this book.

The Nature of Prayer

> When man is praying, he is almost greater than
> the Lord . . . . The greater command, and the
> lesser obey . . . . Man commands when he says
> to God: "Erue . . . ," et "Doce . . . ." Thus in a
> certain way man has precedence over God when
> he prays (351–58).

These remarkable words appear in only two of the manuscripts, the
Altzella and Pegau texts preserved in Leipzig, where they are said to be
derived from many earlier authorities. Whoever their author, they certainly
mirror the philosophical imponderable Peter faced. True, their writer pro-
poses that man is greater than God only on the basis that psalms occasionally
use the imperative mood. In fact, however, his suggestion that supplicants
are powerful throws light on a more pervasive characteristic of prayer, namely that humans plead powerlessness in prayer through words and postures.
By a combination of command and obeisance, humans control God in
prayer.

In the basic long and short versions, Peter the Chanter certainly holds
a not dissimilar view. He does not define prayer as mere intellectual activity, but as goal-oriented artisanal work. He refuses to assign prayer only to the private sphere because he believes that correct prayer should be
seen, as for example, in the author's own verbal and figural images. Directly
to the point, all the manuscripts follow authority in defining prayer ac-
tively, as the individual's capturing (*captatio*) of the benevolence of God (325).

In the study of the manuscript tradition of the Chanter's work, we will
discover that the book on prayer under examination existed as part of a
non-penitential work before it was made part of the *De penitentia*. Without
that knowledge, we would assume that penance dictated Peter's conception of the usages of prayers. Peter does not discuss prayer as thanksgiving
for favors, where "capturing" God's benevolence is not in question. Rather,
prayer is a propitiation for material and spiritual favors such as penitential
forgiveness, where capturing God's benevolence is of the essence. In Peter's
scheme, God plays a largely passive role. This is not a deity with whom
a supplicant carries on a discourse: God either speaks to humans when one
reads or humans speak to God in prayer (349–59), but not both. The communications between humans and God are not conversations. Thus Peter
does not entertain the possibility that through a supplicant's particular corporal or verbal formulation, the God or saint might get the wrong or

unintended message and act on it. This God is merely penetrable: if one "penetrates" to God one has captured his benevolence. Successful at this task, one gets what one has requested, other things being equal (2235–38, 2287–88). If one does not obtain one's will and other things are equal, for good or ill one has simply not penetrated. The rules of verbal and bodily comportment that Peter spells out have as their purpose achieving what one requests.

Peter's penetrating supplicant is always an individual. Though his settings are often public ones, the author nowhere studies prayer as a collective phenomenon, and he nowhere in this work employs the commonplace that collective prayer is more effective in capturing the deity's benevolence than is individual prayer.[21] Thus, prayer is said to be of the individual's and not the collectivity's heart, mouth, and body.

The Types of Prayer

One of the basic tensions in Peter's view of prayer is whether the languages of the body and the voice are one or more. In organizing his book, the author makes body action simply a part of "vocal prayer," the putative subject of the prayer book. Yet the fundamental classification of heart, mouth *and* body, found only in the long version (336, 851–52, 875 ff.), is implied throughout the short text as well. The body does have a separate character apart from the voice. In terminating his description of the body modes of prayer (808–12), Peter speaks of leaving the "material and corporal battle" to examine the "spiritual and mental" struggle of voice and heart. We shall review Peter's conceptions of each of these three types of prayer.

Heart Prayer

To a modern scholar, Peter the Chanter's emphasis on praying from the heart, on meaning what one does, on being sincere, may appear inaccessible to analysis other than as a rhetoric that is itself a comportment. Yet on examination, one finds that Peter describes such heart prayer in terms of the material results of such prayer, and these can be analyzed. For example, he raises the question of whether one's good intentions purge the fault in the performance of the prayer itself (*vitium orationis*; 1995–2010). What is the relation, Peter effectively asks, between form, intent, affect, and efficacy? His answer is seemingly decisive: fault in the form of the prayer is not excused by the intention or affect of the supplicant (2000–2002). Rather, fault in the form throws intent into question.

Let us follow the reasoning. If a supplicant performs a prayer wrong, he is not thinking of and does not understand what he is doing. He has, in one of the Chanter's favorite phrases, "receded from himself." Not being himself, *he* "thus has no affect that relates to prayer, and what affect there is cannot purge" (2002-4). "Just how could anyone's intention or affect excuse that of which one does not think," the Chanter asks rhetorically (2004-5). Making an unwarranted jump from the problem of guilt for and purging of bad action to that of efficacy, he concludes: "The whole power and efficacy (*virtus et . . . efficacia*) of verbal prayer depends and has to come, from the clamor of the heart and from the compunction and devotion and intention of the mind" (2006-7). Elsewhere, Peter speaks of the *vox cordis* (1509). He regularly externalizes what he insists is internal.

Let us isolate certain fundamental propositions from this logical chain. First, as far as prayer is concerned, Peter so closely associates the mind and the heart, or "intent and affect," that they are all but interchangeable, as in the long version where he refers to "mental devotion, and the highest diligence and intelligence or knowledge, and integrity, of the heart" (2147-48). Second, his concept of praying is quite as "clamorously" aural in focus as is his understanding of reading. What is being tested for intent is the form of a prayer said aloud; Peter never analyzes silent prayers, which by definition would have no verifiable form. Third, Peter is obviously talking about prayers that have a canonical form. Although he elsewhere refers in passing to what can be understood as spontaneous formulations of prayer (1743), he does not address himself in this book to the question of whether such prayers do not spring by definition from the "clamor of the heart." Thus Peter's heartfelt prayers are preceded by reflection, they follow a canon, and they are public in the sense that they have to be heard at least by God.

The historical significance of Peter's edifying insistence on the clamor of the heart and the intention of the mind emerges in its relation to post-Hildebrandine, anti-Donatist eucharistic and sacramental theology. In this body of doctrine it is maintained that, whatever the priest's moral or penitential state, by virtue of his status as priest he does confect or make God out of the eucharistic bread and wine by uttering certain words aloud, just as, irrespective of his moral state, he transmits other sacramental graces efficaciously by verbal formulas. Theologians of the rank of Hugh of St. Victor (d. 1141) had quite recently still disputed such a stringent separation between priestly morality and sacramental efficacy, but the stated view was in the ascendancy.[22]

In their purest forms, such doctrines had the effect first of significantly devaluating the traditional, simple insistence upon the celebrant's good intentions in making God in the eucharist and passing on sacramental grace. A debate slowly grew up between those who continued to require an internal intention, as it soon came to be called, for such acts, and those who thought a so-called external intention was sufficient for efficacy. The debate continued as late as the seventeenth century.[23] Secondly and consequently, these verbocentric doctrines tended to decrease the importance one attached to the priest's corporeal behavior at mass, which had once been a central measure of internal intention. Thus contemporaries maintained that quite apart from the celebrant's affect and, to a certain if unclear extent, even apart from his corporeal behavior before and during the transubstantiation,[24] it was the utterance of certain prescribed words that transformed the essentials of the environment. The question for Peter and others was: just where in the full spectrum of devotional life did intention stop being crucial?[25]

True to prevailing ideas, Peter the Chanter said nothing about the celebrant's "intention of the heart" or "of the mind" in his enunciation of eucharistic doctrine. An important contributor to scholastic sacramental doctrine in general, he avoided cavils and stated that the miracle of the host occurred even when the priest's "heart . . . in the canon or secret of the mass, wandered to something else" (1525–26). Referring to the eucharistic verbal formulas, he says that "the whole power [virtus] of the sacrament of the altar" consists in those words (1531–32). In a variant text of his De vitiis et virtutibus, Peter had entered the classic cavil that for the "sacramental forms" to be effective, the priest had to be serious (DVV, 544). But in the present treatise, he avoids such interpretable language.[26]

Eucharistic and sacramental doctrine was a prism through which contemporaries viewed the more general philosophical question of the efficacy of action. Thus the Chanter was obviously aware that the orthodox conception of the celebrant who worked miracles through uttering words, vage mentis or not, could scarcely be brought into harmony with the view that prayers had efficacy only if they were recited with the good and conscious intention of the mind and with the clamor of the heart. Yet it is Peter himself who, discussing the efficacy of prayer and the impediments to efficacy, brings up the subject of the eucharistic words. They too were prayers. Peter might say that the "rules of the dialecticians don't apply to the body of Christ" (k: 31ra). But the logical if not dogmatic conflict remained evident and challenging.

Now it was one thing for Peter to pronounce on the question of whether the celebrant could be efficacious even while sinning. Peter latched on to this penitential question of the effect on the priest of his laxity and decided that a priest who prayed badly and in a depraved fashion sinned mortally even though he might effect the miracle of transubstantiation (1533–34, 1548–49). Furthermore, such a celebrant had not fulfilled his prayer duties ("nec est exemptus ab honere et debito orationis") and had to repeat them (1537; 1215–17).

It was quite another matter, however, for Peter to decide just what it meant to say that only the uttered words were necessary to effect the transubstantiation. How uttered? What precisely was a good and thus miraculous verbal performance? Peter could not satisfactorily segregate the eucharistic prayers from the rest — as if the efficacy of the latter but not the former depended on the *clamor cordis* and the stability of the mind — by merely repeating the accepted doctrine of the sacraments and the mass. For both types of prayer were uttered. A description of Peter's concept of prayers of the mouth makes that clear enough.

Word Prayer

Peter's scorn for the full mouth empty of heart does sound conventional enough. Presumably excluding the sacramental and eucharistic formulas, for example, Peter says that a prayer done only with the sound of the mouth and not the contrition of the heart is totally useless (2007–10). The author speaks often of fraud, hypocrisy and dissimulation, at one point conjuring up the image of the supplicant whose perfect enunciation of a prayer verily proved these sins and was their agent (1549–50, 711–12, 1965–66). Yet in the eucharist, it was said to be precisely and essentially such right enunciations that guaranteed the transubstantiation. What might be mere sound became essential sound in the secret of the mass.

Despite the externalizing thrust of his eucharistic doctrine, in describing the eucharistic prayers Peter does, however, use the word "fraud," meaning defrauding. It consisted in the *imperfect* enunciation or even omission of the key words. The question was: what was imperfection, and could syntactical sloppiness inhibit the transubstantiation? It is a question today's priests still remember from their seminary days. What formal fault might negate the eucharistic miracle, and what should the celebrant do to correct it? Again, that high sacrificial and historically recreative act is a prism for the examination of larger questions about prayer.

We approach this complex problem first as Peter examined it in describing prayers in general. Among four vices or sins that Peter says impede the efficacy of prayer, only speed is behavioral in character: "too great speed, which robs prayer of its effect" (1054). As an example, Peter says that a prayer loses its efficacy when the supplicant leaves out a letter or syllable, or indeed a whole prayer within a series that one is required to say (1072). Thus completeness and correct pronunciation, "which is to devotion what a bellows is to coal," (1148–49) are central to efficacy.

What then of the eucharistic formula? Evidently the matter is treacherous, for the doctrine that the utterance suffices loses its simple borders the moment Peter reflects upon it. He lists, and in the long version elaborates on (1325–27, 1960–65), three types of bad pronunciation: afferism, syncope, and apocope, that is, the omission of sounds respectively from the beginning, middle or end of a word. Interestingly, he condemns systoles and diastoles as well, that is, not only the defraudation of shortening but also the lengthening of "natural" syllabic sounds (1330–31). The Chanter just as facilely refers to vocal barbarism or solecism (1326–27), and negatively characterizes all such departures from norms as "figures" (1953, 1962). He insists that one must finish each word before beginning another (1357–60). Peter does not bother to mention a possible protest that this was over-scrupulosity: that as long as the celebrant *intended* to pronounce, for example, "Hoc est" and not "Ho cest corpu smeum," the miracle would be performed. Such a protest would compromise the doctrine of objective priestly power at its core, and Peter had no such intention.

Peter the Chanter does not try to determine at what point bad pronunciation or omissions prevented the transubstantiation. Nor would any solution he might have proposed have a scientific interest, since the transformation of the essential environment the doctrine of the transubstantiation assumes is based on faith and not observation. But the Chanter does attack the problem of faulty forms by proposing how the celebrant should behave when he is at fault, and his solution is eminently important.

Peter says that in the midst of the mass, after enunciating the eucharistic words or any other prayer, the celebrant should ask himself whether he can remember what he has just said and how well he had pronounced it. He should undertake a "recall of all the dictions of the prayer" ("recordatio omnium dictionum orationis" (699, 1399–1400). Then in the paragraph *De repetitione orationis* and the one that follows (1524–51), the Chanter determines that if the celebrant cannot remember, he should repeat the eucharistic words. This same recommendation is then applied to any words of the mass and indeed to any prayer.[27] Thus at this point, the cognitive skill of memory joins conscious planning as an essential part of the good prayer.

A celebrant repeating part of the ceremony of making God would have been no less strange then than now, and Peter took seriously the scruples he imagined his contemporaries raising: if the celebrant actually repeated prayers, not to mention the eucharistic words, he would scandalize or fatigue the audience (1542–44). Having paraphrased such objections, Peter in fact does not definitively pronounce on their value, leaving us in some doubt as to his ultimate rejoinder to that objection. The most that can be said is that after considering these objections, he does reiterate his original insistence on repetition (1544–46).

Yet why did Peter come up with this remarkable public solution to individual fault in the making of Christ (*confectio Christi*)? Presumably Peter would not have answered that he proposed this solution because if one could not remember one was not "with oneself"; that would have been to compromise the eucharistic doctrine. Keeping in mind that Peter thought eucharistic utterance also required some uncertain measure of correct and precise pronunciation to perform the miracle, it would rather seem that Peter meant to imply that if one could not remember, then one had not performed the words correctly: the eucharist not having been effected, the words had to be repeated. Thus an interpretation of combined mnemonic, intellectual and behavioral procedures led the author to put forth such a startling and, from a practical point of view, impossible mandate. In this reading the faithful's scandal was not just pique, as Peter's words seem to suggest: "nor otherwise can anyone say the secret twice, for then the mass would seem too prolix to the people" (1543–44). Rather, the faithful's awareness that the priest might fail to make God in verbal strokes for body and blood would be the scandal. What else would the faithful have thought if the priest repeated himself?[28]

According to Peter, inability to recall a correct verbal performance should be followed by repeating the behavior. Yet was each word of these verbal formulas really of equal importance? Would not even a merely penetrable God, like any human, attach more importance to the word "corpus," for example, than to the correct pronunciation or even omission of the word "hoc"?[29] The paragraph on fraudulent prayer in the short version of the book affords no help on that score, for it merely brands as frivolous every prayer that is made "with wandering mind and with the omission of some of its parts." But the long version adds an important insert at this point, which is italicized in the following quote:

> Thus if you omit some verse which is part of the whole of the prayer, or some utterance or syllable or letter *which is part of the substance of the execration*, you are praying falsely and evilly (713–14).

With this insert, its presumed author Peter the Chanter obviously meant to qualify the short version by implying that only what was substantial had

to be recalled and thus eventually re-enunciated. In keeping with this im-
plication, the same long version at another point (1235–44) tries to define
the substance of prayer and, as if to say that it is better to pronounce one
completely substantial prayer well than many imperfectly, the author writes
out the Our Father: the perfect prayer that "contains everything necessary
to salvation" (2080–81). The whole Our Father is, therefore, substantial.
Yet this dangerous insertion meant in effect that no binding measure could
be applied to the efficacy of any but the Our Father's performance, nor
to judging the fraudulence or sincerity of prayer.

Christianity is usually defined as a religion of the book, and Peter the
Chanter certainly did return to books for his prayers. Yet like any other,
this religion also was and is importantly one of utterances or verbal
behavior.[30] To Peter, reading meant reading out loud, as praying meant
oral expression. To read and to pray were two most excellent works, Peter
copied Augustine, but if one had to choose between them, prayer was better (343–49, 358–59). Yet how difficult it proved to be for Peter the Chanter
to enunciate what an effective prayer was, and just when it was that one
"penetrated." As we move now toward the author's central study of body
prayer, we can only be sure that not intent but knowledge and action were
the outward signs of the potentially successful supplicant.

Body Prayer

> —That One Should Say the Same with his
> Heart and Body (title, 964).

In Peter the Chanter's own scale of values the behavior of the mouth
was doubtless more important than that of the body. This is not surprising
in a member of the clergy whose business was the utterance of words. Indeed, only recently has modern scholarship modified its traditional ver-
bocentrism and given a proper place to the body as an expressive agent.[31]

Peter's clerical bias leaves a tangible trail in his examination of the body
at prayer. Though the study of body action is the centerpiece of this book,
the body's *modes*, as Peter always characterizes them, are at least formally
included under the species of *verbal* prayer. Second, Peter refers much more
often to the mouth than to the remainder of the body in describing prayer
itself. Right after defining prayer as the capturing or imprisonment of God's
benevolence, he retails the Cassiodoran etymology of "oris ratio" for "oratio"
(326), and he never follows up the former more active image by suggesting
that the supplicant's body was the imprisoning agent. Third, the author

required celebrants to repeat forgotten verbal utterances, but nowhere does he require his supplicants to repeat bodily actions if they cannot remember them. Finally, with the exception of his insistence that the celebrant cross the bread and wine, the Chanter significantly makes no reference to the state of the celebrant's body during the consecration of the mass.[32] Thus while in the long version Peter might say that prayer was "not just what is done with words, but also everything that is done in the devotion of faith in honor of God" ["non solum que fit verbis, vero etiam omnia que geruntur in obsequium dei fidei devotione" (k: 14vb)], the heart, mind and mouth encapsule Peter's conception of prayer's essence much more than does the body.

What is surprising, of course, is that a twelfth-century theologian should bother with a systematic study of the body at all. The treatise attributed to Hugh of St. Victor and titled *De instructione novitiorum* initiated the tradition, but Hugh's brilliant work was concerned with purely human communications. Peter the Chanter, who gives no indication he knew this or any contemporary devotional work, seems to be the first to concentrate on the body in penitential prayer.[33] He was in a good position to do so. Many of the waking hours of the illustrious chanter of Paris must have been taken up leading the boys of the Parisian cathedral school in processions.[34] Before turning to the actual shapes of the body in prayer, I should first clarify Peter's classifications of body prayers.

In his *De vitiis et virtutibus* (DVV, 265) but only in the long version of the present work (2338–43), the Chanter describes certain human body postures by comparing them to animal ones: while standing among humans makes each person equal to the other, before God we fall down to the position of the quadripeds in recognition of our sinful fallen state (2343–46). We are "naturally erect," he says in the *De vitiis*, but just as in human fornication we lie down meanly like animals, so also do we, rightly, to repent our sins (DVV, 265). We copulate with and join ourselves to the earth so as to copulate ultimately with heaven (639, 820, pa: 72vb). Peter rarely if ever considers prayer behavior to be involuntary.

Peter did not, however, associate only the low position with penance. He sought legitimation for his prayer modes not primarily in nature, after all, but in sacred books, and in them standing to pray was common. There are six postures found in the Bible, he says, and a seventh mode of prayer which Peter gleaned from Gregory the Great, creating a symmetry with the seven canonical or vocal hours. Three of these modes are standing ones. Thus while Peter often enough praises descending postures as being particularly demonstrative of penance and sorrow, his basic view is that standing to pray is legitimate because the Bible contains such prayerful postures.

Peter's use of the Bible shows that he tried to avoid one potentially important legitimation for prayer postures. He cites no biblical examples of secular political obeisance or reverence to justify modes of praying to a divinity. This avoidance of the rich information on diplomatic etiquette in the Bible must have been a conscious choice. While never directly saying so, Peter obviously did not feel that the body actions used between human communicants, even biblical ones, could legitimate the postures of one's discourse with God. In what follows, we shall see cases where the influence of twelfth-century diplomatic and political customs and fashions did intrude. But such examples form no principled part of his approach.

That approach, I repeat, recognized that certain postures were "natural," but emphasized the Bible as the source of legitimation. Though Peter might praise Islam generally when condemning contemporary Christianity (pa: 41rb), he never mentions Islamic or other societies' modes of prayer. There is a third legitimating agent implied in Peter's work, and that is his own intellectual authority. As authors often do, this one too suggests to his readers that he is simply passing on the fruits of the Scriptures (7–8; k: 1rab). But Peter did not merely list biblical citations. Instead, he created his own original superstructure of seven modes of prayer, within each of which he cited several historical actions. Further, he introduced a series of norms and paradigms for good prayer that have no scriptural foundation. Peter's work is an intellectual synthesis of elemental body forms of devotion gleaned from his readings of historical events. He wants us to believe that these seven forms are written in the eternal Christian book of order.

As a matter of fact, Peter did not do a good or even an honest job of defending this view, for at times he twisted his sources so that his own exposition made sense.[35] Detailed elsewhere, these instances need not be repeated here. What is important is that this author's product became history. Peter not only repeated, he created. Presumably read to the schools and monasteries after its writing, this book was then an object legitimating itself, and the seven illustrations that accompany each manuscript are a forceful demonstration of the fact that now his words were becoming flesh.

Thus once composed, the book on prayer took on tangible formal properties comparable to the tangibility of other posturing bodies. Peter's performance of his prayer book is sufficient evidence that corporal forms are central to his concept of devotion. It will remain for this study of penitential body shapes to determine just how inexact body prayer could be compared to vocal prayer, yet still penetrate to God.

Shaped Bodies

He was much adorned with natural goods and
graces (490).

All the texts of Peter's work show prayerful activity beginning by having
supplicants "turn [their] face[s] toward Jerusalem" (342), that is, east or
toward the altar of sacrifice. A paragraph of the long version justifies this
behavior at length (900–912). "Turning toward Jerusalem" is a metaphor
for doing penance, one incorporated into the title of the Ottobeuren and
Munich manuscripts. Also in the long version (876, 883), Peter states that
males "qui ad hoc sufficiunt" were to pray with their heads bare; perhaps
by this qualifying phrase Peter meant to exclude male children. Peter adopted
the well-known Pauline text (1 Co 3–4) on head coverings and praised the
"quite durable" Cistercian custom of going hatless even in extreme cold
(880–83). He did not specify, as had the apostle, that women's heads should
remain covered.

The supplicant is then to assume certain positions (*devota corporis positio*;
884), which the long version combines with hatlessness under the rubric
"praying with the body" (*orandum corpore*) as distinct from praying with the
mouth (875, 864). At this point it becomes clear that the modes of prayer
Peter will describe are the postures that result from movements rather than
the movements themselves. Peter states that an efficaciously executed mode
may result in motions, both of the heart or soul (*motus anime*) and of the
body (1912, 2004–10). He follows Augustine in stating that high and sweet
singing is a sign that God has heard one's prayer (pa: 23ra) and Benedict
to the effect that crying and sighing are corporal effects or, as he says earlier,
witness ("testes"; k: 3rb) of such interior movement (2333–34). But he never
defines a motion as a mode of prayer: not flagellation (k: 6va, 10va), and
not even "genuflection." Our study of the manuscript tradition will show
that as used by Peter, this word—like all other words describing prayer
behavior—refers to the already shaped body and not to the process of shaping
it.

Since Peter does not describe motions, he also does not warn his readers
against "gesticulations" or what were said to be excessive gestures in prayer.
As Schmitt has shown, this concept was re-entering the literature at the
time,[36] and in his earlier *De vitiis*, Peter had used the word (DVV, 35).
In the present work, Peter assumes the existence of rules of motion or what
we call grace. He retells Lucan's story of a saint who, in order to avoid
assuming a political office that a visiting official was about to thrust on him,

came forth with "deformed, irregular and uncomposed modes by the gesture and motion of his body, making believe he was ignoble and inept" ("per gestus et motus corporis sui deformes et edendi modos irregulares et incompositos, ignavum et ineptum se simulavit in adventus presidis provincie" (pa: 23rab).

While Peter does not carry over this whole problematic of good and bad motion to prayer behavior, it is significant to this study that he labels the saint's deformed movements, his departure from the fixed rules of motion, as a "false insanity." For far from denouncing motions as madness or sin in his study of prayer, Peter does not even mention them, and the word "gesture" in the prayer book as perhaps also in his story from Lucan means posture: an immobile sign of a stable moral or immoral condition. This is evident in his static characterization of gesture: "The gesture of the body argues for and proves one's mental devotion. For the state of the exterior man tells us about the humility and affect of the interior [man]" (1395–96). But it is still more clear in the fact that his other two uses of the word "gesture" occur with reference to the pictures he wants of his modes of prayer. Peter describes the moral signification of the "gesture of such a prostrate and recumbent man" shown in one picture he has ordained (690–92), and in ordaining another, he says: "Let there be an image which represents the gesture of the supplicant" (494).

Thus, for Peter gesture means an immobile posture of the type captured by artists, who cannot show motion. One is reminded of the *tableaux vivants* of the age, in which live "actors" froze in the prayer postures attributed to the saints.[37] Now the list of the movements Peter does not address can be completed. Though he denounces quasi-theatrical singing in church (982–84), the author mentions neither the liturgical dramas nor the church dances of the time, which were thought of as types of prayers.[38] The author avoids any notion that stability is less moral than movement; for example, the works of mercy he vaunts so highly are by definition mobile procedures. But he clearly thinks that a moral supplicant is an immobile one.

What then are these postural modes of prayer and how scrupulous is Peter in describing their forms? Let it first be noted that the seven modes fit nicely into a category, found only in the long version (884–90), of three "devout positions" for prayer with the body: standing, kneeling, and total prostration. Yet let it also be said that Peter almost certainly did not think the matter through so systematically, for his exposition remains in less than logical order. Four of the seven modes of prayer involve standing, one kneeling, and two reclining. But the modes only generally follow that order in Peter's text.

Of the four standing modes, the first (405–8) envisions having the arms and joined hands over the head "as far as you can extend them." Peter later adds that one's face should be turned toward heaven as well. The second mode (455–57) is cruciform, the hands and arms being extended "similar to a cross." Peter distinguishes the third mode from the first two. It is meant to show "the hands stricken together and contiguous, extended and directed before the eyes" ("habens manus complosas, et contiguas, extensas, ac directas coram oculis suis"; 509–14). Citing Jesus "standing up to read" and Esdra standing up and opening a book (514–18), the author shows he means the supplication to be in an erect reading posture without a book, and the Ottobeuren figure for this mode in fact shows a monk as if reading.

Having listed three standing modes of prayer, Peter pauses in order to praise standing and condemn sitting (525–27). It appears that he is summarizing standing before going on to another "devout posture," and in fact his fourth mode is the kneeling posture (*positis genibus in terra*; 593–94). The fourth standing posture comes later. This order would seem to indicate that the section on the modes of prayer we have before us was never subject to redraftings and remains as Peter first wrote it.

After kneeling comes the fifth mode, full prostration, "when a man throws himself fully onto the earth on his face" (629–32). The biblical texts cited by the Chanter at this juncture as well as in the other texts on "genuflection," which I examine later, indicate that the stomach and feet are to be on the ground, and the mouth and face are to be turned toward the earth so that one can not see upward (632–33, 689–90).

The sixth and last mode justified by the Bible is the fourth standing mode: bowing the head and kidneys from an erect position (720–23). Peter concludes with a seventh mode that Gregory the Great's aunt had practiced. We shall call it proskynesis; Peter himself spoke of the "custom of camels" (*more camelorum*). From a kneeling position, this woman had put her elbows but not her stomach or face on the ground and placed the weight of the torso on the knees and elbows for long periods, her arms obviously bent (769–71).[39]

Peter was aware that describing these modes of prayer was not enough; he also had to rule out other possible prayer postures. Thus the author created a series of boundaries outside of which supplicants were not following his directions, and these boundaries are quite as important to defining the modes of prayers as are the descriptions themselves. We shall first examine bad ways of praying, that is postures that are outside Peter's system, and then the fraudulent or hypocritical body postures that might seem to be but were not within Peter's system.

With the exception of one condemnation of a prone position (2241–42), sitting is the one extra-systemic posture Peter rules out for able-bodied supplicants. In all texts he notes that sitting is proper only for judges or for those at ease, while the correct position of standing is for those in struggle, like penitential supplicants (526–27, 1393).[40] In the long texts, however, Peter spells out at greater length his objections to such "lazy *oratores*" who sat to pray (540–42, 2241–47). The author condemns those who no sooner enter church than they sit down, and those monks who dare defend sitting because it is customary in their order (915–32). Yet his rejection of sitting was not shared by all his near contemporaries; Humbert of Romans, for example, saw nothing fundamentally wrong with it.[41] Nor did Peter himself ever use biblical authority satisfactorily to justify his abhorrence, and indeed he does not mention biblical examples where persons were said to have prayed from a sitting position, the most obvious being the Last Supper and Pentecost. Thus his conventional statement that sitting was reserved to judges becomes all the weightier. Peter seems actually to have denounced sitting in prayer because in state audiences only sovereigns sat. He could have documented that from the Bible as well, but did not.

The other set of incorrect postures are those located within the physical borders of the acceptable modes of prayer. Since Peter speaks of "stealing" from these modes (1329–30), he certainly conceived of the latter as being normatively as well as physically fixed. Since he further brands these intrasystemic behaviors fraudulent, as in the term *fraus genuflectioni*, meaning improper kneeling (2314–15), it is evident that he deduces intention from performance. Peter obviously thought that, within the physical outlines of correct prayer, one could deceive with corporal as well as verbal utterances. The idea that one "spoke" with the body as with the heart is explicit in the long version (964).

In general, Peter's scrupulosity about body postures did not approach his concern for the correct enunciation of verbal formulas. His preoccupation with sloppy verbal syntax was greater than with sloppy body syntax. Yet concern there was, and it emerges most clearly in what he has to say about reclining postures. At one point he dwells at length on what he calls the "true inflection of the knees" (*vera genuum inflectio*). He does not mention kneeling on one knee, but defines true "genuflection" as "when the toes of the feet and the knees are at the same level, so that the knees are no further removed from the pavement than the tips of the feet" (2318–20). A few lines later he insists on correct prostration with equal specificity, calling the position where mouth, knees, and feet all hug the ground "especially . . . sincere and optimal" (*ibid.*). Thus only seeming to bring the face to where it kisses the ground was insincere or, to follow phrases Peter used elsewhere, dissimulative and hypocritical (cf. 1549-51).

But the most characteristic objections Peter has to postures within the perimeters of his gestural system are directed against the use of props to avoid the full rigor of the postures. In all the texts, he regularly denounces the use of kneelers as well as the practice of leaning while in a standing position (407-8, 540-42, 1393-95, 2150-51, 2241-42). He calls kneelers "artificial feet" and says their use is a type of insult or perverse prayer, whose words Peter gives in the long version: "Oh God," you yourself are to blame for my laziness, because you did not give humans enough pedestrian support (2270-74).[42] These denunciations again lack a biblical justification, and once more Peter ignored evangelical documentation that disproved his point of view. Only in another context, for example, did Peter cite the case of Moses leaning on his arms while praying (k: 1rb, 29ra).

Peter the Chanter labels the good ways of praying that I have outlined as true and real, and the bad ones as useless. Yet just as important, he also signifies meanings that are inherent in the acts themselves. Certain "imperfect" postures are insincere and thus dissimulative, hypocritical and fraudulent, while perfect prostration was "especially sincere." This notion of a posture that was objectively sincere is obviously problematical, for at other times Peter espied ostentatious pride in perfectly executed humble postures (1549-51). The solution to this seeming conflict may lie in Peter's observations of the effect of prostration on supplicants. A review of Peter's references to sighing, weeping, and chest-beating shows that the context, especially for weeping, is often a discussion of prostration (1881-98, 2147-50, 2231-38). Thus the Chanter may have thought that prostration was especially sincere because he observed that it produced tears. Even though he knew that some Italians cried at funerals for a living (*ploratorum et ploratricum Longobardorum*; DVV, 97), Peter was not the first or last person to search for a tangible proof of a supplicant's sincerity and find it in tears.[43]

To summarize. Peter is capable of describing and assessing his modes of prayer as denuded physical postures outside time and place. He could judge postures as they physically were and not as they might appear to a devotee. Vestments, for example, might make it appear that a priest leaning on one foot was standing erect. At this level, Peter clearly felt that though all these modes are meritorious, the declining modes were superior. As far as getting what one wanted from God, prostration was just about the best of all the prayer postures (2326-28), though he gives no biblical justification for this ranking.

Second, these denuded postures have distinct moral contents, and again, prostration is the mode Peter characterizes as especially sincere, with sitting, leaning, and using kneelers and walls being objectively insincere. Peter again offers no biblical justification for such assertions, but he wants to make us believe through the force of his rhetoric that something approaching a binding taxonomy of form insuring correct readings of intent exists in the sacred book. Our question now becomes how these readings are affected when Peter discusses showing the body in public.

Showing the Body

— In theatrical scenes. . . , there are as many sins
as there are imitations of persons (DVV, 338).

Peter the Chanter constantly opined that private prayer was better than public or collective prayer. This was true, first because of the temptation to "study vanity" and make a "show of sanctity" ("ostentatio sanctitatis") in the public forum (k: 30ra), and then because—the eye being the ambassador and instrument by which the heart sees and the internal man knows the external (1720–23, 1029–30, 1668–72, 1713–48)—public life distracted the essential supplicant. Sounding vaguely humanistic, the author compared his modes of prayers to physical exercises which, sameness being the mother of satiety, the athletic supplicant should vary along with verbal utterances (822–26, 1755–58, 2100–4). Indeed in his *De vitiis*, the author had noted that when things remain the same, feeling declines: "traditiones implete . . . nimiam pariunt securitatem" (DVV, 236). One can, in short, picture Peter's ideal supplicant, using in private the Chanter's physical postures in a relaxed and functional fashion without the "eyes of the heart" (k: 1rb) being distracted by externals.

Yet that image would be false, despite Peter's undoubted convictions about the value of prayer in solitary places. It is not only that Peter insisted that a church was a better place to pray than a home (416–22, 468–70); but Peter further expected his supplicant to carry out only the approved postures of prayer and the approved verbal prayers in the cell, and not make up his own. He did not produce furtive witnesses to a hero's supposedly solitary behavior as a way of legitimizing new prayers.[44]

Thus Peter the Chanter's goal was to publicize through his work a publicly performed, yet also privately binding, catholic system of devotion rooted in the Bible. There were three reasons to pray with the mouth publicly, he said (864–74). The desire to offer God verbal obsequy was one, and the wish to witness publicly one's devotion was another. But the third reason, the need for instruction, "to teach by word and example" (1666–67) was certainly a pre-eminent reason for corporal as well as verbal prayer. The right modes had to be shown to be learned. That was certainly the business of the lecturer or preacher, but it was also that of a writer like Peter who foresaw illustrations of what he described in words.

Supplicants were to consider the time and place of prayer, Peter now argued, and they must also gauge their prayer according to the object-world around them. In certain of these contexts, supplicants before God should call attention to the modes of body action in which they engage by using prayers whose words refer to them. Thus to a certain extent Peter the Chanter showed his supplicants using an integrated system of prayer in given chronological, spatial, and object environments. This is a different universe than the one previously described, that of absolutely sincere or absolutely fraudulent postures where contexts play no role. Here shame makes its appearance, and it obviously affects the way people pray.

Peter attributes a crucial role to time and place in determining how one should pray and what one should say in prayer. If it is always wrong to pray sitting or leaning, in all Peter's texts it is also wrong to use the first three standing modes if one were required (*debet*) to kneel, bow, or render oneself prostrate (1392–95). The author intended such considerations of time and place to be carried into the private sphere of prayer, but he regularly exemplified them in the public one. The authentic modes of prayer in effect lost their merit if done out of time and place.

Peter meant the norms of time and place to be those of the catholic church, that is, the universal devotional body he described in his work, and not the mere traditions of particular orders. He attacked such small-group norms when they conflicted with what he took to be authoritative ones, entering into specific debates of the time in doing so. For example, the long version (667–83) condemns the conventional view that one should not kneel on feast days, countering that "knees should be bent at all times."[45] The same version considers those monks guilty of reprehensible behavior who sit during the singing of the gradual and during wakes for the dead, even if they plead that it is not their order's custom to stand or kneel for those activities (914–19, 926–28, 934–63).

But we are interested less in these particular debates than in the author's larger sense of conformity in devotional contexts, and we can reconstruct that sense by beginning with Peter's sense of order in purely verbal utterances. Asking in all texts whether there is a right sequence of prayers, he responds that the answer is doubtful and the question therefore licit (2076–78). He then lists his preferred order for seven prayers, beginning with the Our Father and ending with the Credo, and says that only after them should come "all other prayers which are used by the catholic church throughout the world" (2096-97) — regional prayers whose variety Peter praises because they relieve tedium. He specifically states that in ordering the prayers in this way, he does not mean to bind the wise but to show those lacking knowledge and "estranged from intellect" a form and sequence of good behavior (2104-6). For such persons are to be instructed, not followed (2072-73).

Peter becomes less accomodating at the next level. He claims that certain words should be combined with some of the modes of prayer. This refers less to the body postures with which those attending a mass respond to a celebrant's utterances (cf. 723-25), as when one kneels at the "Flectamus genua" of the mass,[46] than to the supplicant's own integration of his or her own words and acts. The prayer book contains two types of such admonitions. First, Peter indicates once that the words one uses with specific body postures should call attention to the latter, just as had his Old Testament sources. Thus in mode 5 he has his supplicant prayerfully explain to God why he is prostrate (632-33). This rare instruction indicates that, just as Peter's own descriptive words were glosses on actual behaviors, he could imagine devotional utterances to be glosses of corporal actions and not vice versa as in the mass liturgy.

The second type of integration automatically associates certain postures with certain words that do not refer to the behavior. This happens once within the very definition of the fifth posture: "when a man throws himself fully on the earth on his face, *saying*: 'Deus propitius . . .' and: 'Ego sum qui peccavi . . . .'" (631-32; my italics). It occurs again when Peter justifies that same body posture by noting that pious Frenchmen performed it at the point of transubstantiation, saying at the same time: "Confectio, tractatio . . ." etc. (730-36).[47] As we shall presently see, the long text goes even further in integrating words to actions.

At a third level, Peter encourages supplicants to integrate words and postures into their physical environment, and first to the objects around them. Thus the author defined the bowing mode six as reserved primarily for altars (721-23), and then for "every place where there is an image or a cross of Christ or a figure of any saint" (757-58).

At the highest level, Peter brings churches into this physical environment of prayer, interrelating spaces to objects, words and actions. Substantial texts on church behavior occur only in the long version, in the first instance where Peter is condemning those false monks who refused to perform the gradual and the vigils for the dead correctly. On entering any church, he

says, true Christians and all persons belonging to religious orders are required to say the Our Father with at least three "genuflections" before the
cross, and to repeat the same before each altar in the church (941–44). Then
they should invoke the Trinity, kneeling at least for the invocation of the
Spirit. Turning next to the bad monks, the long version instructs them on
sequences of standing, prostration, and genuflection (945–60).

The section of the book on prayer that follows the termination of the
ten-book short version (2112 ff.) is largely taken up with elaborating this
theme of a total prayer performance. There are differences from the earlier
account: here, for example, not the Our Father but another prayer is
prescribed for those entering a church. More significant, this elaboration
writes out (2115–19) the various prayers to be said at this point. For example, speaking of a supplicant just inside the door of a church, the long
version spells out the prayers one should say when one "fully throws oneself
flat onto the pavement of the temple on his face," and those when one has
"put his knees to the earth" in the same location. Uniquely in these texts,
Peter says that in this context the prayers, rather than being spoken aloud,
were to be said "in secret and with a low voice of the heart and mouth"
(2121–44). Only when one has done many "genuflections" and, significantly,
only after shedding many tears, could one then stand up and proceed into
the church, assuming mode one, hands over head. Peter prescribes and
writes out a series of other prayers first to God and then to the Virgin for
the various steps on the way (2145–2230).

The long version ends its own prayer book text with a prayer to be said
to the saints of the particular church (2298–2308), but not before it sum-
marizes once more the body behaviors that are effective in pacifying God's
ire and thus getting what one wants. Significantly, this list of comportments includes only one of the prayer modes:

> But those who pray in this way . . . , namely bending their
> knees, beating their breast with their hands, exorting God with sighs,
> irrigating the face of the heart and mouth with tears . . . (2232–34)

will get what they want. Thus while kneeling is mentioned first, that group
of other corporal actions which Peter seems to have associated with reclining positions and seen as their product assumes increasing importance. It
is as if Peter urges supplicants even in the public arena of the church not
to proceed from one step to the next until one has shed many tears.

Peter always describes these various behaviors as taking place in churches, and he recommends them to all Christians because through their performance God sees the faithful's heartfelt dedication. God's eyes, we see,

are the agent through which he is "imprisoned." Yet Peter was by no means oblivious to the eyes of the supplicants' earthly audience. Citing Jesus' statement that he would be ashamed before his father of those who in life had been ashamed of him (841), he leaves no doubt that such public witness is the more precious because people are usually ashamed to perform such actions before other people. He returns to the subject often. We have seen that the Chanter assumed as a general principle that bending and prostrating made one look like a beast, while standing equalized one among humans (2338–43). What Peter the Chanter has to say about the politics of shame offers some solid evidence on the attitudes toward individual postures held by contemporary religious.

Quoting an "insolent and proud blockhead" in all the texts, Peter shows that some contemporaries were ashamed to assume modes 1, 2, and 5: "I am ashamed to pray with my hands extended over my head, or with extended hands, or prostrate on the earth" (838–39). In the long version he adds the kneeling mode 4 as something certain miserable religious "who have become fat, lazy, and removed from the patrimony of the crucifix," disdained to do (607–12). By reminding his fine lay readers that they were reluctant to practice adultery in the presence of lower class people (845–46), the Chanter leaves no doubt that the shame associated with prayer practices comes from being seen in these postures by the earthly audience to the prayers.

Shame obviously had a class component. The opposition of knights to kneeling and especially prostration is today and was even then cited as a cultural characteristic of the medieval West.[48] In a series of uncharacteristic comparisons of prayer postures to postures in civil affairs, Peter confronts such reticence among the clergy. He observes wryly that the same persons who prostrate themselves before a tyrant to avoid punishment refuse that posture in prayer (799–802). In civil affairs people speak clearly before sitting judges so as to capture their benevolence; not so before God (1363–65). Citing Benedict in the long text, the author says that no one presumes to approach powerful men for something without humility and reverence. If clerks did not do so before God, Peter says, "artisans, furriers, farmers, vintners and all other people of whatever profession" when before powerful humans "faithfully, diligently and carefully prepare how they plan to act, so as to achieve" their desires. The vile women weave better than clerks pray (1421–37).

Peter obviously recognized that his clerks were choosing their prayer postures so that they did not express submission. Those monks who refused to kneel on feast days certainly did so at least in part because they did not want to be seen humiliated by the faithful, who usually came to church on those days. Yet the submission modes involved were not just those of the quadripeds. The "humble and reverent postures" to which clerks objected notably included the first two standing postures as well as two reclining ones. Though Peter philosophized that standing made one equal (2340), he did not explore how a standing person performed shameful acts of debasement.

We can. The objection to cruciforming one's arms must have stemmed from the fact that in judicial practice if not theory, crucifixion might still be visited upon the lowest criminals, while to raise one's hands over one's head in public was the sign of surrender. It was a characteristic of medieval life that the humiliations perpetrated upon Jesus were the insults aimed at the most despised criminals.[49]

Peter railed against such supplicants. Of course he condemned those who liked to show off in public and appear saintly, seeking glory from men rather than God (1074–77). Yet one purpose of oral prayer being to show one's humility — to God, presumably, and not to man —, and another being to instruct the people (868–70), a failure to humiliate oneself in public prayer in effect "defrauded" both man and God.

Peter insisted on the need for example to be set — by the best people. In the presence of his followers, Moses had not been ashamed to extend his hands and arms, so Peter's readers should not be reluctant to extend theirs in public (k: 29ra). Had not Peter personally observed a holy man recite the whole psalter in a cruciform posture, even though, he emphasized in the long version, this saintly man "was learned in the science of letters and gifted in the decorum of manners and titled and instituted in the cathedral church, as well as born to nobility, and adorned with natural goods and graces" (487–90)? Indeed, the first, longest, and most powerful justification Peter offers for his sixth mode of prayer is not a biblical documentation, but the fact that professors (those "Frenchmen . . . who have schools of arts and virtues") practiced that mode and even deeper humiliations (725–36) in public.

In the end, the author seems to recognize that his admonitions will fall on deaf ears: many clergy will not perform humiliating acts in public. It is interesting what Peter in all texts does with that conviction (1743–48). Sardonically, he observes that those who plead shame as an excuse for avoiding public humiliation cannot use the same excuse to avoid such humiliating postures in their private prayers. One cannot plead the *scandalum populi* that might result if prayers were repeated in public, and in solitary prayer the excuse is also rendered moot "that he is ashamed to raise his arms above his head or to pray with his arms extended in the form of a cross, or any of the other seven modes" (1746–48).

Thus Peter expects public norms to be transferred to the private sphere. In private one will practice those corporal acts that the community has designated as shameful in public ceremonies. This is not contradictory. It is another evidence of the centrality Peter placed on the importance of public images.

Figuring

> The uncultured come and seize heaven, and we
> with our books descend to hell. — Augustine[50]
> The people should be taught and not followed
> (2072–73).

Peter lived in an age when religious experts might still claim the right to determine correct formal behavior in all spheres of life. Both as writers and as liturgical actors, they were the decorum experts, they still passed as the sole corporate embodiment of comportmental lore.[51] This continuity between written figures and public figures and between author and actors is a key characteristic of Peter's text and its pictures. In the three stages that follow, I want to show that Peter the Chanter viewed his own text as a picture he had painted, and thought of supplicants as painting pictures in their public lives and prayers. I will argue that as a consequence and despite his conventional clerical opposition to picture books, the illustrations Peter introduced into this work were but a natural conclusion to his rich concept of figuration.[52]

The best access to Peter's conception of images or figures is gained through his use of the conventional metaphor comparing the observed forms of daily life to books. In all texts of the second mode of prayer, Peter says that figures, pictures and images were "almost the books of the simple and the lay" (494–97). The long version then elaborates on this statement by saying that the "life of the clerks" is the "book of the common person," wryly adding that it is the clergy's bad actions that the common people read or imitate from this book (497–99). Thus clerics make pictures by acting publicly, and Peter highlights this equation in his *De vitiis* with the phrase "significatio of figures and ceremonies" ("significatio figurarum et caeremonialium"; DVV, 241) as he does here with the words "the decorum of the sacraments" ("ornatus sacramentorum"; 91). Since the "book of the clerks" was obviously the Bible (499), the author clearly assumes a relationship between the biblical "images" of Christ which the illiterates heard about from the performing clergy, the customs they observed in that clergy, and formal drawings. His "book of the common person" is like a repository or museum of such images.

On first reading, it appears that the Chanter believes that illiterates' access to understanding how to pray was fundamentally different from the access of the clergy, because the former only had images, whereas the clergy could read. Apparently catering to the tender feelings of clerical readers whom he thought would resent the illustrations, Peter more than once evoked lay illiteracy in his defense. Using Gregory the Great, he says that pictures and images are the books of the simple or ignorant, that in them those read who cannot, and the ignorant see how they should comport themselves, and so forth (494–95, 520–23). For their part, "idiots" see expressly and openly through figures. Scholars, on the other hand, having exercised their senses ("exercitatos sensus habentes"), easily make mental images of what they read (496–97). Thus pictures were necessary because otherwise the illiterate would not understand.

This justification is suspect because an illiterate wanting to learn or an instructor wanting to teach how to pray from pictures would hardly have used Peter's weighty written tome. Yet Peter has a second and quite different defense of his pictures: humans *in general* need pictures. This is not only because seeing is more pleasing than hearing, as Horace said, but also because Peter's "doctrine" of comportment was more easily and efficaciously shown ("demonstrata") than vocally enunciated (493–94, 687–88: "intellectualis"). In one case Peter went even further, saying that a picture would make what he said *more* understandable *to his readers* (450).

Even when he was not on the defensive with proud clerics, Peter saw the benefits of pictures for the literate clergy. Indeed, I would argue that when Peter called the Bible the book of the clergy, he meant that the latter created mental pictures of its contents. This is the second aspect of the study of Peter's understanding of images. As it pertained to learning comportment, Peter thought of scholars making mental figures of the *Christi actio* (813) or behaviors in the Bible. Thus if the illiterates made mental books of comportmental stances, the literate clergy found similar references by reading texts. Peter seems to have thought that the Bible was the clergy's primary source *for images*. The author had simply visualized all six biblical prayer postures. He had written them down in his own words, and now wanted them reduced to a nutshell, as he said, in the illustrations he ordered (772–73). Mediated by Peter's words, his pictures were to be the final deposit of the mental categories of comportments.

The idea that reducing words to figures could preserve essence should

be explored before embarking on the third aspect of this inquiry, the relation between the author's reduction and the artist's. Peter's ideas on reduction are best grasped in those concentrated texts where he calls for and
justifies his pictures. These texts are present because Peter wanted illustrations, and the same texts could be eliminated without harming the work's
coherence if it were not for the illustrations. Now in these short texts, Peter
leaves no doubt he thought that the words he used to define each mode
of prayer would lose nothing essential by being translated into images. The
image that follows, he says repeatedly, will teach what I have just written;
it will show how to do what has been written above (450–51, 626–27). In
the long text, he cites Gregory to the effect that "idiots" get the same thing
from pictures that literates get from the written word (520–23), that is,
through either medium all end up with equivalent images.[53]

Yet that essence that Peter thought could be preserved in images entailed
more than lines or mere body comportment. Moods and moralities could
also be figured. Thus a picture could teach that supplicants should incline
before any image or cross of Christ or figure of a saint (757–58). A picture
could also teach spiritual duties. By standing erect, says Peter, the supplicant teaches that we have a duty to keep our heart erect; thus the picture
the Chanter wanted of that supplicant would also teach that duty (446–48).
Just as a supplicant in prayer could indicate that he or she has his mind
intent on God, so Peter wanted one of his figures to show that internal
state (690–92). The prostrate supplicant puts his face to the earth because
he fears to raise his eyes to heaven; the figure had to include that human
emotion (688–90). Thus Peter might simply begin: "let there be a figure
representing the gesture of the supplicant." Then he could continue by telling
the artist to "signify" a certain gesture. And then he might explain what
the moral "significance" of that gesture and illustration was (494, 688–89,
690–91). The author used the word "significance" in these texts to indicate
both demonstration and symbolization.

This was a tall order for these artists, and whether any of the illustrations actually achieved such values for their late medieval viewers is, of
course, beyond our ken. What is important is that these concentrated illustrations are supposed to include descriptive, symbolic, and perhaps even
aesthetic qualities similar to those that Peter, like any author, expected from
his own *writing*. The first stage of the examination of Peter the Chanter's
theory of representation found that physical comportment in daily life was
a picture. The second stage determined that this author saw the reading
process as an imaging one and that he viewed himself as creator of a complete set of images. Now we come to the third stage of the examination,

which is Peter's own vision of composing in prose as a process of distillation.

In effect, there is an interesting coincidence between Peter's understanding of his pictures and the characterizations he makes of his own written work. According to him, both are "stripped down" models which include everything essential. Like the *De vitiis*, so the *De penitentia* begins with the words *Verbum abbreviatum* in part to attack sophisticates who have obscured truth (k: 1ra). Peter wants to reduce to essentials. He was an apostle of simplicity — even in this long and complex treatise.

Yet Peter's protestation of his own simplicity is a rhetoric, as is his praise of simplicity in the supplicant, who prays privately not publicly, dresses sparely not richly, etc. This obviously does not indicate that Peter did not mean what he said; many scholars returning to primary sources are motivated to discover simple underlying patterns. On the other hand, such rhetoric is not inconsequential. Viewed functionally, such moods and moralities and the conventional polarities with which intellectual life is still shackled are the very means by which readers and viewers frame, *recognize*, and thus access, discourses. They are also one means by which scholars can discover that a plurality of discussions, in this case talk of pictures and talk of books, are really aspects of one discourse.[54]

Significantly, Peter the Chanter's rhetoric about writing is sprinkled with pictorial terms. The clergy as a whole he characterized as the eyes of society (2063–64); that is presumably why they had "exercised senses" (496). If a supplicant could "depict" sorrow (DVV, 366, 299), so too could writers "paint," "image," "mirror," "color" and "figure" (e.g. 138; k: 14va, 15va). Could one in fact be "true, not typed or figural" ("verus, non typicus sive figurativus"; k: 26vb; pa: 66vb)? Always ready with easy denunciations, for example of those males and females who used cosmetics "to correct the figure God gave us" (k: 15vb; pa: 41rb), Peter could nevertheless bring himself to confess that the writer too had to "color words" to give them significance, seeking only to avoid prolixity on the one side and superfluity on the other.[55]

Bad writers went overboard and "ornamented." In his *De vitiis*, Peter had compared the ornate writer to the goldsmiths and painters who through their meretricious colors and ornamentation seduce others (DVV, 553), and to the thespians who show many faces (DVV, 338). So in the present work he denounces not just the supplicant who shows off (1549–50), but also the pastors or writers who, "like hypocrites and painters" (*more ypocritarum et pictorum*) hold the souls of the simple with sweet words and lengthy benedictions (k: 26vb). Not for nothing then did Peter praise himself in the long version for renouncing the ornate and visually-freighted word "gold" in the titles of his works (k: 8vb–9ra). In my view, Peter's unique call for illustrations in this penitential work was a product of his visual way of comprehending the sources of knowledge and communication.

As an author who defined the *orator* as an artisan, Peter certainly thought of himself as an *auctor artifex* laboring in the vineyards. When then in the *De vitiis* he conflates pictures with ceremonies ("figuris et caeremonialium"; DVV, 241), and in the early part of the *De penitentia* he promises to achieve elegance without ornateness or prolixity (k: 1rab; also 299), or when he polarizes truth and ornament and condemns the "colors and decorum" (*colores atque ornatus*) of words and rhetoric (138), we should recognize not merely a rhetorical technique, but an author's devilishly troubling insight.

This insight—clear, though not stated in so many words—is that form is ornament, in writing as he said it was in woman (k: 30va). Simplicity is possible only through ornament, no matter whether the work is that of the supplicant, the artist, the writer, or indeed the source. As Peter knew from Horace and Ovid, dissimulation was, alas, the handmaiden of art:

'Shunning a fault may lead to error if there be a lack of art' . . . . 'If hidden, art prevails; if detected, it brings shame.'(k: 24vb).[56]

One of the ways that Peter occasionally achieved a *verbum abbreviatum* was, after all, by using figures. We may judge that a work pretending to simplicity that is as long as its biblical source is a contradiction in terms. Peter thought that his illustrations would preserve the essence of his biblical comportments. Alas, as we shall see, there was a rhetoric of showing as well as writing.

Chapter Two

Peter's Pictures

. . . Truth has no edges (DVV, 366).

Peter's remarkable decision to add illustrations to his verbal descriptions of prayer modes has left an important heritage of fifty-eight pictures of seven modes of prayer distributed among eight manuscripts. How should I exploit this unusual resource? Since the Chanter himself definitely intended the pictures to be only translations of his words, it might seem right to begin by seeing how the pictures measure up to the words, especially since the early artists, at least, had to create their pictures in relation to Peter's text. Certainly no artist meant to violate the pedagogic intent the Chanter had for his text and pictures. As we shall see, one illustrator actually redrew a figure that misrepresented Peter's words.

Yet upon reflection, that is not the way to proceed. The right way to begin our exploration is instead to view the corpus of illustrations as distinct from the text. As we shall see, in choosing the forms for representing the modes of prayer, later artists were more often guided by earlier artists than they were by the author. Some artists actually violated Peter's words so as to follow an established artistic procedure. Thus the pictures taken as a whole reveal a continuity of historical development in relation to each other that can seem largely independent of the fixed written text. Especially because the pictures of some manuscripts were done much later than the text copies themselves — as is seen in the chronology given at the beginning of the study —, it will prove quite as legitimate and certainly more economical to ask how late pictures relate to earlier ones as it is to judge how they relate to Peter's words.

What I have in fact described is a tension between the textual and pictorial tradition, even though both share the same pedagogic goal of fostering the correct modes of prayer. I should proceed, then, by studying these pictures as I have Peter's text: as they teach prayer postures. The inquiry will show just how differently texts and pictures teach, and how little the author realized this. *Mutatis mutandis*, I ask the same questions of the pic-

tures as of the texts: what these pictures were meant to legitimate and how
they did it, how the artists meant to attract viewers with their illustrations,
and what scribes and patrons might have found attractive in the resultant
figures. The analysis of these illustrations can best proceed under the
headings of legitimation through words, through past actions, and through
present social reality.

The surest way one can know that pictures legitimate words or utterances
is if the former include references to the latter, and in the present tradition, only one manuscript does so systematically. Each picture in the
Klosterneuburg text, one of only two with significant writing related to
the figures, is accompanied by a scroll, the texts of which are given in this
edition. How do these texts relate to the pictures?

We begin by noting that none of the texts directly describes a corporal
posture. On the other hand, four of the seven texts are fragments of psalms
that do self-referentially indicate the body modes in which the biblical and
figured supplicants prayed and pray. Thus figures 1, 2, 5, and 6 contain
the words "Elevatio Manuum," "Expandi," "Adhesit Pavimento" (not the
descriptive "Adhesio"), and "Incurvatus Sum Usquequaque" from psalms
cited in the previous texts of the respective modes.

The use of the psalms does not end with these figures, however. Figure
3 quotes a psalm ("Deus Propitius Esto"), which is not cited in the text of
that mode. Figure 7 does the same ("Domine Exaude"), but since the mode
itself was non-biblical, these words too were obviously unrelated to it. Thus
six of the modes use words from the psalms, while the remaining figure
4 re-quotes Mark or Luke from Peter's text on that kneeling mode ("Domine,
Si Vis, Potes") without these words referring to a posture.

In all, therefore, only four of the texts mention a body posture; therefore,
describing the postures could not have been the scrolls' primary purpose.
Could the plethora of psalms indicate that the artist intended to legitimate
the postures by calling attention to the historical figure of David as supplicant? Beginning with the fact that neither the Klosterneuburg nor any other
pictures portray any historical person directly, that too will seem improbable
as the analysis continues. What we see in the Klosterneuburg scrolls are
non-individuated yet authentic biblical passages — even for the non-biblical
seventh mode —, which include some psalmodic fragments referring to body
actions.

What then was their purpose? I think the scribe wanted to indicate to
viewers what prayers should be said when they assumed each posture. He
had in mind something close to what Peter the Chanter occasionally indicated he intended: a linkage between particular verbal liturgies and each

of his modes of prayer, both legitimated by the good book.[57] The Klosterneuburg artist and scribe together produced such a linkage.

Nothing in Peter the Chanter's text indicates that he wanted historical figures to be reproduced, and none excepting Jesus was. Not one picture in our corpus shows any historical clothing or customary attributes of the persons whom Peter cited as evidence for his gestures. This is completely different from the storiated sculptures of biblical heroes on the churches of Europe that Peter's contemporaries usually referred to when describing postural training.[58] It also ran counter to time-honored educational theory, called *paideia*, according to which the student sought out and copied successful individuals.[59] Finally, Peter's vision of ahistorical mannequins who, both in the pictures he wanted and in reality, would assume his categorized postures, had little immediate future. As Jean-Claude Schmitt has shown, the next illustrated manual on prayer after that of Peter the Chanter returned precisely to the hero-model, and the Renaissance reinvigorated this traditional paidaic pedagogy.[60]

Clearly, Peter the Chanter's thinking about images was original, and yet comprehensible as a product of a technologically-oriented high medieval culture.[61] But was it not possible that viewers would have read heroic figures and incidents into the pictures? The felicitous survival of contemporary glosses on the pictures of the Prague manuscript provides evidence that some did.

To judge by the writing of its basic text, the Prague manuscript was written in the very late fourteenth or fifteenth century. Further, the hand that glossed the pictures is so similar to this text hand that I believe one scribe wrote both text and glosses. Thus text, pictures and glosses date from the same period.[62] We are then at a two-century remove from Peter the Chanter. The spiritual heroics of individual Mendicants had been part of the European scene almost as long, and now local spiritual heroes like John Hus graced Bohemia. How then did a scribe of the age understand these pictures?

Before he spoke on this matter, the scribe corrected an error of the artist, who had reversed the order of figures 2 (expanded arms) and 3 (hands before the face as if reading), the only such error of transposition in any of the manuscripts. The copyist wrote alongside figure 3 (in the place for figure 2) that "this figure ought to be in place of the expanded hands, and this [place is] for the expanded hands, for the painter has transposed [them]" (variants to 497). Alongside figure 2 (in the place of figure 3) he wrote that "this image ought to be earlier" (variant to 519–20).

Now, the scribe captioned all but the first figure. With the exception of an annotation alongside figure 3, where the author wrote in the title of the following chapter (variant to 692: *Non esse sedere* [sic] *dum oramus*), these captions — all but that for figure 7 lifted from the texts of the preceding modes — clearly aim at describing for readers what the figures represent. In three cases they describe behavior, for example by citing self-referential texts from the psalms, as had Klosterneuburg. Thus the scribe wrote alongside figure 2: "Expandi ad te manus meas," and to figure 6, which shows a supplicant bent before an altar, the scribe added: "Incurvatus sum et humiliatus sum nimis" (variants to 519–20, 763). In one other case, the scribe deserted all biblical legitimation and simply asserted that a mode was right, writing in upside down (!) below figure 5: "Note that the good fall down before the altar," a paraphrase of Bede that the Chanter had included in the previous text (648–49, 692).

But most of the other glosses are different in nature. They describe the representations by stating that particular historical figures had prayed in certain ways. Thus a biblical quotation from the text might authenticate a mode, as on the left of figure 3: "Stetit Finees et cessavit placatio" (variant to 497). Or, as alongside figure 4, the alleged authorial words could be reused to the same end: "Jacob the brother of the Lord prayed thus" (variant to 627; a mistake, as we will see). So determined was the scribe to find individual precedents that a biblical figure was even cited for the non-biblical mode seven. Alongside that figure, one reads: "Mary [Miriam] the sister of Moses prayed thus" (variant to 772), whereas Peter had cited Pope Gregory's *exemplum* of his paternal aunt Tarsilla.

Since Peter the Chanter had emphasized the commonality of each mode to several historical persons, it is impressive how often the Prague scribe drew attention to the behavior of particular historical heroes as that which legitimized the modes. He legitimated in this way quite as often, in fact, as in the Klosterneuburg fashion he cited particular utterances from the Bible to the same legitimizing end. Yet we cannot assess the extent to which viewers of other manuscripts may have seen particular past heroes in these abstract figures, since they do not gloss their figures. And no figure in any manuscript, I repeat, carries any historical baggage.

Having reviewed the available scrolls and marginalia, we are therefore thrust back upon the pictures proper for information on legitimation. In them, we shall find that contemporary reality was a strong legitimizer. Peter the Chanter said more than once in his treatise that his modes of prayer were for every age, sex, and condition, and a measure of his seriousness on this score is that he referred only to the experience of the converted prostitute Mary Magdalene to prove the dignity of prayer (428–33). At times Peter seemed completely indifferent to social indicators, and his instructions for the pictures give no hint that he considered such vital statistics relevant in drawing any particular mode. The artists, on the other hand, did think they were relevant. We can assess the emphases they placed on them by studying the sex, age, and status of the drawn supplicants.

Peter the Chanter overwhelmingly cited male actions to legitimate his modes of prayer, and this was to be expected given his biblical source. Yet there is one interesting exception to this rule which allows us to gauge the attention artists paid to the particular historical instances Peter adduced in his proofs of the prayer modes. The author documented his seventh, non-biblical mode of prayer by referring only to a posture of Gregory the Great's aunt. How often then did the artists show women praying in the whole corpus of illustrations, and how often did they show women in this last mode?

The overwhelming majority of our figures are male, of course: when it came to actually showing figures, the artists did not indifferently represent both sexes. With the possible but improbable exception of Zwettl's figure 4, no woman is represented in any but the seventh mode even though Peter the Chanter did elsewhere cite female supplicants among his authorities (662–63, 856–58). But what happened with the seventh mode, where a woman was the sole authority Peter cited, is significant. Only four of the eight figures in this humiliating stance are women. Still more interesting, the choice of sex is not genealogically predictable. Thus while the ancestral Zwettl text has a figure of a woman, the descendant Klosterneuburg stuck with the young man it had represented in all previous figures. To judge from its figure's hair rather than from its uniquely long gown, the Altzella manuscript stayed with a male child, but the genealogically closely related Pegau manuscript does show a woman. To the south the Venetian manuscript showed a woman, but its Paduan counterpart remained with the young man of all its previous illustrations. Ottobeuren too remained with the monk its artist had finally adopted for that text's pictures.

Now it is possible that in the four cases where the artists showed a woman in the drawing of the seventh mode, some contemporaries may have associated them to female biblical figures despite the absence of historical trappings. The Prague manuscript, we recall, did make such an association. But the fact that four men were painted shows how weak were these historical associations. Thus the artists who painted women probably did not intend to show Gregory the Great's aunt. At most, they were indicating that women should pray in this humble fashion. The distribution hints that the vital statistics of the living were what mattered.

It may be useful to summarize the manuscripts according to the ages of those represented. Male children are clearly shown in Altzella and perhaps in the Prague drawings. The presence of children is hardly surprising because the pedagogic nature of this book of prayer made it particularly suitable for monastic schools and, at least hypothetically, useful for teaching the lay and oblate children in them. What is surprising is how few children are shown. The two non-monkish Ottobeuren figures are youths, not children. Young men dominate five other texts: Padua, Zwettl, and Klosterneuburg show them beardless; Pegau puts short beards on two (4, 6) of its youths, while Venice places such signs of youth on four of its figures (1, 2, 3, 5). Grave men of mature age are completely absent. No matter who was to be the audience, these artists did not intend to sway readers with pictures of seniors.

If it is striking that a majority of our artists chose to represent that generation which, in the view of contemporaries, had the least admirable religious habits,[63] a much greater surprise awaits us when we turn to the status of those represented. According to the author of this work, the clerks *were* the *oratores*, the religious specialists. Yet among the eight manuscripts, only Ottobeuren taught with clerical figures!

It would be unwarranted to jump to the conclusion that the artists and patrons of these manuscripts agreed with Peter the Chanter that the clergy of their time did not serve as a good model for prayer. Contrary to the stereotype of the Middle Ages, contemporaries possessed sophisticated pedagogical theories that at times emphasized the role of peers in teaching correct comportment. If that type of teacher was represented, the absence of clergy would be less significant than might at first appear. Yet let us also be clear that this lacuna extends far beyond the absence of priests and monks. Not one manuscript besides Ottobeuren shows *any* tonsured person!

We recall that Peter had included among the *oratores* not only the religious specialists, but all those who had clerical status. Tonsuring was the mark of that status, and it was bestowed even on monastic oblates at an early age.[64] Thus the absence of tonsured figures in manuscripts mostly associated with monasteries forces us to look elsewhere for clues to the type of youth or child shown. The figures' clothing provides an indication. Peter said only that prayer clothes should be simple (480–81, 1861–62, pa: 24ra, k: 8vb–9ra). The artists were more specific.

The best guess as to the type shown is that some of the manuscripts with uniform clothing characteristics — especially Klosterneuburg and Prague, where the supplicants' gowns almost all reach to the figures' feet, and Altzella, where all the pictures save figure 7 show young boys with gowns ending above their knees — were monastic manuscripts whose artists showed age cohorts of children and youths who were in monasteries for school but not for life, and were therefore not tonsured. The decisive change from boys to monks that we will study in the Ottobeuren pictures becomes understandable from this point of view: the pictures switched from laity to clergy as well as from young figures to older ones.

Along with the absence of clerical status in all but one set of illustrations, the possible presence of confraternal status should also be noted. Again, uniform clothing enables us to hypothesize the presence of such groups.[65] Since the earliest known owners of the Venetian manuscript were members of a confraternity, and of the Paduan text a Franciscan convent, the fact that the figures in these manuscripts have uniform clothing of a distinctly secular cast may have institutional significance. The sometimes-bearded Venetian males wear similar belted gowns that, along with the lip of the belts, end at or above the knees except in figure 4 where the gown falls below the knees. Though figures 1 and 2 of the Paduan text are similar to the Venetian figures, all the remaining ones, done by a different ilustrator, represent a young man whose hemline lies well above the knees, in the mode of youthful dress of the later Trecento and Quattrocento. This was certainly a young man (*iuvenis*) whom one would scarcely associate with the prayerful postures shown in the pictures, but his standardized representation just might indicate a member of a Paduan confraternity or youth group.

Uniform clothing is not a feature of the Zwettl pictures, yet they too give some suggestion of being confraternal representations. Because four of the figures appear to have the letter S on their sleeves, sleeves that remind one of those on the Venetian confraters, the association of the text with some type of early lay penitents cannnot be excluded.

Variety and not uniformity is the keynote in the fine drawings from Pegau. Rather than either clerical or confraternal sameness, these pictures, each set against a lush painted background, all call forth images of courtly life. Among these bearded and beardless figures, gowns of red, white, and brown are encountered (1, 2, 6; 3; 4, 5); they reach to the ankles as well as to just below the knees (2, 6), and are both belted (4, 5) and unbelted. It is even possible that among these male figures, those of modes 2, 3, 4 and 7 are wearing not only hairpins but earrings! What has happened to the abstract penitential supplicants of Peter the Chanter? The exquisite young woman who illustrates mode 7 in this text is no accident. All the figures of this manuscript seduce.

For a reassessment, let me begin again with the ideas of Peter the Chanter about the teaching of prayer. Though he like most male intellectuals of the time conventionally scorned the female sex, Peter had cited women as model supplicants. The pictures, on the other hand, showed very few. He had said nothing about the right age of the ideal supplicant, though most of the examples he gave were of older men. The pictures, however, insisted upon often stylishly bearded young men, a generation associated in the thinking of the time with war and sexuality, not prayer. Peter singled out the clergy as the praying status, yet only one manuscript used clergy to show correct prayer postures. In his work the Chanter showed a conventional respect for station, but having insisted that supplicants dress vilely if not sordidly in prayer (255; pa: 24va; k: 6va, 8vb), he left it at that: he never ordained specific clothing for the figures themselves. The pictures, however, pay great attention to clothing, whether it be that of the monks of Ottobeuren, the confraters of Venice, or the courtiers of Pegau. Peter had distilled seven modes of prayer from a wealth of historical experience for the use of an eternal, ahistorical, asocial, Christian mannequin, and not once did he call for an illustration that took account of status, class, age, or sex. The artists drew social life and reality back in.

I am indicating less a contradiction between writer and the artists than something else. First, I perceive a difference between the media of writing and painting which allows the former but not the latter convincingly to insist ornately on simplicity. Secondly, the writer but not the artist has the ability to attract an audience by denouncing props or contexts.

The patrons of the manuscripts and their artists had to take account of age, sex, and status in a way an author did not. Naked figures were clearly out of the question, so threads of some status had to clothe their figures.[66] Yet that was least problematic. Would a reader or viewer emulate recommended stances if women or peasants portrayed them? Social biases inevitably influenced the form the figures took if the manuscript was to satisfy patrons and other viewers, and if it was successfully to instruct. Decorum and pedagogy were inextricably linked. The author's words might lay claim to subvert such social considerations; his images could not. If they were to be acceptable or emulable, the pictures first had to show the right kind of people.

Furthermore, these supplicants had to be right for specific audiences. If only general social values had dictated the choice of figures, clearly more monks and elders and fewer youths would have been represented. The meager information available about the viewers, not to mention the readers of these manuscripts, reduces us to mere speculation on who they might have been. But if the artists avoided representations of women except in figure 7, they probably did so because corporations of women were not their audience. The male confraternal aura of two or three of the manuscripts may indicate their figures were drawn for such groups. The *oratores* may be represented so poorly because monks were not the ones in monasteries who needed to learn to pray. Yet among the laity so richly represented in our figures, it was the youth and not the children who predominated. Since the idea that children were best taught by youth was part of established contemporary pedagogy,[67] I would suggest that youths are often figured in part because they were thought the best teachers of children. Age superiority was important within limits.

Thus the idea that certain social groups would attract specific audiences certainly played a role in the artists' or their patrons' choices. This is not to ignore the evidence that other principles of attraction or seduction were also at work in many of these pictures. To the end of attracting viewers, some artists followed certain stylistic principles and made certain cultural choices that had impact on the tone of their illustrations and affected at least this viewer much more immediately than the statistics of age, sex, class and status.

The merest glance at the Paduan rake with the fancy hairdo and low hemline, at the beauteous young men of Pegau competing so successfully with the same cycle's blonde femme fatale, at the pompadured tart of Klosterneuburg, and even at the dandy monks of Ottobeuren, shows what I mean. Preachers of this age indeed did look out from their pulpits on just such showy figures, and certainly with words full of ornate figures, Peter the Chanter himself would have condemned them from his pulpit. Yet perhaps to bring the faithful to prayer, just such flashy figures were necessary in church, and in these pictures.

Could the author's wishes have been fulfilled, and the pictures at the same time been rendered attractively? The answer is obviously first contingent upon the technical ability of the artists, which in some cases was clearly limited. Take the prostrate mode 5, where the author called for the supplicant to be lying flat on the ground, his face kissing the earth. In fact, instead of drawing original figures, several artists simply repeated previous standing representations, here merely putting them on their sides. Padua and Venice did their figure 5 from their figure 3, though the latter artist reversed the directions of his two figures. Altzella, whose figure 3 is missing from the corpus, made figure 5 much like its figure 1. The results are most awkward. Also in the Zwettl, Pegau, and Prague drawings of the prostration mode 5, the viewer is beneath the supplicants, whose arms are unrealistically folded beneath them though they lie on the ground. Seen from beneath, the Klosterneuburg figure, vaguely modelled on its mode 2, in a prostrate position condemned by Humbert of Romans,[68] seems almost to be flying overhead.

The representations of this mode suggest that at least some artists might have had trouble drawing a prostration mode independently; a limited formal vocabulary could have affected their ability to show Peter's supplicant realistically. Yet is this so? There is equal evidence that these copies of standing figures were merely shortcuts. Certainly I shall argue later that the Ottobeuren artist redrew mode 1 so as to distinguish it from mode 3 when he discovered that distinction in Peter's text. But the Zwettl and Pegau artists, on the other hand, were satisfied to leave postures 2 and 3 almost indistinguishable, though the author had drawn attention to the difference between them. Again: copying the awkward and unrealistic rectangular body of Zwettl's mode 6, as did all the seven-book texts save Klosterneuburg, was apparently easier than an original effort. Thus though some of the artists' technical abilities were admittedly narrow, I have the impression they generally sufficed to adequately represent the postures mandated by the author.

A second approach to the problem of the artists attractively fulfilling the author's wishes lies in the area of style. We have seen that Peter the Chanter prescribed postures rather than mobile gestures. This emphasis on immobility meant, in turn, that the less tension the figures revealed in their poses, the closer they would be to the author's intentions. Yet we recall as well that the author also wished to transmit various emotions and moralities in the images. An examination of the pictures suggests that to achieve such emotions, the artists violated Peter's wish and mobilized their figures. They used what may loosely be called romanesque and gothic drawing styles to do so.

In the interest of attracting the viewer, some artists tried in different ways to move us by moving their figures' *clothes*. Not particularly avant-garde from a stylistic point of view, the Ottobeuren monks seem to writhe, thanks to the swirls of their Sunday-best religious habits; no less than that manuscript's two charmed boys, these religious specialists have a sinewy sensuousness of motion worthy of Federigo Fellini's processional scene in the film *Roma*. Pegau's glistening young men and woman also show the power of clothes to move figures, fairly tempting us into their opulent settings despite the traditional nature of the drawing. Within limits, one might argue that in the moment such "romanesque" draftsmen took pen or brush to paper or vellum, Peter's exhortation was lost. His instructions, we recall, dealt with the postures of bodies without clothes. These pictures on the other hand conceal those bodies — and their lazy leanings — beneath opaque surfaces of cloth.

In drawings with hints of contraposto, on the other hand, the supplicant's corporal mobility is part and parcel of the essence of the style, inherently moving the supplicant from posture to gesture no matter what the simplicity of his transparent clothing. The fine young man of the Klosterneuburg figures especially seduces by his contraposto. His simple gown, far from convincing us of laical piety, merely emphasizes the dancing figure. Again within limits, it can be argued that this "gothic" style inherently penetrates clothing to reveal Peter's body — in motion.

In their different ways, therefore, different styles violated the decorous calm that the author recommended. Yet perhaps it was precisely a sense of movement which would attract a viewer and involve him in the figured supplicant's action. Perhaps the medieval moralists were right in arguing that the more realistic the figured body, the more seductive *and* the less pious.[69] The more technically at ease the artist in handling his bodies, the less they represented Peter the Chanter's static and thus graceless pious persons.

In the end, however, questions of technical limitations and artistic styles are less significant to my interpretation of these illustrations than are the social mores that restricted the representations. Most of the figures move in recognizable social frames. A renewed glance at the figures of mode 5, the mode of prostration, drives this point home. Not one of the eight representations of this mode shows the face of the supplicant turned toward and kissing the ground, as the author had explicitly required (688–90). There are other cases where individual draftsmen violated the author's wishes because of contextual or aesthetic demands, but here all the manuscripts avoid his instructions. The fact that these faces are not turned toward the earth can hardly be explained by these draftsmen's technical limitations.

How then? My previous exposition has laid a groundwork for an answer. The face was an especially critical facet of honor, and in these figures even monks saved face: the Ottobeuren monk reaches his arms and hands out to hug the ground, but the artist turns the face of that monk toward us.[70] The Chanter had specifically condemned those professional supplicants who would not assume certain prayer postures because of the same shame laymen felt. Noting that many people felt shame when they grovelled on the ground, a shame he condemned, Peter said that the shame one felt in public would be no excuse in private for not praying with the face to the ground as his picture would show (1746–48).

Yet how would one learn private postures if public instruction was not offered by attractive persons? An apostle of elegant simplicity, our author no less than his contemporaries understood the topos of the penitential king wearing sackcloth in public (1861–62). One had to believe a supplicant or an author was respectable before his rags became exemplary.

Thus since these pictures do not show heroic persons but, rather, universal types, they had to be animated. High social status—here of the monk, there of the liberal youth or beauteous woman—overcomes technical limits and styles and draws us to pray. For what faceless human could instruct others? And uninstructed, how could supplicants reach God? Perhaps almost by definition, images, public once they are seen, must look out at us. They must seduce us by power, class, or sex before we will follow them.

THE MANUSCRIPTS

Chapter Three

De penitentia et partibus eius

The first part of this study analyzed the work on prayer. The task now is to justify my attribution of the work to Peter the Chanter and, through a study of the manuscripts, to create the basis for sound judgments about the development of the manuscript tradition and thus the attribution of particular words and ideas to this writer. The second part begins with a study of the work as a whole, and that requires a more generalized approach than the more detailed study of the *De oratione* that comes in chapter four. The task of determining the authorship of particular passages begins, therefore, with external problems raised by the provenance of the manuscripts and continues with the titles and then the incipits of the different parts of the work. Only then can we turn to prose proper.

Provenance

The central problem raised by the provenance of these nine manuscripts, none of which has autographic traits, is clear from a glance at the map: no manuscripts of this work have been found in France, and none of the nine known copies of the *De penitentia* is of unquestionable French origin. Certainly this fact must be kept in perspective. Despite Peter's great reputation, the long version of the *Verbum abbreviatum* — that is, the work I will show that Peter called *De vitiis et virtutibus* — is preserved in only three complete texts, one of which, though of French origin, is now in Rome. In the case of the *De penitentia*, however, not three but nine manuscripts have survived, seven manuscripts along the eastern and southern borders of the Empire and two in the Veneto. The peculiarity of these locations is heightened when we compare them to the well-known short version of the *De vitiis* as studied by Baldwin: of 41 known texts of the latter, only one copy is found to the east of France, in the Vatican Library. With few exceptions,

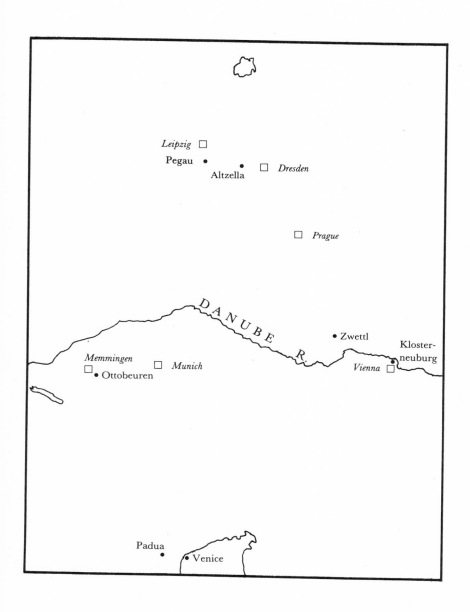

one can say that the *De vitiis* is found in France and England, the *De penitentia* only to their east and south.[71]

Is it possible, however, that the provenance of one or the other of the codices is different from its present location? Let me examine the sparse information on origins, consigning general bibliographical information on the codices to the introduction of the edition. The Zwettl codex (= "z") was definitely assembled after 1190 and probably after 1203.[72] The Ottobeuren copy now in the British Library (= "o"), which is an immediate source of the much later manuscript kept in Munich (= "m"), is contained in a codex that preserves the only hard chronological information in any of our nine copies: it was written for the monastery between 1227 and 1246, during the time that the abbot Bertold headed this famous Benedictine house.[73] One of the two manuscripts preserved in Leipzig (University Library 433) has ownership information: probably in the fourteenth century, a librarian wrote across three facing folios (ff. 1v–2r; lii v–liii r; ciiii v–cv r): "Liber Veteris Celle Sancte Marie," thus identifying the Cistercian monastery of Altzella (= "a"), as it was known after 1250, in the town of Nossen near Dresden. In a personal communication to me, Susan M. Dupont, a specialist in Altzella manuscripts, thinks that Altzella procured the copy rather than producing it itself. On the other hand, based on an analysis of initials she believes that a second Leipzig University manuscript (n. 432) was produced by a local scriptorium, that of the Benedictine monastery of Pegau (= "pe") near Leipzig.[74] This idea withstands the art historian Bruck's unsubstantiated opinion that the manuscript is French, for the Leipzig cataloguer Helssig had already observed that the manuscript contains a crook-cross of the type found on Pegau's abbatial coins.[75] I found no further contemporary information on the date or early locations of the manuscripts from the Empire.

At first, information seems even more sparse for the Veneto manuscripts, both obviously written at an early date. The Venetian antiquary Cicogna did assert that the text in the State Archive of that city (= "v") was "della ... scrittura della scuola [confraternity] di Santa Maria della Misericordia," but he gave no reason for his statement.[76] The cataloguers of the copy of the *De penitentia* owned by the Franciscans of Padua, the only one preserved by or known ever to have been associated with the Mendicants (= "pa"), hazarded no guesses as to provenance. Abate and Luisetto did however describe an unusual characteristic of the codex containing our work.[77] Just before the beginning of the *De penitentia* are four pages (two folios) of text placed there to protect the *De penitentia*, three written in double columns and one in a single column. They contain a history of near eastern affairs written in old *French*. Our manuscript tradition is, therefore, not completely free of French associations.

The sheets of French text turn out to be two separate, but internally continuous, segments of William of Tyre's (d. 1186–90) History of *Outremer* describing events of the year 1182. The latter sheet contains the end of chapter 15 and part of chapter 16 from book 22, the former the end of chapter 22 through part of chapter 24 of the same book.[78] French texts of William's *History* existed at the end of the twelfth or by the beginning of the thirteenth century, the time of Peter the Chanter's death.[79] Unless indeed it was actually written in northern Italy, two plausible routes exist by which such a text could have arrived in Padua. It could have come by sea from the Near East to Venice and thence to nearby Padua; indeed, according to Mayer, the Venetians had their Tyrian headquarters in the archepiscopal palace of that city.[80] Since French was the *lingua franca* of the crusades, perhaps this is the most probable route. But it could also have come from some part of present-day France, whose inhabitants' lust for romantic details about *Outremer* had insured the success of the French narrative and now explains the large number of manuscripts that still survive. It is not hard to imagine that the cosmopolitan order of the Franciscans, which owns the sheets today, was also the original agent for their transmission to the Veneto.

But the question is: when were these French sheets placed in the Latin codex? In my view: early. Written in a different but perhaps equally ancient hand as the *De penitentia*, these fragments of William of Tyre *are* significant to the early history of the Paduan *De penitentia*. The key lies in an early table of contents of Peter's work done with arabic numerals on one of these loose sheets.

Yet before examining this table of contents, let it be noted that it was not the first reference system used in the Paduan manuscript. In all probability before the *folios* were numbered (arabically), certain *paragraphs* in the work already bore sequential roman numerals, ones that readers were in fact using for cross-referencing.[81] They had been put in place by a scribe likely working from a complete roman numeral list of the paragraphs that may no longer exist. Thus the Paduan *De penitentia* was in use for some time before it was paginated or provided with a table of contents.

The Paduan pagination is, I think, an early example of the practice of numbering with arabic numerals. The table of contents with the same digits soon followed. Once the scribe had written such numbers onto the corners of the folios, he or a contemporary prepared a list of the titles of the first part of the work based on the early folio numeration (ff. 1r–24v). This table of contents was written on the page opposite the first page of the *De peniten-*

tia, that is, in the left margin and at the bottom of the last, single-columned side of the French text of William of Tyre.[82]

Certainly the modern cataloguers exaggerated in postulating a possible twelfth-century date for the Paduan codex as a whole.[83] My estimate is that the Paduan *De penitentia* itself was written about 1220. Yet I think it immediately came to bear the roman numerals used for cross-referencing and, not much later than 1250, was outfitted with the arabic characters on its folios and the partial table of contents written on the fragment of William of Tyre.

Thus even if the different elements of the codex were not written and bound together in some part of present-day France, as is possible, the French association of this *De penitentia* was established by mid-thirteenth century, when the table of contents to a Latin work was written alongside a French text. While the Latin tractate of the French scholar Peter the Chanter may not be found in his native country today, it is associated with a French historical text in a codex preserved for centuries in a Franciscan friary in Padua. The absence of a copy of the *De penitentia* in France no longer compels one to doubt, as did Baldwin, that the tractate was actually written by Peter the Chanter.[84]

The absence of this text in France can be explained in another way. What if Peter wrote the *De penitentia* abroad and died before the work could be established in France? There is some reason for such speculation, since we shall see that the work was composed after the *De vitiis et virtutibus* and thus about the time Peter travelled to Rome, shortly before his death. He could have written the *De penitentia* during that trip, leaving texts behind as he went. The evidence that Peter had associations with the Empire, where so many of the manuscripts are located, is admittedly tenuous. Did Peter stop at Prüm near Trier on his way to Italy in late 1196 or early 1197? That might explain why the prelates of that church requested his appointment as executor of a decision in Prüm's favor that had earlier been reached by judges in Cologne. Pope Celestine III acceded to the wish while the Chanter was in the Eternal City.[85] But it is not known whether he visited the Veneto, whence come two of the manuscripts, during this Italian trip.

The only support within the text for this speculation that Peter wrote or deposited his *De penitentia* in the Empire or in Italy is just as tenuous. A passage in the *De penitentia* that describes a French prayer style sounds like a Parisian *en provence*, bringing the latest fashions to the hustings:

Galli vero, apud quos viget religio, ubi floret studium, qui habent scolas artium et virtutum, quorum fides adhuc fervet aliquantulum, quoniam refrigescit caritas multorum, illi autem viri dei et timorati non solum flectunt caput et renes, immo, remotis capuceis et pilleis omnibus a capitibus, prosternunt se et cadunt in faciem suam in confectione et perceptione carnis et sanguinis Christi, taliter secum orantes: 'Confectio . . . .' [725-30][86]

Clearly, the slimness of this evidence seeking to place Peter abroad makes the question of the authorship of the present work the more problematic. This is especially the case because not only Baldwin but Artur Landgraf, who examined the two Leipzig manuscripts, came to the conclusion that apart from the sections copied from Peter's earlier "Verbum abbreviatum," the work was not written by the Chanter.[87] However, by examining the titles and then the texts of all the manuscripts, I can demonstrate that Peter did indeed author a work called *De penitentia*.

The Titles

The work bears two distinct titles in medieval script, of which *De penitentia et partibus eius* is the more common. It occurs in similar forms in several manuscripts. Thus Zwettl and Klosterneuburg have identical beginnings: "Incipit primus liber operis cantoris Pariensis ["pariēsis"] magistri Remensis de penitentia et partibus eius. Verbum abbreviatum fecit deus super terram. . . ." The Prague text generally follows, but omits the word "primus" and uses an "s" to spell Paris conventionally. The Veneto texts are similar. Both lack the phrase "magistri Remensis"; the Venetian text omits the word Paris; Padua, using Zwettl's and Klosterneuburg's spelling "Pariensis," inverts two word couplets, reading "liber primus" and "eius partibus."[88]

The two manuscripts that do not have the title *De penitentia et partibus eius* are two whose introductory words do not follow the above format. Ottobeuren and Munich begin identically: "Incipit liber magistri Petri cantoris parisiensis qui dicitur Viaticum tendentis Ierusalem"; the Ottobeuren text also calls the work "viaticum liber" in its explicit, that is, a guide book on doing penance.[89] The beginning of this format is, in turn, identical to that in the Altzella text, but the latter stops after the word "Parisiensis" and thus does not name the work. The other Leipzig manuscript has no introductory words at all.

Authorship

Let me move now from the title to the author, beginning with some characteristics limited to certain manuscripts. Zwettl, Klosterneuburg, and Prague are the only manuscripts to identify Peter in their incipits as a *magister Remensis*. For its part, Padua's incipit is like those of Zwettl and Klosterneuburg: it identifies the author as of "Pariensis," a spelling the latter two texts repeat in their explicits.

Otherwise, however, the texts correctly identify the author as the chanter of Paris, usually in their incipits but sometimes in the explicits as well. All but the Munich and Paduan explicits attribute the work to the chanter of Paris (Zwettl and Klosterneuburg: "Pariensis"), Ottobeuren repeating the name "Peter" which all but the Venetian and Paduan texts had given in their incipit as well. The Venetian incipit is singular. It introduces the opus on penance as written simply by "the chanter" ("Incipit primus liber cantoris de Penitentia . . ."), in the explicit more formally identifying him as the chanter of Paris. As Baldwin has noted, the practice of identifying Peter simply as "the Chanter" was not unknown.[90] It seems that there was only one famous chanter when this manuscript was written, so that only the familiar appellation "cantor" was necessary to introduce his work. This is a strong argument for an early date for the Venetian text.

Four of the manuscripts identify the author at a third point, in the middle of the work. In the Zwettl and Klosterneuburg texts, the book on prayer I edit here begins: "Incipit quintus liber cantoris Pariensis de oratione et speciebus illius. Confortame. . . ." Prague, and the Pegau text of Leipzig, have the same re-introduction of the author but spell Paris conventionally. Such a re-identification of an author in the midst of a tractate is not customary, and argues for a relation between these texts, especially between those of Zwettl and Klosterneuburg. It raises the possibility that the text that follows was once a separate entity, a possibility to be pursued at a later point. But of importance at this point, this intervening naming of the chanter of Paris reinforces the incipits' and explicits' insistence that Peter the Chanter was the work's author and specifically the author of this prayer book, most of the contents of which are not found in Peter's other works.

Yet these skeletal identifications could easily have been added by copyists or compilers. It is in the text proper, really, that authorship can best be determined, and there in fact that Peter's authorship becomes certain. For in all nine manuscripts of this *De penitentia* the author thrice refers to the earlier and well-known *De vitiis et virtutibus*. Thus in the last book or tractate of the work (pa: 73va; k: 29ra) under the rubric of the enemies of man, the author explains that he will abbreviate his exposition of the vices of pride and envy because they have been dealt with extensively elsewhere:

> Tertius hostis tuus est Lucifer, a quo persequeris superbia et invidia, de quibus vitiis est dictum et difusius, pleniusque in opere quod inscribitur de vitiis et virtutibus. Et etiam ideo hec sunt omittenda in presentiarum, ut aufertur illis occasio murmurandi, qui sunt ad resistendum potius quam ad obediendum preparati et pronti, querentes nodum in scirpo, incrustantes vas sincerum et infundentes luci tenebras.

This discussion is indeed found in two long chapters of the short "Verbum abbreviatum" (Migne, 205, 44–54). Since, therefore, little doubt exists that Peter is referring to the latter, I have abbreviated this edition and work as "DVV."

Again in the middle of the *De penitentia*, shortly before the book on prayer which I edit here (pa: 40vb; k: 15va), the author while commending alms backs up an assertion by referring to the earlier work (DVV, 273, 286):

> Item caritas, elemosina, misericordia sunt quasi nomina sinonima, hoc est idem significantia, de quibus tractatum est plenius in libro qui inscribitur de vitiis et virtutibus.[91]

But it is the author's first reference to his earlier work (cf. DVV, 250–55) which is most important, for it goes beyond revealing its intended title. This reference characterizes his goal in the present work and, in a translucently authorial fashion, distinguishes its quality from the works of an unnamed adversary or adversaries. I cite the text in the consecutive rubrics *Contra vestem pretiosam* and *De sacre scripture utilitate*, which is found in all nine manuscripts early in the work (pa: 24va; k: 8vb–9ra):

> Quare autem fideles et salvandi tenentur iacere vestiti et precinti, lumbos atque calciati pedes et crura, vel quo habitu debeant uti viri dei . . . , hec omnia dicta sunt supraplenarie in alio nostro opere quod preintitulatur de vitiis et virtutibus, ubi sunt ponita et exponita multa ad bonos mores pertinentia et plurima ad veram salutem necessaria. Est autem totum pondus nostre intentionis et omnis affectus nostri sermonis inducendi lectorem ad expetendam eternam beatitudinem in cunctis scripturis nostris. Quelibet sane scriptura que non tendit ad hoc, ut extirpet vitia et inserat virtutes, potius est scientia vanitatis et curiositatis quam . . . pietatis atque sanctitatis. . . . Scire namque te volumus, karissime, quod scriptura sive opuscula nostra carent titulo

lucrativo auri vel argenti quemadmodum immensa volumina sacre
pagine et universi codices theologie. Non enim est pure divinus liber,
neque est tantum scientia dei, in qua agitur de divitiis et de pecunie
inventione. Unde liquet illum esse falsum theologum, et constat eum
non esse verum Christi imitatorem, qui laborat ut ditetur, et qui est
cupidus et avarus. Fuit autem caput nostrum, scilicet Christus, doc-
tor paupertatis, magister humilitatis, exemplum patientie, amator
castitatis et honestatis. Non est autem ille predicator seu preco Christi
verus qui pecuniam cumulat et eius questum docet, immo verius
pseudopropheta et nuntius Antichristi. Contra cupiditatem ait
Augustinus. . . .

I have little idea who the prophet of the Antichrist was whom Peter condemned because he titled his works with the descriptive term "golden" or
"silver."[92] What is certain is that the Chanter thinks the titles of his own
works characterize his intellectual efforts. Both the present work on penance,
and the earlier one on the vices and virtues, aim, he says, at extirpating
vices and replacing them with virtues. The author claims that he is the real
imitator of Christ because, like certain theological codices and the Bible
but unlike the works of his adversary, his works have avoided "golden titles."

These seem to be the words of a man justifying a lifetime of intellectual
effort during a pause in a late work, one he hoped to finish, he says at
different points (985, 1702), God willing.[93] Certainly he attained his goal.
Claiming as his own a *De vitiis et virtutibus* that we know to have been authored
by Peter the Chanter, this author refers to it, *if not in the prayer book proper*,
then at three other points near the beginning, in the middle, and toward
the end of this *De penitentia*.

Peter the Chanter is the author, if not necessarily the definitive compiler, of this work. Although Artur Landgraf's other findings are not without
value, his denial of Peter's authorship collapses if only because he remained
unaware of Peter's three references to his earlier *De vitiis et virtutibus*.[94] A
scribe who was probably the copyist of the Venetian manuscript did notice.
In the margin alongside this longest authorial reference to the earlier work,
he wrote: "Auctor scripsit feceritque librum de vitiis et virtutibus."

The Work as Characterized by the Author

The authorial self-reflections and advertisements quoted above are found
in all of the manuscripts, so there is no reason to doubt that the polemical,
self-confident personality they betray is a product of Peter's own words.

It is important to keep this in mind as we now review some even more confident self-references that are found in a majority but not all of the manuscripts. I move from the question of authorship to that of the author's understanding of his work. In the three northern (Altzella, Pegau, and Prague) and two eastern or Austrian manuscripts (Zwettl and Klosterneuburg), in a block of text just before the illustrated prayer book, the author sums up what has been said and what remains to be said. In this bridge segment, Peter the Chanter is made to utter a series of self-commendations which merit close attention. The present text edition begins with these commendations (1–264).

Embrace "our little work," the author instructs his "diligent reader," for it contains a just, holy, and pious rule of life with admonitions for people of every age, sex and social condition. The wise will be exercised by its solid food, whereas the Bible, the author implies, might leave them intellectually unsatisfied; the simple will be instructed by its drink, where the simplicity of the Bible could mislead them (49–56). His own work, Peter brags, is a paradise of all delights, a drugstore of the Holy Spirit where are found the fruits of the whole Bible (7–8). The fundamental purpose of his work of theology is to drive out vice and stimulate virtue, and Peter places rubrics between his self-advertisements to suggest through metaphor that just as his previous sections on penance can bring people back from spiritual death, so the materials on verbal and real prayer (called here "hours") that are yet to come can lead to their resurrection if these people will only "enter the church" (229, 245).

"Do not ever let this book fall from your hand," Peter admonishes his reader (47–48), for it is sufficient in itself. Earlier in the work, he had justified his use of the *bene dicta* of the ancients, and later he defends the liberal arts curricula against obscurantists.[95] But here, clearly addressing the work of his contemporary Parisian competitors, Peter has other ideas. He is ready to recognize that rhetoric and dialectic, astronomy, geometry, music and arithmetic are subtle, but, thinking that these subjects are of little use for moral ends, he encourages his reader to reject them (216–26). The obscurantism is quite impressive in the texts of these five manuscripts. Yet in the last sentence of the rubric "On the Effect of What has been Said and What Remains to be Said," the two Leipzig manuscripts, and they alone, have the author actually vaunt his superiority to the ancients. In the ornateness of its words, and in the utility and weight of its judgments, this text says, the present work excels the sayings of the gentiles and all the volumes of the pagans (211–14).

While this last turn of phrase may not be Peter's since it is found only in two closely related manuscripts, its general tenor is, I think, in keeping with the self-assertiveness found in all the manuscripts, and especially the five northern and eastern ones. Indeed the whole long bridge seems a unified conceptual whole, insisting at different points that it is a superb work of moral theology aimed at converting sinners to penance.

The Audience

The same consistency emerges when we listen to the author address his intended audience. Going beyond the ubiquitous address forms "karissime" or "diligens lector," this bridge text in fact contains the best indication of Peter's primary audience. Nothing indicates that any of the text ever had the form of a public sermon to the faithful. The work is, rather, a source book for the minister. "In our work," Peter twice says in the five long eastern and northern texts, there is fertile and copious material for private admonition, spiritual exhortation, public preaching, and for instructing and teaching everyone (8–12, 209–11). Obviously Peter intended the people of God to benefit from his text, but they would do so through their ministers, who would first have studied it.

Thus Peter's self-advertisements are directed to ministers who should find his work useful. Since these advertisements come just before the section of the work that contains pictures of prayer modes, the question arises whether the author thought his proud, presumably literate ministers needed pictures, or whether the author thought these illustrations would benefit only the "simple" illiterates, perhaps including young students. Yet to raise this central ambiguity in the work regarding the author's attitude toward his audience is to say more than is necessary at this point. What is clear is that Peter insists on the work's pedagogic, its "how to," character.

Indeed, so much does Peter the Chanter consider this work a manual for practical use that, in these five manuscripts, he positively encourages his readers to change the text as they find necessary! It is an unusual and significant admonition. True, the Ottobeuren and Munich texts, and they alone, end the text of their prayer book by making Peter admit the work's faults:

> Negare non possum nec debeo sicut in ipsis maioribus, ita in multis opusculis meis, multa esse que possent iusto iudicio et multa temeritate culpari. [variant 2110–11]

But in the northern and eastern texts, readers are encouraged to correct those errors, supplement his dicta, eliminate what is superfluous, and clarify the obscure and the difficult. "For the insights of masters," Peter asserts, "should be used so that they are ground up by the tooth of disputation, [and] expounded in the schools with much questioning" (171-72).[96] The author has in mind, it seems, a text that should be shaped by classroom experience for the needs of future students. Indeed several of its arguments take the form of academic questions and responses (1533, 1751, 1995, 2079). Comparing himself to a smith working on iron, Peter encourages the artisanal creativeness of his reader as well.

It remains to be seen if this humble stance of the proud intellectual, this positive encouragement to his readers to revise the work partly explains the fact that the text tradition is so varied. Nor can it be excluded that such encouragement to revise the work, found only in the long version, is an insert of later emenders seeking to justify their actions. What is clear is that while this work was intended for ministers, Peter the Chanter was too much the intellectual not to want it to become the food and drink of the academic banquet as well.

Construction and Organization

Having ascertained the author by an examination of the texts themselves, what he considered to be the character of his work, and for what audience it was written, I stay with the same internal textual evidence in turning now to the study of how the author constructed the work.

Questions of text construction are certainly not easily divorced from ones concerning the manuscript tradition, especially when, as I shall argue, the author may himself be responsible for a fundamental division between two groups of texts. Before embarking on the study of the work's construction, then, it is necessary to re-emphasize some important facts about the manuscript tradition.

All manuscripts of the work are divided according to books. As is seen in the table of incipits and explicits, the three northern (Altzella, Pegau, Prague) and two eastern (Zwettl, Klosterneuburg) manuscripts are divided into seven numbered books. The two western (Ottobeuren, Munich) and two southern (Padua, Venice) manuscripts I shall say to be divided into ten books, the last of these being identified in Ottobeuren and Munich as the "ultimate book," but in the Venice and Paduan texts as a "tractate" forming a continuation of book nine.

If readers now peruse my edition of the prayer book, they can see that

TABLE OF INCIPITS AND EXPLICIT

	PEGAU		ALTZELLA
	(ff. 9r–127v)		(ff. i–ra — cvi–ra)

f. 9r	Incip: Verbum abbreviatum . . .	f. i–ra	Incip: Incipit liber magistri Petri cantoris parisiensis. Verbum abbreviatum . . .
f. 13r	*peccati sodome. Incipit de penitentia. Ubicumque est compendium* . . .	f. v–rb	*peccati sodome. Incipit de penitentia. Ubicumque est conpendium* . . .
f. 17r	*unde certamina tolleramus. Sicut enim repente nemo fit summus, ita nemo repente fit turpissimus. De Gradibus Vitiorum et Virtutum. Quemadmodum tribus gradibus* . . .	f. ix–vb	*unde certamina toleramus. Sicut enim nemo repente fit summus, ita nemo repente fit turpissimus. De Gradibus Vitiorum et Virtutum. Quemadmodu tribus gradibus* . . .
f. 21v	Expl: custodit eam. Explicit liber I. Incip: Incipit II de cautela sacerdotis. Consequenter agendum est de officio sacerdotis sive confessoris . . .	f. xiii–vb	Expl: custodit eam. Explicit liber primus. Incip: Incipit liber secundus de cautela et offitio sacerdotis. Consequenter agendum est de offitio sacerdotis sive confessoris . . .
f. 29v	*opera sua. De Labore Penitentie. Consequenter agendum est de fructu penitentie* . . .	f. xxi–vb	*opera sua. De Labore Penitentis. Consequenter* [f. xxii–ra] *agendum est de fructu penitentie* . . .
f. 36r	*predantur euntes. Item Augustinus in libro qui dicitur Omeliarum: De Verbi Dei Dignitate. "Interrogo* . . .	f. xxviii–ra	*predantur euntes. Item Augustinus in libro qui dicitur L Omeliarum: De Verbi Dei Dignitate. "Interrogo* . . .
f. 40r	Expl: Ypolitum pone priapus erit. Explicit liber II. Incip: Incipit liber III de modis peccandi. Sciendum est quod peccatum . . .	f. xxxi–vb	Expl: Ypolitum pone [f. xxxii–ra] priapus erit. Explicit liber II. Incip: Incipit liber III de modis peccandi. Sciendum est quod peccatum . . .
f. 43r	*De Genuflexionibus.*	f. xxxv–rb	*De Genuflexionibus*
f. 52v	*muliere mala. Explicit tractatus penitentie. Possemus ad huc plura dicere* . . .	f. xliiii–ra	*muliere mala. Explicit tractatus penitentie. Possemus ad huc plura d cere* . . .

| | | | | IV. | | f. 39ra |

"
nse-
st
eius,
atione et
m trac-
quod est
tis in
eiunium

f. 65vb Expl: Fuge pluralitatem, non solum voca-
bulorum verum et hominum et om-
nium rerum. Nam ut deus: "Unum
est necessarium."

Incip: Incipit liber quattuor. Consequenter
agendum est post penitentiam de
partibus eius, videlicet de ieiunio et
oratione et elemosina. Inprimis tractandum de ieiunio et oratione, quod
est potissima pars faciei euntis in
Ierusalem. De Ieiunio Generale. Ieiunium generale . . .

f. 69ra *sine labe notes.*

Toto . . .   f. 69vb [Commendatio] *Toto* . . .

liber IIII.   f. 71vb Expl: consonet ymo.
toris   Incip: Incipit liber V cantoris parisiensis
oratione   de oratione et speciebus eius. Con-
orta me   forta me . . .

V.   VIII.   f. 42rb Ex
             f. 43ra In

esum   f. 86ra Expl: sedeat maior. Unde dixit sapiens:
"Regnat in exiguo magno pro cor-
atur de   pore virtus."
ibus   Incip: Incipit VI liber ubi tractatur de reali
n vocali   oratione atque partibus eius. Hacte-
                     nus egimus de vocali oratione . . .

VI.   IX.   f. 60vb Ex
                      in

Expl: caritas in te non est.

quo   Incip: Incipit VII liber in quo agitur de
efata,   missa. Post prefata, hoc est, tracta-
t voca-   tum orationis realis et vocalis, est
amento   agendum de sacramento altaris . . .

VII.   (X.)   f. 69ra

xplicit   f. 100rb Expl: premium perfectorum. Explicit liber
Laus sua   cantoris parisiensis. Laus cantori sua
us opera.   fuit actus et sone. Explicit cantoris
                    liber parisiensis.

f. 77vb Ex

PADUA		VENICE	
turba facit turbationem. Fuge multitu-dinem [f. 39va]. *Sequitur ut tracte-mus post penitentiam de partibus eius, videlicet de ieiunio et oratione et helymosina. De Ieiunio. Inprimis agendum est de ieiunio, quod est potissima pars faciei euntis in Iherusalem. Ieiunium generale* . . .	f. vb	*turba facit turbationem. Fuge multitu-dinem. Sequitur ut tractemus post penitentiam de partibus eius, videlicet de ieiunio et oratione et elymosina. De Ieiunio. Inprimis est agendo de ieiu-nio, quod est potissima pars faciei euntis in Ierusalem. Ieiunium vero generale* . . .	f. 188r
			f. 192v
: sine labes potes. »: Speciebus eius. Incipit liber VIII de oratione et. Conforta me . . .	f. vb	Expl: sine labe notes. Incip: Incipit liber VIII de oratione et speciebus eius. Conforta me . . .	f. 192v
: maiori sedeat maiori. »: Incipit liber IX ubi tractatur de reali oratione et partibus eius. Hactenus egimus de vocali ora-tione . . .	f. rb	Expl: maiori sedeat maior. Incip: Incipit liber VIIII ubi tractatur de reali oratione et partibus eius. Hactenus egimus de vocali ora-tione . . .	f. 204v
voracitatem oblationum. De Multiplici Causa. Post prefata, hoc est tractatum orationis realis et vocalis, est agend[f. 69rb]*um de sacramento altaris* . . .	f. vb	*voracitatem oblationum. Post prefata, hoc est tractatum orationis realis et vocalis, est agendum de sacramento al-taris* . . .	f. 209v
: premium perfectorum. Finito libro, gratia referamus Christo. Qui me scripsit, deus illum benedicat et in pace cum domino vivat, amen.	f. vb	Expl: premium perfectorum. Explicit opus cantoris parisiensis. Deo gratias, amen.	f. 216r

OTTOBEUREN		MUNICH

<table>
<tr><td>

turba facit turbationem. De Partibus Penitentie. Sequitur ut tractamus post penitentiam de partibus eius, videlicet de ieiunio, oratione et elemosina. Inprimis est agendum de ieiunio, quod est potissima pars euntis in Iherusalem. Ieiunium generale . . .

</td><td>

f. 141va

</td><td>

turba facit turbationem. De Partibus Penitentie. Sequitur ut tractamus post penitentiam de partibus eius, videlicet de ieiunio, oratione et elemosina. Inprimis est agendum de ieiunio, quod est potissima pars euntis in Iherusalem. Ieiunium generale. . .

</td></tr>
</table>

	f. 146ra	
sine labe notes.		*sine labe notes.*

Expl: ad finem hominis.
Incip: Liber(8)de oratione et eius dignitate. [f. 193r] Conforta me . . .

f. 146va Expl: ad finem hominis.
Incip: Liber[blank]de oratione et eius dignitate. Conforta me . . .

Expl: maiori sedeat maior. Unde dixit sapiens: "Regnat in exiguo pro magno corpore virtus."
Incip: Liber VI(III) de reali oratione et eius effectu. Hactenus egimus de vocali oratione . . .

f. 158rb Expl: maiori sedeat maior. Unde dixit sapiens: "Regnat in exiguo pro magno corpore virtus."
Incip: Liber sextus de reali oratione et eius effectu. Hactenus egimus de vocali oratione . . .

Expl: voracitatem oblationum.
Incip: Liber ultimus. Ut Sacerdos Sit Crucifixus. Premisso tractatu de oratione vocali et reali, consequenter agendum est de sacramento altaris . . .

f. 164rb Expl: voracitatem oblationum.
Incip: Liber ultimus. Ut Sacerdos Sit Crucifixus. Premisso tractatu de oratione vocali et reali, consequenter agendum est de sacramento altaris . . .

Expl: premium perfectorum. Per omnia secula seculorum, amen. Finit Viaticum liber magistri Petri parisiensis cantoris. En pater, ad finem duxi scribendo volumen. Fac caput inclinem fessum requiscere lumen. Si perfectorum sequimur sacra dogmata morum, Possumus astrorum rite subire chorum. Hoc Berhtoldus abbas fieri iussit varium vas legum. Qui legis has leges, imitando triumphas. Librum cantoris et Alanum continuavi, Berhtoldi iussu, coeunt quia nectare suavi. Scribere qui iussit, qui finem fortiter ussit. In patria celi potiatur sede fideli. Sint sibi mercedis celestis gaudia sedis. Sit pretium fidei gratia summa dei.

f. 171vb Expl: premium perfectorum. Per omnia secula seculorum. Deo gratias.

the northern and eastern manuscripts are longer than the western and southern ones: italics identify text found in all the manuscripts, while roman type identifies text found only in the northern and eastern manuscripts. What is true for the prayer book holds for the work as a whole: the seven books of the northern and eastern manuscripts are substantially longer than the ten books of the western and southern ones.[97] Thus henceforth, I use the terms "seven-book" and "long version" indifferently to refer to the Pegau and Altzella manuscripts at Leipzig, to the Zwettl and Klosterneuburg texts, and to the late Prague manuscript. The terms "ten-book" and "short version" refer in the same way to the Ottobeuren and Munich, Venetian and Paduan texts, although the latter two actually have only nine books.

By a demanding "walk through" of the incipits and explicits table, that outlines the work as a whole, I now try to identify internal, prose signposts of Peter's construction. There are, it transpires, three fundamental turning points that Peter made in constructing these texts, and these are shown in the incipits and explicits table. Numbers one and two concern us forthwith. First, the introductory section of the work ends when a tractate on penance begins. The second turning point ends that tractate and begins a study of the parts of penance. Thus, in all nine manuscripts the usual title of the work, *De penitentia et partibus eius*, is reflected in the texts proper. I will conclude that the work must have been envisioned by Peter the Chanter as an integrated whole.

After examining the Leipzig manuscripts, Artur Landgraf decided that what he called the prologue of the work ended and the first book proper began with the rubric *De tribus modis regendi populum*.[98] But in the Leipzig manuscripts and all others, the introductory matter actually extends much further. Long declamations against sexual crimes, first against those of bad priests and then against male and female homosexuality in general society, follow this title. These paragraphs are clearly meant as a rhetorical device to show how God's (gender) order has been compromised, to be set aright by the penitential practices Peter will recommend (k: 2rb).

Only then do the two Leipzig manuscripts read: ". . . peccati sodome. Incipit de penitentia. Ubicumque est compendium . . . ," while Zwettl, Klosterneuburg and Prague differ only in having the word "tractatus" after the word "incipit." Thus the five northern and eastern manuscripts — all but the Leipzig manuscripts of which have the title *De penitentia et partibus eius* indicated externally — clearly mean to distinguish the introductory matter from the proper beginning of the tractate on penance. None of these texts starts a new book 2 at this point. They rather continue in book 1.

The four ten-book manuscripts have similar text, but do begin book 2 rather than identifying the beginning of a "tractate." Venice and Padua read: ". . . peccati sodome. Incipit liber secundus de penitentia. Ubicumque est compendium . . . ," while Ottobeuren and Munich differ only in omitting the word "incipit."

Note now in the summary table that the tractate on penance takes up the remainder of book 1 and books 2 and 3 in the seven-book northern and eastern manuscripts, but consumes books 2 through part of book 7 in the ten-book western and southern manuscripts. With the exception of the Prague manuscript, the seven-book type ends book 1 and begins the second book as follows: ". . . custodit eam. Incipit liber secundus [or: secundus liber] de cautela sacerdotis. Consequenter agendum est de officio sacerdotis. . . ." By this time, however, the ten-book type, which began a new book 2 for the tractate on penance, has divided the remaining material of book 1 of the seven-book type into two further books. Thus Venice and Padua begin book 3: ". . . sed simulant. Incipit liber III de gradibus vitiorum aut virtutum. Sicut nemo repente . . . ," while a short time later Munich follows Ottobeuren with: ". . . lucrum. Incipit liber iii de confessione. Contritione cordis. . . ." All four of these manuscripts then end book 3 (with the same explicit of "custodit eam") and begin book 4 at the same point that the seven-book manuscripts end book 1 and begin book 2. And while the Ottobeuren and Munich texts then begin their book 4: "custodit eam. Liber iiii de officio sacerdotis. . . ," the Venice and Paduan texts begin that book with the same title, *De cautela*, as do all the manuscripts of the seven-book version. To summarize: book 1 of the seven-book type is equivalent to books 1 through 3 of the ten-book type.

The same combination in one book of the long version of several books of the short one is evident in what follows: book 2 of the seven-book model (*De cautela sacerdotis*) is equivalent to books 4 through 6 of the ten-book model. Beginning book 4 with the words "Post prefata, agenda est de officio sacerdotis" (and not "Consequenter agenda est . . ." as in the seven-book type), all four of the ten-book manuscripts end it and begin book 5 similarly: ". . . opera sua. Incipit V de operis satisfactione," Venice and Padua lacking the word "operis." The four then end this book at different points, but begin book 6 identically with "Liber sextus de dignitate verbi dei. Docet Augustinus. . . ." The Ottobeuren and Munich codices end their book 6 with the words "posse iacere cadunt," at a slightly different point than the Venice and Paduan texts, which end with the words "Ypolitum pone Priapus erit."

This is precisely the explicit of book 2 of the seven-book northern and eastern manuscripts, so that essentially, their book 2 is equivalent to books

4 through 6 of the ten-book version. Henceforth the matter is simpler: with
the exception of the idiosyncratic Ottobeuren and Munich texts, which call
their book 7 *Quot modis dimittitur peccatum*, the ten-book and seven-book
manuscripts begin their new books (7, 3) with the same title *De modis peccandi* and with similar initiating words.

Let me summarize the tractate on penance to this point. The seven-book
variety began it within its book 1, as if that were proper for a work most
of its manuscripts call *De penitentia et partibus eius*. The ten-book version,
on the other hand, began the tractate with a new book 2 called *De penitentia*. We then found that book 1 of the seven-book type is equivalent to books
1 through 3 of the ten-book type, and book 2 of the former is equivalent
to books 4 through 6 of the latter. This means that at this point, the ten-
book model already has four more books than the seven-book model, whereas
the whole work differs in the total number of books only by three, seven
as against ten. Since, as we shall see, both traditions divide the latter part
of the work into three books of similar content, that one book too many
was not "made up" in the later part of the work. Where then was it
recuperated?

The answer lies in the way the two traditions handled the end of the tractate on penance. Whereas the seven-book model ends its book 3 and begins
a new book 4 at the end of that tractate, the ten-book model continues on
in the same book 7 right up to the book on prayer which is edited in this
volume.

To unravel this, one must first note that all the manuscripts clearly mark
the end of the tractate on penance and define the rest of the work as concerned with the parts of penance. The end of book 3 of the seven-book type,
for instance, is identical in all five manuscripts: ". . . peius muliere mala.
Explicit tractatus de penitentia." This is followed by one paragraph
("Possemus ad huc plura dicere de penitentia . . . unum est necessarium")
that brings book 3 to its conclusion. The slightly varied incipits of book
4, then, clearly identify the future text. Zwettl, Klosterneuburg and Prague
read: ". . . necessarium. Incipit liber IIII. Consequenter agendum est post
penitentiam de partibus eius, videlicet de ieiunio et oratione et elymosina. . . .
In primis autem tractandum est de ieiunio, quod est potentissima pars faciei
euntis in Ierusalem." Pegau and Altzella read: ". . . necessarium. Explicit
liber iii. Incipit liber iv de partibus penitentie. Restat ut agamus post penitentiam de partibus eius, videlicet de ieiunio, oratione, et elimosina. In primis
. . . de ieiunio. . . ."

The western and southern manuscripts indicate the end of the tractate
on penance in a different fashion, with the Ottobeuren and Munich texts

being most helpful in this regard. Eliminating the statement about bad women in the seven-book model *and* in the Venice text ("vermium. Nichil autem est peius muliere mala"), they precede the paragraph beginning "Possemus" that ends the book in the seven-book model with the following designation: "Brevis epilogus ponitur huc de penitentia. Possemus...."

The Venetian and Paduan texts do not follow the western texts in characterizing as an epilogue the paragraph beginning "Possemus," nor do they indicate that the tractate on penitence has reached its end, as do all of the seven-book manuscripts. But like all but the Leipzig texts, they do incorporate a statement to the effect that after treating penance itself, they will now turn to the parts of penance. Because Padua did not copy a section of text before the beginning of what Ottobeuren calls the epilogue, it leads into the paragraph "Possemus" as follows: "sitis altera crevit. Possemus...," whereas Venice, like the seven-book texts, reads: "muliere mala. Possemus...." Then Venice and Padua, but also Ottobeuren and Munich, end this paragraph beginning "Possemus" at a slightly later point than the "necessarium" of the seven-book version, Ottobeuren and Munich with the words "facit turbationem," Venice and Padua more prolixly with "facit turbationem, fuge multitudinem."

But at this point, both Venice and Padua mark the passage to the new subject of the parts of penance with the words: "multitudinem. Sequitur ut tractemus post penitentiam de partibus eius, videlicet de ieiunio et oratione et elymosina," to then immediately begin a new rubric: *De ieiunio. In primis est agendum de ieiunio....* Similarly, Munich follows Ottobeuren in marking the end of its epilogue on penance and the beginning of its study of the parts of penance as follows: "... turbationem. *De partibus penitentie.* Sequitur ... et elymosina.In primis.... ieiunio."

Thus all the manuscripts use prose to mark the transition from the study of penance to the study of its three parts, fasting, prayer, and alms, and all but the Venetian and Paduan texts separate the end of the tractate on penance proper from what the Ottobeuren and Munich texts characterize as an epilogue, namely the paragraph beginning "Possemus." At this point, the work does begin to look as if it was conceived by Peter the Chanter as an integrated whole.

Once having laid out that course, all the manuscripts terminate their examination of fasting and bring their works up to the study of prayer (the second part of penance) with texts of three distinct lengths which afford some valuable information on genealogies. The seven-book version begins a new book 4 on fasting, and ends it with the long *Commendatio istius operis* that begins my edition. The texts of the short version, on the other hand, which begin their study of fasting in the same book 7 in which they terminated their examination of penance itself, fall short of that commendation, but at two different points. Ottobeuren and Munich end book 7 after paragraphs on the ages of the world and then of man, but Padua and Venice end the same book far short of those paragraphs, at the common point "sine labe notes." Thus the Ottobeuren tradition has more of the long version at this point than does the Italian one.

But why? The Paduan text provides an important answer. It comes to the words "sine labe [n]otes" in the middle of its folio 42rb and then breaks off abruptly, failing to signify that this is the explicit of book 7, as it had identified the ends of previous books. The rest of that column is then blank, and the whole of folio 42v, though later used for extraneous matter, also has no text from the *De penitentia*. Obviously, more text was intended — perhaps the paragraphs on the ages of the world and of man. Indeed the odd fashion in which the scribe entered the title of the following book on prayer at the beginning of the next folio, 43ra:

> Speciebus Eius. Incipit Liber
> VIII De Oratione et,

suggests that he had intended to begin the introduction to the new book at the bottom of folio 42vb, and that he may have measured the blank space to accommodate the intended text. I shall shortly develop this hypothesis. In any case, Venice almost certainly simply copied Padua or its copy at this point, but left no hint that its Paduan source had intended to enter more text: it eliminated the blank space in the text and straightened out the incipit of the book on prayer. This is a strong argument that the Paduan text is older than and a direct source for the Venetian one.

Having strengthened the hypothesis that the work was conceived as an integral whole, I turn now to determine if Peter actually executed that conception in the remaining books, that is, if after fasting he next examined prayer and then alms. Generally speaking, in this latter part of the work there is no overlapping of the type we have worked through in its earlier segments. While each book of the ten-book version is shorter than the corresponding book of the seven-book version, almost everything that is in the former is also in the corresponding book of the latter in the same order. Thus:

> Ten-book: book 8 = book 5 of the seven-book version;
> Ten-book: book 9 = book 6 of the seven-book version;
> Ten-book: book 10 = book 7 of the seven-book version.

Now, a study of the contents of these three books shows that these books do cover precisely prayer and almsgiving, the last two parts of penance. Even if its stated topic or rubric is *verbal* prayer, the core of book 8 (= 5) is a study of the *corporal* modes of prayer that left no trace in the *De vitiis*. Next, even if its stated topic is "real prayer, that is, the works of mercy" (k: 24ra, 26rb), the subject of book 9 (= 6) is also almsgiving. For, as the Chanter repeats, almsgiving, the works of mercy, and charity are synonymous terms.[99] Thus, here as in the *De vitiis* (chs. 129–33; DVV, 324–27), paragraphs on alms follow ones on prayer, though the treatment of alms here is very different than it is in the older work.[100]

Finally, even though the title of book 10 (= 7) refers to the mass or sacrament of the altar, the conceptual framework is actually, as the Ottobeuren and Munich texts lucidly show by their variant title "Ut sacerdos sit crucifixus," the perfect charity or real prayer of Jesus. Indeed, recall that the Paduan and Venetian texts do not begin a new book for this subject, but append a "tractate" on the charity of Jesus to their treatment of earthly charity or real prayer, and thus conclude the work within book 9. The subject matter of this book or tractate, as distinct from its conceptual framework, does not follow the order in the *De vitiis*, but rather harks back to that work's earlier chapters.[101]

Thus there can be little doubt that Peter the Chanter both conceived and executed the *De penitentia* as one work. Yet how he executed this latter part is open to question. Did he write these last three books after he had written the section on fasting? That appears unlikely for three reasons. First, Peter does not provide prose to mark the passage from prayer to almsgiving — from the second to the third part of penance — , a process he would certainly have followed if he were writing the parts in sequence. There is no book entitled "De elemosina."

A second reason lies with the title of the prayer book. In all but the Ottobeuren and Munich manuscripts, its subject is given as prayer and its species. On reading the first part of the book, one finds that there are two species of prayer, vocal and real, of which the modes of prayer are subdivisions (276–78, 396–401). Thus though the title *De oratione et speciebus illius* stands at the beginning of only one book, that on vocal prayer, it actually covers in concept the subsequent book on real prayer as well, which in the present text is separately titled.

This contradiction is resolved and Peter's actual procedure clarified by a third reason why it is unlikely these books were written after the tractate on penance. Recall that earlier in the work the author furnished a second major transition in prose when he moved from penance to its parts. A third major prose transition occurs at the beginning of the final book on the mass or, in the case of Padua and Venice, of its concluding tractate. After their incipits, all but the Leipzig manuscripts read with minor variations: "Post prefata, hoc est tractatum orationis realis et vocalis, est agendum de sacramento altaris."[102] Thus these texts refer to both preceding books as a unified whole from which they are now exiting (the two Leipzig texts omit the words "et vocalis" and envision only a transition from real prayer to the next book on the mass).

If we combine this third prose transition with the first and second ones, a different structure for the work appears. It seems that the work consists first of a tractate on penance, then (after a wedged-in treatment of fasting) of a tractate on the two types of prayer, and finally, of a tractate on the mass. Yet such a division conflicts both with the logic of the title *De penitentia et partibus eius* and with Peter's stated intention to examine the *three* types of penance in the second part of the work. Indeed the text of this transition to the tractate on the mass does not include fasting among the subjects the author had examined since his previous summing-up.

The problem can be resolved if the following hypothesis is correct: that the two books on verbal and real prayer already existed as a separate work when Peter plugged them into this one *without revising their introductory prose so as to conform to his previous organization of the parts of prayer*. Thus verbal and real prayer became the second and third parts of penance. But the bridge to the mass book continued to emphasize their unity outside the penitential schema, making the banal distinction between verbal prayer or what one says, and real prayer or what one does.

There is persuasive evidence that this was precisely Peter's procedure, beginning with what is missing from these books on verbal and real prayer. First, for a work on penance, there is little attention given that subject in these books. A computer search for "peniten" in the prayer book edited here shows, for example, that excluding three quotes, Peter used this stem only 13 times. In fact, excluding three usages in introducing the subject of prayer (272–74), he used the stem only once in the whole section on the modes of prayer (567). Second, at the beginning of the book on prayer, the author says that he will study prayer because he has already studied fasting and alms "elsewhere" (276: *alias*). He does not say he has studied fasting above and will study alms below, as called for by his organization. A third argument from silence is that in a work that has its share of cross-references, there is none in the prayer book, while the two cross-references to this book on prayer from outside it are found only in the long version of the work.[103] Finally, none of the three references to Peter's earlier *De vitiis* occurs in this prayer book: two were found in the earlier tractate on penance and the latter turns up in the last book or tractate on the mass. Neither the book on prayer nor the one on alms-giving or real prayer contains such a reference.

What is present in the prayer book is quite as important as what is missing. Four of the five seven-book texts, including the Prague text that has antecedents pre-dating Zwettl, re-introduce Peter the Chanter at the beginning of the book on prayer with the words: "Incipit quintus liber cantoris Pari[s]iensis de oratione et speciebus illius." The four short version texts do not, but the absence of this unusual re-introduction may be ultimately traceable to the ancient Paduan text, which as noted has a blank page before it begins the title of the prayer book on a new folio with the curious format:

Speciebus Eius. Incipit Liber
VIII De Oratione et.[104]

Thus the bottom of the previous empty folio might have been the planned locus for the reintroduction found in the seven-book texts as well as that part of the title of the new book that precedes the words *Speciebus Eius*.

Taken together with the third transitional passage analyzed above and with what is absent from the prayer book, this real or latent presence of a text reintroducing Peter the Chanter as the author strongly indicates that the books on prayer and alms already existed as a separate work, distinct and separate from the tractate on penance. We shall later study the question of the date of this original work on verbal and real prayer in relation to the *De vitiis*.

The last piece of evidence that the two penultimate books of this work were originally separate is complex yet compelling, and it is important because it relates directly to the study of corporal prayer. The subject is genuflection. One would expect that all the systematized information on corporal forms would be either reserved to this book, or at least repeated there if such information were also found elsewhere. This is not the case. For while the long version does argue that "genua sint flectenda" (606 ff., 667 ff.), none of the manuscripts includes the word "genuflection" among its modes of prayer, while all but one of the manuscripts do have paragraphs on *genuflexiones* earlier, within the tractate on penance (7 = 3). These paragraphs are published at the end of the edition. The Paduan text, finally, does not have these texts. It does not categorize genuflection anywhere! These facts leave us with definitional, organizational, and genealogical problems of some import.

The problem of definition arises from the fact that Peter the Chanter does not unequivocally use the word "genuflection" as we do, to mean bending to or on one knee. In the early Christian centuries genuflection had been out of favor in certain parts of the west because it evoked the mockery of Christ during his passion. It first reappeared as a reverence for lords, including popes and bishops, but by Peter's time the one-knee genuflection is said to have been widely used in prayer contexts as well, even if it did not become part of the mass liturgy until the sixteenth century.[105] To be sure, caution is called for in discussing "genuflection," because the word "genuflexio" literally means flexing one knee but commonly refers to bending both. In Latin, this imprecision springs from the fact that there is no one noun or verb for kneeling — 'positis genibus" being a common circumlocution. Half a century after the Chanter, Humbert of Romans almost uniformly meant kneeling on both knees when he used the word "genuflection," and he insisted on that posture before God because of the greater reverence due a creator: kneeling on one knee was only to be done before secular magnates.[106]

In his tractate on penance, Peter the Chanter seems to have included under his rubric "genuflections" every non-erect posture *except* a one-knee bend. One might believe the contrary on noting that the author uses both the singular and plural nouns, the first arguably referring to genuflexion on one knee and the second to kneeling on both. But other evidence makes that improbable. First of all, Peter sometimes breaks "genuflectiones" into two words indicating both knees: "genuum flexiones" (pa: 17vb). More significantly, like Humbert of Romans the Chanter uses the plural noun whenever he elaborates on or exemplifies such flexings and, as a reading of the paragraphs *De genuflexionibus* and *De utilitate genuflexionum* makes clear, his examples of genuflections do not describe the modern genuflection. In the former, the author moves from saying that genuflection is a principal part of external penance to condemning the use of kneelers and then to praising genuflection as "especially sincere and optimal" when the mouth, knees and toes are all on the ground. This is not our modern genuflection. Peter follows the same rhythm in the latter paragraph on utility. Temptation recedes, he begins, when repeated genuflections are mixed with invocations. But he immediately follows by praising a fully prostrate position, with the chest, stomach, mouth, shins and toes on the ground.

As noted, Peter does not use the word "genuflection" in his description of his modes of prayer. But in later usages (942–43, 952–53), he again moves quickly from the word "genuflection" to describing different forms of prostration but not modern genuflection. This "principal part of external penance" seems on balance to refer to a general declension of the body rather than to a particular one. Although Peter's long version does once make a distinction between "flexis genibus" and full prostration (883–85), Peter seems to have used the word "genuflection" in the more general sense of "bending the knee" and intended merely to distinguish that general corporal stance from one in which the supplicant was erect. In this reading, the absence anywhere in the text of a reference to moving toward, or of being on one knee, means that Peter took for granted what Humbert of Romans would spell out: in prayer, one did not genuflect in our modern sense.

One final observation on this question of definition: even if these texts do not refer to "genuflection" in describing the modes of prayer, the choice of language here and earlier leaves no doubt that both the genuflection texts in the tractate on penance and the later descriptions of the modes of prayer are by the same author. Thus in the former, after exemplifying genuflection by prostration, he characterizes the latter as perhaps the best "inter omnes modos orandi." And in fact, prostration is the fifth among those postures called "modes of prayer" that Peter identifies in the following book on prayer.

But what can this tell us about the way that Peter put the two parts of his work together? Here is the organizational problem these texts represent: even if the choice of words shows one author to have been at work, the paragraphs on genuflection on the one hand and the modes of prayer on the other occur in very distinct *contexts*. "Genuflections" and various types of prostration are examined in the earlier passages within the context of a polarity between exterior and interior penance. The later texts mention no such polarity. Instead, Peter places the modes of prayer within the context of verbal prayer, which he contrasts with real prayer. With all due tolerance of the medieval penchant for classification, I must conclude that if Peter had written the two sections in sequence he would have kept the study of "genuflection" for the book on prayer. Two separate tractates must have been joined together to produce such varied contexts.

Yet a genealogical problem stands in the way of this solution: alone among the nine manuscripts, the ancient Paduan text has *no* paragraphs on genuflection, and thus no reference in the tractate on penance to "modes of prayer." Setting aside for a moment the larger problems this poses, one immediately wonders if the Venetian manuscript, usually so close to Padua, added the passages on genuflection that are missing in the Paduan text, or if the Paduan text subtracted them from the Venetian. This is a particularly interesting query because of my impression that from a paleographical point of view as well, the Paduan and Venetian manuscripts may be the two oldest manuscripts of all.

I have already presented some evidence for the precedence of the Paduan manuscript, and that is confirmed by what is absent in the Paduan text at this juncture. Note in my edition that in all other manuscripts, the texts on genuflection appear at two different points separated by other texts (e.g. k: ff. 12rb, 13rb). Now it transpires that the Paduan text (38ra–39rb) does have most of these intervening texts as well as most of the texts immediately before and after the texts on genuflection. Indeed, in the Paduan manuscript are *all* of the intervening and immediately preceding and following texts that are necessary to coherence, for those that are missing are indirectly related to the discourse on genuflection found in the other manuscripts.[107] Thus the Paduan text reads more coherently at this point than does Venice or any other manuscript, and could have been written by one author sequentially.

As Baldwin has pointed out, consistency is often the product of reducers, not enlargers,[108] but this does not seem to be the case as regards the matter of genuflection. The only one among our nine codices with any association to Peter's native France — bound as is the *De penitentia* with a fragment of a French version of William of Tyre's *History* — , *Biblioteca Antoniniana* 532 again seems older textually than the Venetian text.

We are thus confronted with an insoluble choice as to the chronological order of the texts on genuflection in this work. On the one hand, all but the Paduan text show the same author referring to the "modi orandi" in two very different contexts, suggesting that two separate tractates by the same author, one on penance and another on verbal and real prayer, were melded together in the *De penitentia*. On the other hand, the Paduan text, hypothesized as chronologically and textually older than the Venetian and perhaps the other texts, has no such repetition and is more coherent, as if the genuflection texts were not there in the first place and Peter the Chanter originally excluded systematic attention to "genuflection" from the whole work. Obviously, a final ordering of these manuscripts will have to await the accumulation of all the evidence.

Yet I decided to examine Peter's handling of "genuflection" less for text/genealogical reasons than to understand Peter's construction of the work. Confident that Peter conceived and executed an integral work, I reviewed genuflection along with other characteristics of the texts to defend the proposition that the books on verbal and real prayer already existed when Peter conceived his *De penitentia*, and that he then integrated them into it. Taken with the other evidence, to which the Paduan manuscript conforms rather than departs, this study of the genuflection passages does strongly affirm that view.

Thus real prayer in this earlier work was the pole of verbal prayer. In the *De penitentia*, however, it functions as a study not just of the works of mercy but of the synonymous alms-giving, the third part of penance. To conclude this study of the organization of the work, we should examine more closely the question of whether the last book or tractate on the altar was itself part of this original work on verbal and real prayer, or whether it was an independent tractate appended to the *De penitentia*.

The conceptual relation of this book to the earlier one, as I have said, is the charity of Christ in bearing his cross. Its actual contents, however, are distinct enough to make us believe that the book was not a part of the original work on vocal and real prayer. It is divided into two parts. The first deals with priests who say repeated masses and sell them; several of these paragraphs have strong echoes of early chapters of the *De vitiis*, though only a limited amount of text duplication.[109] The second section of the work emphasizes the confection and reception of the eucharist within a framework of the three crosses of Christ. Together, the whole book is an invaluable addition to Peter's eucharistic theory as expounded in his *Summa de sacramentis*.[110] But generally speaking, the subject matter does not seem a logical conclusion of a tractate on vocal and real prayer. Once we recall that, unlike the books on verbal and real prayer, this section does refer the reader back to the *De vitiis* (and was thus written after it), it may be suggested that it was fashioned apart from these books on verbal and real prayer.

An important variant in text organization between the short and long traditions that occurs at the beginning of this last book or tractate confirms my hunch that this concluding book or tractate was originally independent of what went before. Arguably the oldest manuscripts in each tradition, Padua and Zwettl, both had at their disposal the long introductory paragraph of this new section, dealing with the eucharist. Yet the two manuscripts insert the same paragraph into their texts at different points. They do so in such a way as to make it clear that the rest of the work existed distinct from the original work on verbal and real prayer. We see that in some instances, the oldest ten-book and seven-book texts ordered more or less identical pre-existing texts in different fashions.

Note in the tabular outline of the work that in keeping with the caritative conception of the book on real prayer the seven-book version ends its treatment of real prayer with the words "caritas in te non est," while the ten-book version concludes with "voracitatem oblationum." Since both versions contain these words and the texts that precede them, this variant is not caused, as are others, by the greater length of the long version. Instead, the single long paragraph in the Paduan text (69ra–70rb) at the beginning of its final tractate (". . . voracitatem oblationum. De multiplici causa. Post prefata, hoc est tractatum orationis realis et vocalis, est agendum de sacramento altaris") is found much later in the Klosterneuburg manuscript (k: 27rb; cf. z: 39rb ff.), after the words "caritas in te non est" (cf. pa: 71ra), where it is subdivided into several paragraphs. Therefore the intervening paragraphs of Klosterneuburg, which come later in Padua, are found still within its book 6, following the words "voracitatem oblationum." Klosterneuburg begins its book 7 much later than does Padua its corresponding tractate.[111]

This introductory paragraph on the eucharist had to exist separately in order to have been differentially inserted in this way; it is the sole major variant between the two traditions in this final book or tractate, so the rest of this section on the mass and eucharist lay before the compiler in a presumably integral form. Just as significant, the place the Zwettl tradition inserted the passage makes for much more coherent reading than does the Paduan insertion,[112] whereas in the matter of genuflection I found the Paduan text more coherent.

Clearly, coherence or its absence is by itself no proof of relative antiquity. In the Paduan and Zwettl manuscripts, which I will argue is as far back as we can look in the text traditions, the compilers of both the long and short versions inserted identical texts into the work at different points. We shall encounter this phenomenon again. *The long version is not simply the result of an expansion of the short version.*

In all the manuscripts, Peter concludes his work by again emphasizing charity as its capstone, and by referring for a last time to himself as author. What he says seems intended to soften the tension between a work conceived as a penitential tractate and one executed in part by incorporating a previous, nonpenitential tractate. Wedged in between a chapter on the significance of the mass and the concluding chapter of the work, in which he quotes Prosper's definition of charity, are the following words (my italics):

> Item quoniam omnia suprascripta sive prelibata ideo sunt observanda fideliter et custodienda diligenter ut contingamus illam metam que est finis perfectionis et non consumationis, videlicet caritatem, sine qua cuncta sunt insufficientia et imperfecta. *Hic autem plurimum habet convenire cum penitentia.* Sicut enim caritas alia est incipiens, alia est proficiens, alia est perfecta, ita et penitentia alia est incipientium, quedam est proficientium, tertia est perfectorum. Et quoniam caritas est finis preceptorum, que est quasi tectum, id est, consumatio et

perfectio spiritualis edificii, cuius parietes spes erigit, in quo fides quasi iacit fundamentum, idcirco eam velut conclusionem et finem nostri laboris vel opusculi constituentes ad ultimum inserimus diffinitionem de qua ait Prosper in libro de contemplativa vita: 'Caritas est. . . .' (k: 32ra).

Let me summarize the construction of the *De penitentia*. Three key elements of an understanding of this work now seem well founded. First, Peter the Chanter authored essentially the whole work. Second, he conceived and executed it as a whole. Third, the parts of the work on verbal and real prayer pre-existed as a separate opus; Peter inserted them here as studies of prayer and almsgiving, the second and third parts of penance. Fourth, compilers assembled certain parts of the work into two different traditions of ten (v and pa: 9) and seven books, that are already fixed in the oldest of the short and long versions.[113] Fifth, neither of these traditions fully follows the dynamics and turning points projected by the author. Whether Peter the Chanter established either of these models is unclear, but it is unlikely that the first texts of either division are among our extant codexes.

Genealogy

The previous section has deepened our understanding of the construction of *De penitentia* as a whole, within the limits imposed by an undertaking whose primary task is to analyze and edit Peter's book on prayer. Within those same limits, I turn now to the task of determining the genealogy of the manuscripts. Certainly the most persuasive evidence of the relations between texts are variants in prose, and these will be abundantly demonstrated in the apparatus of variants to this edition of the prayer book. In the present overview of the whole *De penitentia*, we shall satisfy ourselves by the construction of a genealogy suggested by the external characteristics of the nine manuscripts.

The incipits and explicits long since began to yield information about the relationships between these manuscripts. To review only the most obvious one: the western manuscripts Ottobeuren and Munich are related because, having the same incipits and similar explicits, they alone bear the variant title *Viaticum tendentis Ierusalem*. Munich was definitely written later, a close but perhaps not immediate descendant of Ottobeuren. These two manuscripts obviously form a distinct set. So do the Paduan and Venetian manuscripts, the other short texts, with my nod going to the Paduan text as the source of Venice.

Likewise, titles and incipits have already allowed us to construct relationships among the manuscripts to the east and north. First, the almost
contemporaneously written Zwettl and Klosterneuburg texts could be closely
related because both consistently refer to the author as the cantor Pariensis. The late Prague text is in turn related to this set because, though it
refers consistently to the cantor Parisiensis and not Pariensis, all three bear
the title *De penitentia*, all re-identify the author at the beginning of the book
on prayer, and all are alone in referring to Peter as the Master of Reims;
my analysis will presently show that Klosterneuburg and in part the Prague
manuscript are descended from, but not copies of, Zwettl.

The explicits enable us at this point to link all five eastern and northern
manuscripts into one packet of texts. Zwettl ends as follows: "Explicit liber
cantoris pariensis. Laus sua cantori fuit actus et consonat ori." This laud
was omitted by Klosterneuburg (the explicit is otherwise identical), but it
is found with variations in the Prague text and in the Altzella and Pegau
manuscripts preserved at Leipzig (the Pegau text also re-identifies the author
at the beginning of the prayer book as do the Zwettl, Klosterneuburg, and
Prague texts). Thus a concluding laud (cf. W, 34176) not found in the
western or southern manuscripts is found in four of the five eastern and
northern manuscripts.

The question of the disposition of marginal inserts finally permits us to
ascertain the relations between this bundle of five manuscripts. The Zwettl
and Klosterneuburg texts are the only manuscripts among the nine whose
owners added in the margins not merely omissions but inserts. We will
search out their fate in the other texts. That of the Zwettl marginalia is easy:
all of the three in question are found within the texts proper of all the other
long versions save Prague, which has part of one Zwettl insert in its text
proper but not Zwettl's two significant additions to its prayer book.[114]

The marginal inserts to the Klosterneuburg text, on the other hand, are
only found within the two Leipzig texts.[115] This indicates first that from
a genealogical viewpoint the Zwettl text is older than and a source of the
Klosterneuburg and Leipzig manuscripts, and perhaps of Prague as well.
Second, the manuscripts from Leipzig but not from Prague derive from
the Klosterneuburg text. Third, the fourteenth- or fifteenth-century Prague
text has a Zwettl-type text for at least one model, but was relying on another
manuscript tradition as well, one still to be determined. Thus the two
Austrian and two German manuscripts seem to fit into a sound descent,
with the Prague manuscript — chronologically the youngest of any of the
nine save Munich — providing a "wild card" that hints at a tradition older
or at least different than Zwettl.

Four clear couplets of manuscripts have emerged. It is clear that among the western and southern manuscripts of the ten-book short version, Munich derives from Ottobeuren, and Venice either descends from or is very close to Padua, to whose content I have assigned the greater age. Two of the sets among the five eastern and northern manuscripts, all having a seven-book organization, are just as certain: Klosterneuburg certainly derives from Zwettl, and the two Leipzig manuscripts of Pegau and Altzella are closely related, although I am not sure which of these is the older. The late Prague manuscript clearly derives in part from Zwettl and not from either Klosterneuburg or the Leipzig texts, but perhaps also from still older manuscripts than Zwettl.

How then do the short and long versions relate to each other? Doubtless their differences extend well beyond length and the number of books. None of the western or southern manuscripts reidentifies the author at the beginning of the prayer book. None has a laud in its explicit. None of the western or southern texts integrates the marginal inserts of the Klosterneuburg text and precious little if any of the Zwettl text. The only relationship between the four western and southern texts on the one hand, and on the other the five eastern and northern ones that a study of the fate of the Zwettl and Klosterneuburg inserts allows, is that the former may, like Prague in part, be older in inspiration than the latter.

And yet there are genealogical relations between certain of the long and short texts. We have seen, for instance, that the Italian manuscripts share their texts' titles with the seven-book texts, and that the Paduan text shares the variant formulation Pariensis with the Zwettl and Klosterneuburg texts. Two peculiarities of the Ottobeuren and Munich manuscripts associated to the titles and numeration of their prayer books allow me now to prove that Ottobeuren has a relation to the Zwettl manuscript.

The Zwettl text has already revealed its special interest as a seed text in the fact that it has important text inserts added at the bottom of certain pages. The texts of these inserts, I noted, were integrated into Zwettl's seven-book descendants (except Prague at times), but they are not found in the ten-book manuscripts. The titles of the Zwettl text provide a second example of this type. Many Zwettl titles were added in the margins rather than being within text borders; that is, a fixed body of text was thus subdivided by more titles (e.g. z: 15ra–16ra). These titles were then integrated into Zwettl's descendant texts but are not found in the same places in the ten-book texts.

A seemingly unexceptional example of such a title is "De orationis dignitate" (427), which the Zwettl scribe inserted into the margin after his description of the first mode of prayer: it is found integrated between the margins of the texts of Zwettl's descendants, but is not found at that point in the ten-book texts or margins. Yet with a slight variation, the title "de oratione et eius dignitate" does appear elsewhere in the Ottobeuren text, indeed as the very title of its prayer book, which in all other texts is "De oratione et speciebus eius" or "illius" (variants: 265–66). Thus a title which appears for the first time as an addition to the Zwettl text, and is not in Ottobeuren's sister texts Venice or Padua, emerges slightly varied in the Ottobeuren manuscript, whence Munich copied it. This hints at a relation between Ottobeuren and Zwettl.

The relationship is enhanced by a second peculiarity of the Ottobeuren and Munich texts. In terms of the sequence of books, Ottobeuren's and its derivative Munich's prayer book and the book on real prayer are misnumbered, but their false numbering corresponds to the actual numbers of those books in the seven-book tradition.

Up through book 7, both manuscripts number their books in correct order with roman numerals. Yet where Ottobeuren begins the book on prayer (192v–193r), it reads: "liber 8us de oratione et eius dignitate," the "8us" being an insert into a text that originally had no number or space for one. Significantly for once, Munich departs from Ottobeuren, leaving a blank at this point (146va) for the book number, so that it reads: "liber [blank] de oratione et eius dignitate." It seems obvious that Munich copied the Ottobeuren text or an inextant copy before the "8us" of Ottobeuren, in arabic cipher rather than the customary roman numeral, was added.

This is confirmed in the sequence at the end of the prayer book and the beginning of the book on almsgiving. The Munich text (158rb) reads "liber sextus de reali oratione" — whereas the book should be numbered "novus" —, while the older Ottobeuren text (204v), ending the one book with the same explicit as Munich, begins the next with roman numerals as follows: "liber VIusIII de reali oratione." This text is repeated in the margin, where it reads: "liber VIus (III". This curious numeration is quickly explained: the characters "VIus" are in one ink and hand; Ottobeuren originally numbered this book as the sixth, and its scribe thus thought the previous book was the fifth. The three strokes "III" are a later addition, as one sees by the different ink and by the intervening "(" in the marginal repetition. What seems to have happened is that at the same time Munich copied Ottobeuren's or an inextant copy's unnumbered text introducing the prayer book, it copied Ottobeuren or a clone while that latter text in introducing its book on real prayer still read "VI." In the Munich text the wrong number "sextus" remained, but a later Ottobeuren scribe recognized his manuscript's error and inserted the additional strokes to correct it.

The significance of this false numeration in one pair of ten-book manuscripts is that the numbers 5 and 6 are the right numeration for these books in the seven-book model. Thus while the Ottobeuren text certainly used a ten-book source (its idiosyncracies exclude its being the original of that form), it used a seven-book text as well, probably one close to Zwettl, despite the fundamental differences between the two groups of texts in terms of their length and book organization. By originally leaving a blank space at the beginning of the prayer book, the Ottobeuren scribe managed to avoid the error of wrong number there. He committed the error however in the book on real prayer, copying from his seven-book source the term "liber VIus de reali oratione," to then change the following "et eius effectu" to "atque partibus eius."

Ottobeuren's use of a seven-book text is finally confirmed by the very fact that it has a tenth book. Since it adopted the term "liber ultimus," and Munich followed, the numeration problem does not recur. But as noted, neither Padua nor Venice, indubitably the older texts in this tradition, separated this last section into a book; instead they attached it to their book 9 as a "tractate." There can be little doubt, therefore, that Ottobeuren created a separate final book following the example of a seven-book text.

Why would the scribe of Ottobeuren have chosen the ten-book text and then have consulted a text from the seven-book tradition as well? The central peculiarity of Peter the Chanter's whole *De penitentia* puts one answer close at hand: the scriptorium at Ottobeuren decided to model its prayer illustrations on those of a manuscript of the *De penitentia* that was divided into seven books. To determine if that manuscript was Zwettl, however, we must await an examination and comparison of the illustrations themselves.

Chapter Four

De oratione et speciebus illius

The purpose of the present, as of the past chapter, is to determine the genealogical relations between the nine manuscripts. The findings of the present inquiry, however, will perhaps rest on a more solid base than did those earlier findings, because I have subjected the *De oratione*, alone among the books of the Chanter's *De penitentia*, to close textual examination. The significant verbal variants between these manuscripts are to be found in the apparatus of variants to the edition. Several of the more substantial variants in the placement of texts, as well as variants in the corpus of pictures of the modes of prayer, will be analyzed here.

An analysis of these variants absolutely confirms, while enriching, the genealogy already postulated by the study of the work as a whole. This confirmation is particularly important because, as shown in the last chapter, the books on vocal and real prayer existed before Peter used them as part of the larger *De penitentia*. While there is some reason to believe that these two books were originally written after the author's *De vitiis* (c. 1191),[116] proof on this score is elusive; only very limited evidence on the earlier history of these texts has emerged.[117] Thus it is comforting to find that the genealogical studies of the whole work and of this single, peculiar part arrive at similar conclusions. This allows us to conclude that the manuscript tradition we possess developed after all parts of the *De penitentia* had fallen into place. With all due caution, we may generalize about the whole work from what we now learn about this part.

Text Variants

Faced with this uncertainty about the date of the text of the original books on verbal and real prayer, we are thrust back on a comparison of variants in the manuscript tradition of the *De oratione* to seek greater certainty about the shaping of that tradition. We begin by analyzing five subjects that are addressed in all the manuscripts, at varied points and in different ways. The first three of these variants boil down to these points: Padua and Venice refer at the beginning of the description of the prayer modes to six rather than seven modes. The textual reference to the illustration of the seventh mode seems to be an insert into an earlier text, so no illustration of this mode may have originally been intended. After describing the seven prayer modes, a Paduan title refers to six "iamdictorum" modes. Taken together, these three variants will almost conclusively demonstrate that the Paduan text is the oldest in content.

Certainly the most important variant in the texts of this book concerns numbers. All nine manuscripts begin their exposition of the various prayer modes by saying that the church observes seven canonical hours, and seven of these manuscripts immediately follow by saying that there are seven modes of prayer, *approved by the Bible*, which the book intends to examine. Venice and Padua, however, say that there are six such biblically approved modes to be examined (401–2). Another distinction at this point is that all the ten-book manuscripts plus Prague characterize their modes as "authentic and meritorious," but the remaining four seven-book manuscripts also characterize them as "regular," presumably meaning monastic. Since among those manuscripts which refer only to "authentic and meritorious" modes the Prague manuscript is late and the Ottobeuren and Munich ones are regularly idiosyncratic, one suspects that originally there was one tradition which introduced six authentic and meritorious modes, here preserved by the ten-book Venice and Padua texts. Another tradition introduced seven authentic, meritorious *and* regular modes, here extant in the seven-book manuscripts minus Prague. In any case, this first variant is no scribal error. As we shall see, the Venetian and Paduan manuscripts point to a different conceptual organization of the exposition than in the other manuscripts and, in this part at least, to an earlier time of origin for those texts than for the other seven.

We recall that alone among the manuscripts, Venice introduced the whole opus familiarly as written by "the chanter," which could indicate a very early date for this copy. One arrives at the same conclusion after the number of prayer modes is studied. A glance at our plates shows that Venice and Padua, like all the other texts, illustrate and describe seven modes of prayer. Whence then the seventh mode, since these manuscripts introduced only six?

The answer is clear once we overview the texts of all the prayer modes. Our examination will show that Peter in fact went on to document *biblically* only the first six prayer modes. Presumably wanting to achieve symmetry with the seven canonical hours, he then incorporated a seventh mode of prayer, unrelated to the Bible, from the *Homilies* of Gregory the Great. Since in introducing the numbered prayer modes (six for Venice and Padua, seven for the rest), all texts uniformly refer to modes found in the Bible, this study will leave no doubt that the number six used by Venice and Padua is correct, and the number seven used by the other seven texts is wrong. The Bible did not authenticate seven prayer modes.

This reading is driven home by closer examination. First of all, after the exposition of the first six modes, all texts uniformly summarized these "said six modes" authenticated by "the New and Old Testament" (760–61) before proceeding to the seventh. This leaves no doubt that after the prayer modes authenticated by the Bible, the author intended to make a transition. Second, alone among the manuscripts, Venice left no space and has no title for that chapter which in all the other texts is introduced as "De septimo modo orandi." This chapter says that, in addition to the previous six modes, there is another one found in the writings of Gregory—that is, not in the Bible (766–67). Thus Venice titled the six modes of prayer it had mentioned at the beginning as being authenticated by the Bible, but not the seventh, which is not authenticated by the Bible.

A second significant variant in the manuscripts of this prayer book follows immediately after the description of the seventh mode of prayer, and raises the possibility that Peter the Chanter did not originally intend to illustrate this last mode. To understand this variant, however, we must first review the procedures that Peter the Chanter followed in referring to the pictures of the first six modes, and survey the relation of these referential texts to the pictures as they appear in all but the Ottobeuren manuscript, an exclusion I shall explain at a later point.

In all manuscripts, Peter the Chanter either directly ("sequens," "fiat," etc.) or indirectly calls for or requires illustrations of the first five modes to follow those referential words. Five illustrations do in fact come after these indications, though sometimes at different removes from the words requiring them. A first glance at my edition shows one reason for this latter variation. In the first three modes, the seven-book models entered texts unknown to the ten-book manuscripts after the calls for illustrations (450–51, 497, 519–20), delaying the appearance of the illustrations. The origin of this difference is particularly clear in mode 2 of the Zwettl manuscript, direct ancestor of three later seven-book texts. There the illustration follows immediately after its text referent, as in the ten-book texts, but twelve lines of text are written in at the bottom of the page as an insert to follow that referent. By integrating Zwettl's insert into their texts, Klosterneuburg and then the Leipzig texts caused a delay in the appearance of their illustrations.

In such cases the ten-book model clearly reflects an older, inextant text tradition, since the pictures follow the call for them, whereas Zwettl and its descendants moved the illustrations away from the call by adding text. In mode 4, for example, where there is no difference in the texts after the call for illustration ("imago presens ostendit"; 627), the figure follows immediately in all texts.

Yet it is not so that the oldest texts *always* place their illustrations right after the words calling for them. Thus in mode 5, it is the seven-book texts that place their illustrations just after the instructions calling for them ("species ista depingitur . . . ad deum mentis"; 688–92). Venice and Padua, on the other hand, go clear to the brink of the text of mode 6 before entering their mode 5 illustrations, traversing several chapters of text found in all manuscripts, but which come after the illustrations of mode 5 in the seven-book texts. Nor is it the case that the ten-book texts always place their illustrations just before the beginning of the text of the following mode. For the illustration of mode 3 in the ten- as in the seven-book manuscripts is followed by substantial texts that precede the beginning of the text of mode 4. To summarize: while in the first five modes Peter the Chanter called for illustrations that he explicitly or implicitly meant to follow immediately, not even the oldest texts always adhered to this clear intention. This alone shows that in-extant texts that followed the authorial intention preceded the oldest texts we possess of both the long and short versions.

A short observation about the text of mode 6 brings us directly to the variant in mode 7 which is the point of this discourse. While all the texts of this mode place their illustrations in the identical place, as they had in mode 4, the author himself almost certainly did not originally call for that illustration as he had for all the previous ones. To be sure, he did paint an image in words, to the effect that whenever one saw the "imago vel crux Christi aut figura alicuius sancti," one should pray bent over. But none of the ten-book texts has the words that follow this admonition in the seven-book manuscripts: "sicut docet hec ymago" (758). In these texts at least, Peter the Chanter does not call for an illustration of his sixth mode.

Now we can turn to the second major variant in our text, the import of which is that Peter certainly did not originally intend an illustration of the following and final mode 7. The variant occurs after the description of that mode. If readers consult the text and variants, they will see that the seven-book placement of lines 777–86 ("In iamdictis . . . corporis") after lines 773–74, a placement followed by my edition, was not followed by Prague or the ten-book model. These five manuscripts place lines 777–86 before 773–74. That is, if lines 773–74, which occur in all texts, were eliminated, there would be no text variation. What surely happened, therefore, was not a transposition of lines 777–86 but a differential insertion into a previously identical text of lines 773–74, which refer to a picture rather than to an argument. This is the second time we have encountered this practice of differential insertion.[118]

There is an important variant even within these two inserted lines, however. The words "antea hic" found with insignificant variations in all the long versions ("Hec figura septima quam habes *antea hic* preoculis docet enucleatus quod dictum est a Gregorio superius") are absent from the short version. Thus the long text speaks of a previous picture, while the short texts say only that the picture of mode 7 is present "before our eyes."

With this double variant in mind, we should note the peculiarities of the texts that result before quickly returning to the essential. First, from a textual point of view, the place where the short texts and Prague inserted these two lines (at the end of line 791 of the present edition) is awkward, because it is in the midst of a complex argument which is senselessly interrupted by the insertion. Thus on its face, the placement of lines 773–74 by the four long texts is better, since it avoids that irruption. The fact that all the long texts refer to a preceding picture, however, caused a problem in the four long versions that followed the order in this edition: the picture of mode 7 comes after and not *antea*. In fact the only text of the long version that uses the word *antea* and actually has the picture before it is Prague, which is the only one among the long texts that placed these lines later — awkwardly, in the midst of an argument.

Here again, the Prague manuscript obviously draws on a pre-Zwettl tradition among the seven-book manuscripts. It would appear that the word *antea* was adopted by that Prague ancestor, but that Zwettl's immediate ancestor and in turn its descendants then relocated the whole two lines as they are found in the edition, before the picture. This was a more coherent place for a reference to a picture, but the words *antea hic* were never deleted. Zwettl and its three ancestors blindly kept this reference to a previous picture while placing the picture itself at a later point.

But let us not miss the most important point. The manuscript variants in these two lines, which refer to a picture rather than an argument, confirm that they were originally inserted into a previously standard text. What then might explain a later insertion of these lines, which refer to the illustration of this seventh, non-biblical, mode?

A third significant variant in the text of the prayer book almost certainly answers that question. It occurs immediately after the interrupted complex argument referred to above, and thus after the discourses on the seven modes of prayer and after all the references to the pictures illustrating them. The variant occurs in the Paduan text, one whose hand may be older than any manuscript other than that of the roughly contemporary Venice. At this point (808), Padua begins with the title: "Cum sit orandum aliquo iamdictorum *vi* modorum." Venice has no title for this chapter and, as indicated by the edition, all the other manuscripts, though their titles are otherwise similar to that of Padua, say simply "iamdictorum modorum." They do not specify how many modes have just been described. The Paduan title refers to *six* modes of prayer described above, whereas Padua itself had described seven!

The reader rightly cautions that though space for the Paduan title was provided by the original scribe, the title is in different ink and could have been written later; also, the number "vi" might just be a mistake for "vii," the actual number of previous modes of prayer. The latter possibility does not, however, prove out. The paragraph that follows the title in all texts shows that the number "vi" is correct, whenever the title was written.

This paragraph argues that the *actio Christi* should be our instruction — already seemingly referring to the six modes authenticated by Christ in the Bible rather than to the seventh mode. What follows confirms that reading. Peter justifies his argument by saying that many (early) saints followed Christ's behavior, and he identifies modes 2, 5, and 4 as examples (817–22). This saintly diversity is good, he proceeds, for when one becomes tired of mode 1, one can turn to 6, and then to 3 (822–26). Thus Peter lists the six biblical modes of prayer that are the *actio Christi*.

In the preceding text regarding the fourth mode, the long version had, it is true, already referred to five modes (1 and 2, 4–6) used by such saintly heroes (612–16), but in this *actio Christi* paragraph, Peter unmistakably directs us to use the first six (of the seven) modes because they are biblical, an admonition that is present in all the texts. Thus the title of the Paduan text is quite precise: preferentially, one was to pray in *six* ways.

Let me repeat the three variants analyzed above: at the beginning of the description of the prayer modes, Padua and Venice refer to six not seven modes; the text reference to the illustration of the seventh mode was probably inserted into an earlier text; a Paduan title refers to six "iamdictorum" modes after describing seven. That done, we can, I think, explain the later insertion of lines referring to the illustration of the seventh, nonbiblical, mode.

Perhaps we should first dismiss as unwarranted the notion that Peter the Chanter originally thought unsymmetrically to balance seven canonical hours with only six modes of prayer. Certainly from the beginning, Peter's scheme called for the six modes he could document in the Bible plus one un-biblical mode to achieve symmetry. Yet the fact that he ends by saying that one should follow the *actio Christi* (that is, the first six modes) strongly argues against the proposition that he wanted all seven illustrated: the whole point of these figures being to instruct, why show a mode that was not particularly recommended? We are drawn to the conclusion that lines 773–74 referring to the seventh illustration were Peter's afterthought, as was the picture itself.

Let us return to basics. It is clear that in his introduction to the prayer modes, Peter meant to refer to six biblically authenticated prayer modes, as in the Venice and Padua texts, and not to seven, as in the others. What is just as certain is that at the end of his description of the seven prayer modes, Peter urges the reader to use the first six. What happened is now clear. Some scribe whose manuscript later served as a source for Prague and Zwettl, faced with seven illustrations, achieved symmetry with the seven canonical hours mentioned in the introductory text by saying right off, if erroneously, that there were seven biblically authenticated, meritorious, and "regular" modes of prayer. Perhaps the addition of the word "regular" was in fact meant to "cover" the seventh, non-biblical mode. In doing so the scribe lost sight of the clear superiority Peter assigned to the first six, which all the texts emphasize in the paragraph that Padua titled with reference to those "vi."

The correct reference to six biblical modes of prayer gives further evidence that either the short Venetian or the Paduan text is genealogically the oldest of all the manuscripts, just as they are probably the oldest chronologically. They are older on the one hand than the other ten-book text from Ot-tobeuren, which by 1246 refers erroneously to seven modes of prayer, and on the other older than Zwettl, the oldest manuscript of the seven-book model in terms of its writing and content. It is at this point that Padua's and Zwettl's assignment of authorship to the chanter of "Pariensis" ("pariēsis") takes on a new significance. Padua must have passed on this variant to a Zwettl-type manuscript.

I have already shown a textual influence on Ottobeuren of Zwettl, the oldest known manuscripts to change the introduction of the study of the prayer modes from six biblically authenticated modes to seven. I will later show that a pictorial relationship as well existed between these two manuscripts of different book organization. But for now, I conclude with the hypothesis that the Ottobeuren book on prayer is younger than Padua and Venice at some points, and Zwettl younger than Padua at many others. This is not to say that the long version of this book is a simple elaboration of the short version. That we have already seen to be false.

Lest it be thought that these labors have led to a definitive and unproblematic genealogy regarding these particular manuscripts, I pass now to a fourth significant variant in the book on prayer, the only one that deals with the substance of the texts themselves. Beginning with line 622 of the present edition, one reads in all save the Ottobeuren and Munich manuscripts first that James the brother of Jesus knelt while he prayed 100 times each day and each night for the sins of the peoples, and second, that as a result his knees were as hard and calloused as the feet of camels. These statements are followed by a reference to the pending picture of the fourth mode of prayer. As seen in the apparatus of variants, however, Ottobeuren followed by Munich has significant variants to this text. They add up to this: not James, but Bartholomew, who goes unmentioned in the other texts, is the one who is said to have prayed 100 times each day and night on his knees. The scribe then indicates in a general fashion that James and Bartholomew did similar things.

We are clearly dealing with Ottobeuren's additions to the text of the edition, rather than with an elimination by all but the Munich manuscript of the reference to Bartholomew in Ottobeuren. This is probable first because only Munich copied any of Ottobeuren's idiosyncratic text, but also because Ottobeuren has not one but two variants at this point, both of them clearly additions to another text: the first allowed the Ottobeuren scribe to enter Bartholomew into the text, the second permitted him to exit from his insert and return to the discourse on James in his sources. This procedure explains why Ottobeuren necessarily repeated the story of James' callouses and ends up by saying that both he and Bartholomew did the same thing. It is evident that Ottobeuren added to its source.

The Ottobeuren scribe had good reason to make the change. In the relevant ancient texts, it was in fact Bartholomew who prayed 100 times day and night, as Peter the Chanter also knew (DVV, 321c), and James who had the hard knees. In the mid-thirteenth century, Humbert of Romans (II, 165) also described them in this way.[119] Thus Ottobeuren and Munich are the only texts that copied the stories correctly. Since Peter the Chanter hardly made the mistake, and Ottobeuren's awkward solution to the error rules out that *its* wording represents the original text, I conclude that a scribe writing before any extant text miscopied a more elegantly formulated correct text of this passage. Since it is also clear that any of our extant manuscripts would have kept the correct reference to Bartholomew and not the incorrect one to James, it is again evident that Munich alone used Ottobeuren as a direct or indirect textual source.

A last significant variant in the text of the prayer book occurs in the

Venetian and Paduan manuscripts under the title "De quarto vitio eiusdem" (1219 ff.). With allowances made for the shortness of the ten-book manuscripts and, in this case, also of Prague,[120] the sequence of the edition before the reader is the same for the seven-book model and for the Ottobeuren and Munich manuscripts. But the two Italian manuscripts place lines 1233–44 ("Quod sit fideliter orare") after line 1324 of the edition, to then return to the sequence of the other manuscripts. The careful student will note that in the edition this chapter on what it is to pray faithfully follows logically a first mention of faithful prayer at lines 1226 of the other manuscripts in this edition, whereas their position in the Venice and Paduan manuscripts — but not by the other two short manuscripts Ottobeuren and Munich — is less coherent. For the third time, an insertion in the short Italian manuscripts makes less sense than the order of the long versions. But the fact itself of the insertions is quite as important. Here again a sequence of lines (1233–44), surely by Peter the Chanter himself since this sequence too is in all the manuscripts, was fitted into an established text. What we appear to have before us, therefore, is a book compiled from loose sheets.

Several of the variants just studied involved texts that are in all manuscripts but in different locations. This is quite a different phenomenon from texts that are found in some manuscripts but not in others. It is to variants of this latter type that we now turn our attention. Usually, of course, such texts are in the long version, and the edition distinguishes that fact by its type faces. Time and again, the long seven-book version not only elaborates upon materials, but has whole chapters that are not found in the short ten-book version. Studying just the titles from the first through the seventh modes of prayer in the most important manuscripts, for instance, one sees that while the short-version more or less limited itself to titling the seven modes themselves, the long version went much further. Here are the total number of titles in this space:

v: 6   o: 7   z: 23 (including 1 marginal title)
pa: 8   pr: 14

Readers can verify that more is involved here than just a subdivision of a given text into several titled rubrics: there is also much text in the long version that is not in the short one. As one might expect, the basic instructions for praying are in all the texts and the long version does not add to those instructions. Rather, the further texts of the long version usually contain other proofs that such modes are found in the sacred writings. If we did not already know better, we might, to judge only by this section on the modes of prayer, conclude that the long version is just an enlargement of the short.

The evidence to the contrary can now be further enriched. First, some seven-book texts are found in one but not both of the subsets of the ten-book model.[121] Much weightier is the fact that in later parts of the prayer book, the short version contains some quite extensive texts that, with one significant exception in the Prague text, are not found in the long version:

> lines 1100–86: in o and m only;
> lines 1281–1324: in o and m,
> v and pa;
> line 1907–43: in o and m, v
> and pa, *and* pr.

The presence in the Prague text of lines 1907–43 once more verifies that this seven-book Prague copy relies in part on texts genealogically older than Zwettl. But the absence of all three of these texts from Zwettl and its three descendants suggests that Zwettl or an ancestor may have renounced certain texts already available in the shorter, older manuscripts.[122] It would seem that already in the earliest extant manuscripts, the recommendation of the author that people add and subtract as they thought best was put into practice.

Nowhere are the results of this recommendation more easily observable than in the Ottobeuren manuscript and its Munich descendant. Not only were hundreds of lines rewritten by the scribe or scribes of that monastery into a form that only Munich copied. But the Ottobeuren writers also adopted fundamentally different oral prayers from those in the Italian manuscripts or those in the seven-book texts, variants again absorbed by Munich alone. The prayers from lines 730 to 755 in this edition, for example, were recommended to the faithful as mass prayers because they were the prayers said at the consecration of the mass by the pious men of the French schools. These are replaced in Ottobeuren and Munich by litany and other prayers that presumably corresponded to the mass order of that particular monastery.

After reviewing the major variants in the prayer book, it is evident that determining Peter the Chanter's role in fitting particular texts into the whole is a risky business. Clearly, at least one compiler other than Peter worked at it. Did such a compiler or compilers add text? For example, it might seem plausible to argue that the scattered additions that the Leipzig manuscripts made to the Klosterneuburg text are genealogically late enough not to have been written by Peter, or at least not to have formed part of the work he conceived and executed. Yet can we deny that words which we have seen the Leipzig texts put into Peter's mouth came from his pen?[123] Again, the Ottobeuren scribe undoubtedly subjected substantial parts of the whole manuscript to rewriting. Yet to whom if not to Peter are we to attribute the Ottobeuren/Munich passage where the author pleads his imperfection?[124] These are serious, open questions, and there are others which could be raised.

The basic long and short versions, however, are another matter, and I am persuaded to assign both of them to our author. Certainly the problem of attribution must be kept in perspective. The basic texts describing and analyzing the modes of prayers themselves are very similar in all the manuscripts, so that the problem of authorship has been a limited one for studying Peter's views on prayer.

There is a final perspective to be adopted regarding the texts other than those on the modes of prayer which are at the center of our concern. We have been discussing a short and a long version of this work whose texts were *both* generally fixed if not by Peter's death, then surely while some of his students were still alive and spreading his fame. Ottobeuren, we recall, has a terminus post quem of 1246, and Zwettl is probably older, as I hope to show again in the following examination of the pictures. Thus even if later scholars discover that some of the texts in Zwettl or Prague but not in either of the Italian manuscripts are additions that Peter did not write — a position my texts, my focus on the prayer book, and my decision to limit my manuscripts studies to this *De penitentia*, makes it impossible to defend —, my mistake would not affect the view that the words of the Chanter's circle were being described.[125]

The Pictures

At an earlier point in this study, we examined the illustrations accompanying eight of the manuscripts largely out of time and with little attention to their relations to each other. Now we approach their actual history, especially emphasizing the pictures' relations to the texts of their individual manuscripts, and the relations of the pictures of any one manuscript to those of others.[126] My concern is to compare the family relations that have emerged between texts to those that may emerge between pictures. But as I promised at an earlier point in this study, this genealogical study will also enrich our knowledge of the illustrations' relation to Peter's wishes.

The media in which our pictures were done should first be summariz-ed: the Venice, Pegau, and Altzella manuscripts are illuminated in several colors. Ottobeuren and Prague have finished drawings in sepia, which is also the color of the Paduan, Zwettl, and Klosterneuburg sketches.

Next, the chronological relation of pictures to texts in these codices must be explored. I can say flatly that there is no one manuscript in which all the illustrations were drawn before the relevant text was entered. Rather, most of the manuscripts followed the standard procedure of the time: scribes left spaces for the pictures while writing, to be filled in by the artist at a later time. This is clearly the case of the pictures planned for the Munich manuscript, where the scribe left spaces with indications like "hic debet esse figura" for pictures (and initials) that were never executed (m: 146vb–150va), and it is certainly the case in the Zwettl manuscript as well, where figure 2 is squeezed in between pre-existent texts. Pegau's figures 2, 3, 4, 5 and 7, and Altzella's figure 2 definitely postdated the text.

Clearly, an artist did the Venetian manuscript's figures 2 and 3 before the chapter *titles* that followed them. Conversely, Pegau's figures 2, 3, and 6 were definitely done after the following titles, and the Altzella artist did his figure 7 after the large initial that followed; these figures partially cover those titles and initial. But these titles and initials could themselves have been inscribed long after their texts. As regards the relation between figures and texts proper, however, most of the scribes wrote the text and then the illustrators added the pictures.

Let us turn now to the shapes of the spaces that scribes left for later pic-tures. They fall into patterns, the most common practice being to leave a whole block of column space for each figure. This procedure was fol-lowed by the two Italian manuscripts, Zwettl and Prague — four of the seven manuscripts with double columns of text —, as well as by Pegau, one of the two manuscripts written in a wide single column.

Other manuscripts combine such whole blocks with narrower ones bor-dered by text. For example, the double-column Altzella text left whole blocks for all but its third figure, which it placed to the left of a narrow slice of text. The Munich text, whose pictures were never executed, has one whole block for the planned illustration of prostration (mode 5), combined with seven narrower blocks to the left of texts.

Klosterneuburg, another double-column text, falls mostly into this same pattern: whole blocks of space were left for figures 5 and 7, and narrower blocks alongside narrow texts for figures 1, 3, 4, and 6. Only its second figure, showing the prayer mode with extended arms, offers a third option. Here there are three wholly blank lines to accommodate the arms, but text on both sides of the lines level with the head and lower parts of the figure. If it were not for the fact that Klosterneuburg's figure 1 was certainly drawn after the text was written, we might think that this figure 2 was drawn before its text was inscribed. It was not. Rather, the scribe left the missing lines and narrow blocks for a subsequent figure — after he had seen a drawing of the same mode in another manuscript. A comparison of this Klosterneuburg figure 2 to its Ottobeuren counterpart shows that the former is almost certainly an elegant copy of the placement of a less happy Ottobeuren figure. In both, figure 2 comes *after* and is surrounded by the title and the beginning of the description of *mode 3*.

This first evidence of the influence of one set of pictures on another draws our attention to the single-column Ottobeuren manuscript, one which bears a *terminus post* of 1246. It is the most interesting of the pictorial documents, in part because it is the only text most of whose pictures were drawn *before* the scribe wrote the surrounding texts. Thus the plates show that the figure for mode 3 clearly preceded the text transcription: it extends its reach from the left margin into the thin slice of text to the right, three lines being still further shortened to accommodate the gesture. Figures 4 through 6 are also anterior to the text, for they are enclosed by text lines of unequal length so as to conform to pre-existent illustrations. Figure 7 is also enclosed, but in a rectangle. All these figures feature monks as supplicants.

Yet the Ottobeuren figural cycle is not that easily understood. For example, the illustrations for modes 1 and 2 require close attention if we are to explain not only why none of the figures of mode one is surrounded by text like most of the others, but why modes 1 and 2 are multiply represented (three for mode 1 and two for mode two), and finally why these figures show young schoolboys as well as monks.

A merely cursory review of these peculiarities shows that the Ottobeuren manuscript changed course in mid-stream, with the most evident result being that the Ottobeuren scribe, slavishly followed by the Munich copyist, left eight spaces for seven modes of prayer. The Klosterneuburg copyist committed a comparable error: alone among the manuscripts, this text erroneously entered a chapter title "De octavo modo orandi" (776), which is another possible indication of Ottobeuren's influence on Klosterneuburg. Thus an explanation of the peculiarities of the first Ottobeuren figures may give us insight into the artistic procedures of the Ottobeuren scribe and artist, but it can also illuminate some of the figural procedures of other scribes and artists.

If we move backwards from figures 3 through 7, all of which show monks within the borders of the text, we begin to understand what happened. First, note that figure 2 (extended arms mode), the first representation surrounded by text, is not a monk but, like the figure within the margin just above him (mode 1, figure 2), a schoolboy with a full head of hair. Monks are there for modes 1 and 2, but they are drawn outside the margins opposite these youthful figures, obviously added after a decision was made to represent all the figures as monks. Thus implementing a judgment that mature monks best represented supplicants meant abandoning an earlier decision to show innocent young schoolboys praying.

The Ottobeuren scriptorium reached a second decision at this point. It decided to draw subsequent figures of monks within the body of the text, just as the now-replaced schoolboy of mode 2 had been drawn. But why in the first place had that schoolboy been drawn *and then* surrounded by text? To answer this question we must first try to shed light on the peculiar fact that mode 1 was represented twice within the margins of the text before it was done for a third time outside the margin.

Note first of all that the copyist created the first two spaces in the text for figures that were to be drawn in later by narrowing the length of text lines: the second blank block, which comes at the end of the text for mode 1, was rendered much smaller than the first blank block, which is located in the middle of the text for the same mode. This first block was larger, I suspect, because the copyist originally envisioned for this title folio an auspicious maiestà: a double figure of a supplicant and a pompous Christ. Among the extant manuscripts that might have been available to him, such a double figure is found in Zwettl's figure 1; among later texts, it is found in the Pegau and Prague manuscripts. Perhaps the Ottobeuren workshop knew the Zwettl manuscript or one like it, just as the Klosterneuburg one certainly knew Ottobeuren or one like it at a later point, the artists of ten-book and seven-book texts easily copying their opposites' pictures if not texts.

Why then did Ottobeuren abandon this alleged plan for a maiestà? There are two possible answers, both of which assume that while the Ottobeuren scribe and artist may have seen the Zwettl pictures, they had not noted or no longer remembered the position of those pictures in that text. First, the answer could be that only on reaching the end of the text of mode 1 did the copyist find that that text ("Ad hoc ut melius intelligatur quod dictum est, figura oculis subiecta evidenter et manifeste demonstrat") called for the appropriate illustration there, on what was a new folio, and not earlier, on the previous title folio. So the artist drew into the correct space for the figure on the second folio and then, almost certainly as a throwaway, drew a solitary tonsured clerical figure into the large space on the previous page, its sleeveless gown different from that of the monks in later modes. Both figures show the same awkward and, as it turned out, incorrect posture with heads faced straight ahead but arms up.

A more probable explanation for this change in plan was that, no figures having yet been drawn, the correct placement of figure 1 was not actually determined until the scribe had written out the text of mode 2. In my view, he originally intended the large block on the previous page for figure 1, and the narrower block opposite the introductory title of mode 2 for figure 2. Thus he began to write out the text of mode two opposite the narrow block he originally intended for its figure. This becomes plausible when we discover that the first figure of mode 2 that was actually executed was drawn in the center of the page at the end of the text of that mode — which like the previous mode concludes with a call for an image ("ydiote advertunt in figuris expresse et aperte") — *before any further text was inscribed.*

By this time the scribe had grasped that the picture for each mode belonged at the end whereas, if he had understood this before writing the text of mode 2, he would presumably not have written it alongside the schoolboy representation of figure 1. Now however, there was no choice. The illustrator drew in that schoolboy of the first mode alongside the pre-existing narrow beginning of the text of the second mode, and then the schoolboy of the second mode at the end of that mode's text. As in other manuscripts, the presence of these figures at the beginning of the following modes, often juxtaposed to the following titles, could only confuse readers. At first glance, one often incorrectly thinks that the title refers to the nearby figure.

Perhaps aesthetic considerations led the artist to draw this latter figure in the center of the page before any text was entered: a figure with extended arms is handsomer there than on the left margin that had been used earlier. Yet the artist had obviously drawn the picture without consulting the copyist. Since the text of mode 2 was finished, the scribe now either had to leave the bottom of the page empty of text or enter the text of mode *3* around this mode 2 figure. Confusing though it turns out to be for readers (note the horizontal line that positively commits this figure 2 to mode 3), he chose the latter option for either aesthetic reasons or economy. He was unwilling to leave blank the space to the left and right of the schoolboy, the only way to avoid a confusion of the picture of mode 2 with the text of mode 3. Almost surely, it was this spacial arrangement that the Klosterneuburg artist adopted for his figure of mode 2: it too is ensconced in the text of mode 3. In the Ottobeuren manuscript, this embarrassed solution led in turn to the artful, planned enclosure of subsequent figures within texts.

Thus in the earliest stage of the Ottobeuren text, the copyist preceded the artist. For the later figures, all of monks, the two men obviously worked in tandem on and around each figure. Yet before that synchrony first becomes evident in figure 3, someone decided that monks were, after all, better figures to induce emulation than schoolboys. While I cannot say what brought on that decision, I will now show the context in which it was made. It involved the discovery that mode 1 had been misdrawn in both earlier blocks. The content of the texts themselves, once correctly understood, led the artist to redraw monks as figures 1 and 2 in the margins.

Peter the Chanter's verbal description of mode 1 does not state how the head should be positioned, so the artist had shown the figures facing straight ahead but with their arms directed toward heaven, an awkward stance if for no other reason than that two distinct objects of supplication were thus evoked.[127] But in the textual justifications for mode 1 that followed the description of the mode, Peter the Chanter cited Martin of Tours as having his eyes as well as hands and arms turned toward heaven (444–46). It was upon noting this disparity that the copyist and artist presumably decided to correct the pictures. A glance at the second space for mode 1 shows what happened next: the artist now drew a monk opposite the schoolboy, this time with the figure's eyes turned to heaven as required by the later text. And once this monk had been drawn, the artist drew monks in the subsequent drawings, beginning with a new monkish figure that "replaced" the schoolboy of mode 2.

Thus the fundamental question of the proper social status to represent for edification was answered by the Ottobeuren artisans in the context of correcting a prayer posture so that it corresponded to the author's intent. We started with a description of how different artists placed their figures in relation to their texts. My examination of the ten-book Ottobeuren production, finished within half a century of the *De penitentia* itself, hypothesized that for its first figure, Ottobeuren had been influenced by the triumphal first figure of Zwettl or a copy, and thus postdates that manuscript. Further study confirmed that at least one of the Ottobeuren drawings inspired the later seven-book Klosterneuburg drawings in the placement of its figure and in the shaping of the text around it. And I have shown just how dependent the late Munich copyist was on its ancestor Ottobeuren when it also provided eight spaces for its seven figures. Studying the placement of these figures and the shapes of the spaces for them demonstrates that existing visual traditions influenced later pictures.

But answering the simple problem of figural placement in the Ottobeuren text showed that those placements were embedded in decisions of greater import. First, the Ottobeuren artisans did attempt to represent what the author had written, even if it meant redrawing a figure, an event we find in no other manuscript. Second, the Ottobeuren artist and his patrons obviously were concerned enough about the figures' social status to change it, yet Peter the Chanter had said nothing about the social status he wanted in the pictures. These textual and sociological findings are important leads in an inquiry that will end by suggesting that with the best of wills, the social context of the artist did not permit him to convert words into pictures precisely.

We turn now to a comparison of the physical postures the figures assumed in the different manuscripts, for the purpose of relating and thus dating the different sets of drawings. Whereas Peter the Chanter said little or nothing about the placement of the figures, he did mandate physical postures with different degrees of specificity. Therefore the study of these postures has the Chanter's words as its backdrop. Yet we will find that the illustrators of the extant manuscripts did copy their postures from each other as well as being aware of Peter's words, and it is these artistic similarities which will permit further genealogical progress. In what follows, the question of the correspondence between the author and the artist vies for attention with the question of the correspondence of the new artist with the old.

The first problem regarding postures that one should address comparatively is what directions the figures faced; those directions can reveal possible families of illustrations. The Ottobeuren and Klosterneuburg figures will soon emerge as significantly different from the others. But almost all the figures of the other manuscripts face to the left, including all the Paduan and Leipzig figures. Indeed among these seven manuscripts, all exceptions to the left-face rule except for Venice's female figure 7 are in one mode, that of the prostrate figure 5: in addition to the late Prague drawing, the early and remarkably similar figures of Zwettl and Venice also face right, alerting us to the possibility of a relation between them.

Yet all the Klosterneuburg and eight of the ten Ottobeuren figures (the exceptions being figures 5 and 6) face as resolutely right as most others do left! This confirms the previous evidence that the Klosterneuburg artist consulted the long-finished Ottobeuren text before he set to work, even though his text was derived from Zwettl. It will remain a general rule: the two sets of images that seem least related to the other figures in their respective seven- and ten-book traditions have significant affinities with each other.

Examining now the shapes of the figures themselves, we begin by noting certain affinities between those whose texts are also related. Not surprisingly, there are obvious similarities between the Venetian and Paduan drawings. The postures in modes 1–4 are almost identical, as is mode 5 except that the two figures face in opposite directions. The Paduan illustration of mode 6, meant to show a standing figure bowing, is however quite different from the Venetian: the Paduan supplicant is kneeling, the Venetian one not; the former is before an altar, as was suggested but not mandated by the uniform text, but the latter is not.

Postural similarities are also common between Zwettl, Pegau, Altzella and Prague, all seven-book manuscripts. Striking similarities link whole sets of drawings: if not all the Pegau and Altzella figures (1 and 4 are different), then most of their drawings of postures are as similar as their texts, even when the figures are of different sexes as in their mode 7. But nowhere is the similarity of this family more evident than in mode 6. All four drawings show the standing supplicant in a deep, awkwardly rectangular bow with the hands and arms hanging straight down in the first three, less so in Prague. This athletic posture shows a close dependence of these illustrators upon each other quite apart from the text, which does not call for such an improbable rectangular bow. Since Peter did not mandate such a pose and I could not find it in other sources,[128] it seems that Zwettl or a copy was the ultimate authority for the posture's replication in the latter three manuscripts. The unlikelihood that supplicants would actually imitate this pose is another matter, one that we shall later address.

To summarize, strong visual evidence corroborates the relations already established in the text traditions themselves between the two Italian manuscripts on the one hand, and, with the exception of Klosterneuburg, between the seven-book eastern and northern texts on the other.

Yet while these illustrations do demonstrate genealogical similarities in the poses, particular modal figures within genealogically related manuscripts also reveal how strikingly artists within a given tradition might vary those poses because they or their scribes read Peter's ambiguous text differently. In turn, accomodations of those readings could affect the figures themselves. Let us probe one example of this variety, the text and figures of mode 6.

After describing the bow, Peter says that one should use this mode before any altar. We recall that here for the first time the short text does not call for an image. Only the long version follows the admonition regarding bowing before altars with the words "sicut docet hec imago," which encourages, but still does not mandate the presence of an altar in the illustrations. The result was remarkable variety: some of the illustrators but not others in the same family of texts drew in an altar. Padua did, but Venice did not. Zwettl did not, but Prague did. Of the two Leipzig manuscripts, Altzella has no altar, but Pegau does.

Where introduced, this altar placed pressure on the figures' loyalty to the text. We turn therefore to the impact of added visual details on text fidelity. Thus the Paduan artist, given an available space that apparently prohibited realistically representing the supplicant standing at the foot of a higher altar, pulled his supplicant to his knees. This directly violated Peter's mandate to stand, but here the posture of the supplicant, though uppermost in the author's mind, was less important to the artist or his employer than the presence of an altar, to which the supplicant had to be accommodated.

Pegau and Prague also thought an altar was called for, but under similar constraints of space as Padua, their portrayal of the supplicant was nevertheless dictated directly or indirectly by the awkward rectangular posture of the supplicant already done by the Zwettl illustrator, who had not thought an altar was called for. Thus having determined to include an altar, the Pegau painter drew it higher than the bent supplicant, but with the unfortunate result that the latter's torso, arms and hands, then eyes and head tend to face in three different directions. The Prague illustrator avoided just this problem by reducing his altar to an unrealistic miniature at the feet of the supplicant.

Thus the Paduan figure is realistic but the illustrator either deliberately misrepresented the author's instructions or misunderstood the scribe's instructions. The Pegau and Prague figures do not violate the author's instructions, but the pictures are certainly unrealistic. The culprit in the latter cases was the slavish copying of a Zwettl model that was an unrealistic elaboration of Peter the Chanter's simple instruction. All three artists drew figures that Peter the Chanter probably would have found ridiculous.

If the figures of mode 6 have allowed us to see the range of figural variety possible in families of texts and pictures that are generally consistent, the figures of mode 1 permit us to further explore the visual relations between these families. It is true that the most unusual feature in the pictures of this mode is limited to textually related manuscripts: only in the Zwettl, Pegau and Prague texts is the supplicant shown praying to or with a life-size Christ whose presence is not even hinted at by Peter the Chanter. Yet an analysis of this supplicant demonstrates that the Christ of the seven-book tradition was a later addition to a supplicant whose shape is first found in the ten-book tradition.

There is every reason to believe that the artist employed for the Venetian manuscript painted all its illuminations contemporary to, if after, the text. This is also probable for the first two figures of Padua, although its figures 3–7 were done by a different artist at a later time. Now the Paduan and Venetian mode 1 illustrations show what is certainly the oldest extant supplicant representation: the supplicant's only slightly bent arms and his hands point almost straight up, while head and eyes rise to gaze on the same heavenly spot. There is no Christ.

On examination, the Zwettl supplicant has precisely the same posture. Yet here a Christ of equal size stands opposite the supplicant and logically demands his bodily attention. Given the Zwettl supplicant's posture with head, eyes, arms and hands raised to heaven, however, the picture shows a problem of communication between the two. Christ seems almost an interloper, the supplicant being enclosed within a space whose frame Christ's arms are made to overlap as the latter reaches into the supplicant's space. The Zwettl artist's solution to the lack of communication was awkward: for no apparent reason other than the stance of the supplicant, Christ's arms are made to reach up to heaven just as do those of the supplicant. As in the study of the altar in mode 6, here again the introduction of an object of prayer created a problem because of the avowed imitation of the supplicant from an existing manuscript, in this case one of the Italian ones.

The two later manuscripts that have a Christ opposite the supplicant are Pegau and Prague, the same two that introduced an altar into mode 6, whereas the model for their supplicant, Zwettl, had no altar. Prague avoided the problem of communication that Zwettl raised, simply turning the supplicant's face to the viewer and thus creating two distinct greeting directions. The Pegau artist tried to solve the problem. He dropped the head and pulled in the elbows of the supplicant so that head and face are turned level to the magisterial seated Jesus. Yet this directly violated the instructions Peter the Chanter gave in the text of mode 1, which said that the arms were to be extended as far up as possible.

But because of its antiquity, the Zwettl illustration remains the most interesting of these maiestàs. For the first time among the extant manuscripts, Zwettl added a Jesus figure, one that could have had no other purpose than to increase the decorum of the text at the first illustration, as is evidently the goal of the monumental Pegau illumination. Yet the Zwettl artist as good as copied the supplicant of the Christless Italian drawings of this mode. He seems also to have been influenced by the clothing, to have copied the armbands, and to have imitated the hair style of the Venetian manuscript in other figures. The evidence is strong, I think, that Zwettl's drawings descend from those of Italy.

Zwettl's introduction of a triumphant Jesus figure not only influenced subsequent manuscripts in the seven-book tradition; the influence of its drawings can also be seen in the ten-book Ottobeuren text. The production of the Ottobeuren manuscript, finished by 1246, included two distinct spaces with drawings of figure one. The first of these is so large that it may originally have been intended for a double figure of Jesus and supplicant. The copyist or artist may have gained this triumphal idea from Zwettl or an intervening inextant manuscript.

Nor is this the only evidence that the Ottobeuren artisans may have examined the Zwettl text or a copy, different though the drawings are in other respects: the triangular flare of clothing in figures 4 and 7 of Zwettl is quite similar to that in figure 4 and, to a slight degree, figure 5 in the Ottobeuren manuscript. If these links are correct, therefore, here is another case of influences between text families, this time from the seven-book tradition to a ten-book one. In this view, the Zwettl production of text *and* pictures was finished before 1246, the terminus post quem of the Ottobeuren text.

We come finally to an elaboration of the cross-family tie between later Klosterneuburg and earlier Ottobeuren, which I earlier established by their similar placement of figure 2. How striking has been the absence of Klosterneuburg from everything said above about relations between the seven-book texts in modes 6 and 1. Despite its undoubted textual descendance from Zwettl, and Pegau's and Altzella's undoubted textual descendance from it, Klosterneuburg has neither the altars nor awkwardly rectangular figures in its mode 6, nor a Christ figure in mode 1.

Yet when we compare Klosterneuburg's drawings to Ottobeuren's figures, the similarities go beyond the placement and stance of the cruciform figure 2. The stance of the two males in figure 7 is also strikingly similar. Figure 6 of Ottobeuren, instead of being in the rectangular position of other manuscripts, shows a monk certainly with a bow slighter than that of Klosterneuburg, but with its arms bent and hands up in similar fashion. Combined with the fact that the figures of these two manuscripts mostly face right and not to the customary left, it can be suggested with some confidence that the Ottobeuren drawings influenced the Klosterneuburg draftsman.

Let me summarize the readings of the history of these images. While there are strong similarities among the Italian manuscripts on the one hand and among the northern and eastern ones on the other confirming the textual similarities, there is strong evidence of influences across family borders. First, the Venetian figures and perhaps figures 1 and 2 of Padua influenced Zwettl. Second, the Ottobeuren artist seems to have seen the Zwettl drawings; we noted the similar triangular flanges on the dresses of certain figures, and that he seems to have left space for a triumphal double figure 1. This reading yields a terminus post quem of 1246 for the Zwettl production, the date by which the Ottobeuren production had definitely been terminated. Third, perhaps more than a century later, the Klosterneuburg artist consulted the much earlier illustrations of Ottobeuren. Combining all this information, I here superimpose the findings regarding the relations of these illustrations upon the genealogy of the texts:

Genealogy Table

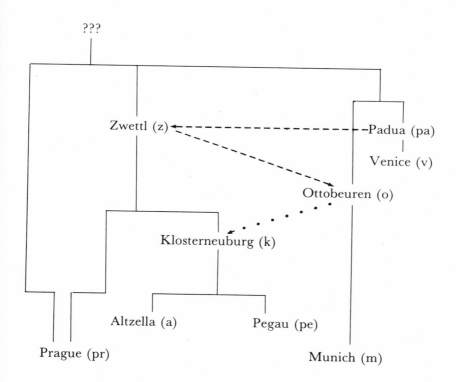

Legend

Dashes = text and pictures
Dots   = pictures

Conclusion

Finit Viaticum liber magistri parisiensis cantoris. En pater, ad finem duxi scribendo volumen. Fac caput inclinem fessum requiescere
lumen. Si perfectorum sequimur sacra dogmata morum, possumus astrorum rite subire
chorum.[129]

The Ottobeuren text of Peter the Chanter's penitential opus proves its unique character one last time. The codex in which it is found, we recall, fur-
nishes the only picture of the author. Now the text itself closes with an Ottobeuren scribe's comprehension of the work. In this striking encomium,
he characterizes Peter's work as concerned with the "holy rules of manners"
and asserts that, once we have mastered these rules as they are practiced
by the perfect, we will be able to enter heavenly society. In modern translation: this reader of Peter raises the question of the relevance of manners
to one's ultimate identity not just among the heavenly but within earthly
societies. With more insight than the Chanter himself, our scribe discusses
the place of the body in the medieval scheme of things.

Hopefully the present study and the text of Peter's book on prayer will
help draw attention to this neglected question. Mine is a modest contribution, to be sure. Constrained by the demands an unstudied text tradition
placed on me, I have spent as much time deciphering and explaining that
tradition as I have commenting upon it. To do that for a work ascribed
to Peter the Chanter hardly needs justification. And as the complexity of
this tradition has shown, without this effort no assignment of texts to particular persons would be possible.

What then has been shown about these texts? A first result: we may be
confident that Peter the Chanter conceived and executed the plan of the

De penitentia. This included the incorporation of an earlier treatise on vocal and real prayer. The book on prayer published here, with its accompanying figures of prayer supplicants, was originally the first of a separate, two-part treatise on vocal and real prayer, as the author came to label it. On being inserted into the new work, vocal and real prayer became prayer and almsgiving, the second and third parts of penance.

Next, the best evidence suggests that Peter the Chanter authored most of the texts of both organizational forms this *De penitentia* took—a long and short version of respectively seven and either nine or ten books. While at times the long version did add some texts to the short version, elsewhere it dropped texts in the short version. Thus no easy rule of enlargement or contraction allows us to deny Peter authorship, for example, of the longer texts of the long version.

On the other hand, I am less confident that the author was responsible for dividing the work into these two book structures. To be sure, it has been shown that these two versions existed in more or less canonized form, if not by the time of Peter's death in 1197, then certainly by the early thirteenth century, and the genealogy I have constructed assigns the earliest extant manuscripts from each version to just such early origins. But the turning points in the construction we discovered in the prose reveal an earlier organization with no hint of books. It is at times at odds with the organization by book, which seems later and less authentically authorial.

Perhaps the genealogical finding that a treatise on body prayer existed in the late twelfth or early thirteenth century will be more important to readers than the assignment of authorship to Peter the Chanter. This is no great work of the master of the boy singers and processors of the cathedral of Paris, the leading intellectual light of late twelfth-century Paris. Certainly he had few brilliant insights about the body at prayer: Hugh of St. Victor's few pages on the comportment of boys, indeed the Ottobeuren scribe's platonic couplet suggesting that good earthly comportment mirrors the ultimate order of things, both outshine the usually conventional truisms of the chanter of Paris.

Yet, in two ways Peter the Chanter did achieve remarkable breakthroughs. The very idea of the book on prayer is one: Peter clearly conceived of basing Christian prayer, a particular type of comportment, not on his age's conventions but on prayer as described in a sacred book, the Bible. The fact that he often failed in constructing this synthesis does not detract from the originality of the undertaking.

Through his call for illustrations, Peter made a second and even more remarkable breakthrough in the study of the body. Forget for a moment

that he never did directly address the tension and the comparability between the language of the mouth and that of the rest of the body; still today, we can only begin to explain that dynamic interrelation. Remember
rather that, defining prayer gestures as immobile postures, he was the first
clerk who dared to suggest that a catholic comportment could be taught
by illustrations devoid of historical referents. Pedagogy and images are linked
in this work in an unexampled way.

By accomplishing this, Peter the Chanter brought to the surface a series
of questions about the forms of action and the means by which the environment can be transformed through action. Can behavioral forms be recap-
tured from written sources as Peter was sure they could from the Bible?
Can they then be reduced to a crystalline verbal form by an author, as
Peter was sure he had done? Can verbal forms be considered as identical
to pictorial ones, as Peter at times thought? What then was the relation
between living and dead images, and their relation to the supplicant
hypothetically revivified through them? Even if his contemporary clerical
ideology and the inherent blocks of authorial rhetoric made many of his
answers contradictory, Peter did raise these questions.

Let me conclude by reconsidering the pictorial tradition in these
manuscripts. With notable exceptions, the artists who illustrated these
manuscripts give the lie to Peter's idea that his words could be translated into figures. Through the freedom Peter's words afforded, through
the artists' own commitments to existing figural forms, and through
the pressure of their own patronal ambience, the artists created a tradition somewhat apart from the constraints of the author's text. To the
extent these pictures taught, they taught both more and less than what
Peter had said.

I have argued that this was the result of the difference of the media, but
even more important, of a conflict that is inherent in the description of
what is taken to be meaningful behaviors among humans. To mean,
behavior must be transparent. For Peter the author, that meant describing the body posing without clothes — although *of course* supplicants did not
go naked. For our artists, meaning began with clothes — although *of course*
their figures meant what their clothes said.

Then and now, viewers of supplications made to gods or humans recognize
meaning first through reading the social status and other vital statistics of
the actors. Only through clothes — Peter called it coloring — , does the process of legitimizing behavior begin. The fact that Peter was describing the
particular comportmental setting of prayer only apparently stands in the
way of such an understanding, for Peter seemingly imagined that his God —

so illusory to many moderns — recognized and read messages using the same dictionaries as did humans.

Thus many of the pictures shown in this edition begin with statements about status, age, and gender. Otherwise, no patron divine, monastic, confraternal, or princely would have "bought" them, would have paid attention. We may leave Peter the Chanter with his idea that the Christian God knows no preference of person. What remains for us from his words is that right action comes from those who know. What remains in the pictures is that right action comes from those who dress in the threads and gestures of their patrons.

Notes

1. J. W. Baldwin, *Masters, Princes and Merchants. The Social Views of Peter the Chanter & His Circle*, 2 vols. (Princeton, 1970), 1:3–17; F. S. Gutjahr for O. Schmid, *Petrus Cantor Parisiensis. Sein Leben und Seine Schriften* (Graz, 1899); *Histoire Littéraire de la France*, 2nd ed., 15 (Paris, 1869), pp. 285–303.

2. The picture from the Ottobeuren ms. now in the British Library is also reproduced by Baldwin, *Masters* 1:frontis. See further below for data on the ms.

3. *Summa de Sacramentis et Animae Consiliis*, ed. J.-A. Dugauquier, 3 vols. in 5 of the *Analecta Mediaevalia Namurcensia* (Louvain, 1955–67).

4. Baldwin, *Masters* 2:248 f. The long version I use is in *Biblioteca Apostolica Vaticana, Reg. lat., ms. lat.* 106 (hereafter *BAV*).

5. J.-P. Migne, *Patrologiae Cursus Completus . . . Latinorum* (hereafter "PL"), 205 (Paris, 1855).

6. Baldwin, *Masters* 2:241–65.

7. P. G. Molmenti, *La Storia di Venezia nella Vita Privata* 1 (Trieste, 1973), p. 124, with the two prostrate among the seven figures reproduced wrong, in an erect position; Trexler, *Public Life in Renaissance Florence* (New York, 1980), p. 23, with the prostrate male figure reproduced wrong.

8. Baldwin, *Masters* 2:253 f. On Peter of Poitiers, see A. Teetaert, "Le 'liber poenitentialis' de Pierre de Poitiers," in A. Lang *et al, Aus der Geisteswelt des Mittelalters* (Festschrift Martin Grabmann), (Münster, 1935), pp. 310 ff.; the biographical entries in *Dictionnaire de Théologie Catholique* 12 (Paris, 1932), esp. c. 1905; P. Michaud-Quantin, *Sommes de Casuistique et Manuels de Confession au Moyen Age (XII–XVI siècles)*, (Louvain, 1962), p. 24, n. 14.

9. For the documentation, see below. C. Miroux characterized it as a Vice and Virtue work; C. Langlois, "Les Manuscrits du Verbum Abbreviatum de Pierre le Chantre. Projet de Publication par C. Miroux," *Journal de Savants* n. s. 14 (1916): 310. It is listed in M. Bloomfield, *Incipits of Latin Works on the Virtues and Vices* (Cambridge, Mass., 1979), pp. 548f. Early thirteenth-century writers, however, already referred to it by the title *Verbum abbreviatum*; Baldwin, *Masters* 2:8.

10. In addition to White's classic (Oxford, 1963), see also his *Machina ex Deo* (Cambridge, Mass., 1979). On the Ottobeuren ms., see below.

11. "Between Text and Image: the Prayer Gestures of Saint Dominic," in J.-C. Schmitt (ed.), *Gestures (History and Anthropology* 1 (Paris, 1984): 127–62. In the same volume, see my "Legitimating Prayer Gestures in the Twelfth Century. The *De Penitentia* of Peter the Chanter," pp. 97–126.

12. See the list of the manuscripts below, in the Introduction to the Edition. The

only known manuscript of this work I could not obtain is the Gdansk ms. referred to in Baldwin, *Masters* 2:253. The catalogue Baldwin mentions indicates that this ms. is an abridgement of the prayer books 7 and 8, taken from what I call the long version of the work. No illustrations are referred to.

13. Cf. 323–94 to DVV, 318. Note that the selections from the DVV bring our text up to the section on the species of prayer, and thus to the brink of the seven modes of prayer. None of the cases of conscience concerning prayer in Peter's *Summa*, and thus none of their language, recur in the present work; cf. Dugauquier, *Summa*, vol. 3, pt. 2 b., pp. 465–70.

14. The emphasis of the texts shortly following the modes of prayer is upon the vices of prayer (986–1232); after that point, however, it is hard to discern more than the "wild profusion" Baldwin somewhere refers to in characterizing the DVV.

15. G. Duby, *Les trois ordres ou l'imaginaire du féodalisme* (Paris, 1978), pp. 384–403. Duby cites the use of the word *genus*, or rather its French equivalent "maneria," only once (p. 341). On the popularity of the scheme later, see pp. 327 ff. On the same subject in the early modern period, see O. Niccoli, *I sacerdoti, i guerrieri, i contadini. Storia di un'immagine della società* (Turin, 1979).

16. On the liberal arts, 139–46 against the trivium, Aristotle and civil law, and 216–28 against the quadrivium. Cf. this to k: 30rb, where, on the basis of a famous papal letter establishing diocesan schools, the author favors the trivium and quadrivium against those attacking them, On the schools, see Baldwin, *Masters* 1:77 ff. For Peter's work *De tropis loquendi*, see F. Guisberti, *Materials for a Study on Twelfth Century Scholasticism* (Naples, 1982), pp. 87–109.

17. The very rigor of scholastic classroom presentations, of course, taught "pious" behavior; a work on comportment as a goal of the medieval schools seems to be absent, however. Note the formulation: "Magis valere doctrinam rerum quam verborum"; k: 25ra. The word "doctrina," like the word "schola," was a common word for a group that shared the same behavior or rule. On the role of schools in forming modes of "praying" either to Gods, lords, or academic opponents, see M. Dufeil, "La prière implicite dans les texts universitaires," in *La prière au moyen-age (littérature et civilization)* (Aix-en Provence, 1981), esp. pp. 225 f., 236 ff.

18. See B. Smalley, *The Study of the Bible in the Middle Ages* (Oxford, 1952), p. 208. Baldwin, *Masters* 1:91 distinguishes *legere* as reading from the "more restrictive" usage "to lecture." But in this work on vocal prayer, I could find no clear use of the verb indicating reading with the mouth closed, not even when Peter discusses private prayer.

19. To my knowledge, no one has considered corporeal engineering within the general rubric of medieval technology. On the latter subject see White, *Medieval Technology*; on what might be called "verbal engineering," see Dufeil, "Prière implicite," pp. 223–53.

20. Interestingly, the furtive witness' oath on what he saw and heard remained central even though he was often said to have sinned by intruding; on the subject, see Schmitt, "Between Text and Image," pp. 131 f.

21. He glosses Jesus' words to the effect that unified identical prayer was important if collective prayer was to be efficacious (703–5). At 1741–43, he says that communal prayer is often useless. On the coordination and power of collective prayer, see Trexler, *Public Life*, index, "prayer."

22. On Hugh's and Peter Lombard's claim an excommunicated or heretical priest could not effect transubstantiation, see F. Margott, *Der Spender der heiligen Sacramente nach der Lehre des heiligen Thomas von Aquin* (Freiburg, 1886), pp. 75–89; J.-A. Chollet, *La doctrine de l'Eucharistie chez les Scolastiques* (Paris, 1908), p. 41; A. Landgraf, *Dogmengeschichte der Frühscholastik*, 4 vols. (Regensburg, 1952–56), vol. 3, pt. 2, pp. 223–43; the soon-

classicized formulation of the *substantia sacramenti* is studied *ibid.*, vol. 3, pt. 1, pp. 158–68. Most recently, see G. Macy, *The Theologies of the Eucharist in the Early Scholastic Period* (Oxford, 1984), pp. 53 ff.

23. Simply, external intention is the appearance a performer's actions give about one's internal intent; the internal intention of a celebrant, on the other hand, is unverifiable by human society. The intention in question since the later twelfth century was to "want to do what the church did," which did not necessarily mean "doing what others did"; Landgraf, *Dogmengeschichte*, vol. 3, pt. 1, pp. 133, 135 ff. The opposed terms ("interior et mentalis . . . exterior et vocalis") are first found in the work of Durandus of Saint-Pourçain (c. 1270–1332), but the idea and debate is, of course, ancient; Landgraf, for example, was led to organize his exposition of twelfth-century intention theory around the polarity; *Dogmengeschichte*, vol. 3, pt. 1, pp. 119–45. Peter came close to describing the polarity; Dugauquier, *Summa*, vol. 3, pt. 2 b, pp. 467 f. See further L. Renwart, "L'intention du ministre des sacrements, problème mal posé?" *Nouvelle Revue Théologique* 81 (1959): 469 f. For example, Peter the Chanter's contemporary, Innocent III, taught before his election to the papacy that Jesus had consecrated the bread (and by extension priests might do so) without words; J. Pohle, "Eucharist," *Catholic Encyclopedia* 5 (New York, 1909): 585. On the early modern history of the debate, see Renwart, *loc. cit.*, and his "Intention du ministre et validité des sacrements," *Nouvelle Revue Théologique* 77 (1955): 800–21, esp. 811; H. Bouësse, "Intention du ministre et validité des sacrements," *ibid.*, pp. 1067–74 (esp. 1072 on external and internal simulation!), and Renwart's response on pp. 1075ff.

24. The classical formulation revolved around the ideology that the Jews had been external but the Christian dispensation superseded ceremony and followed the internal law; thus much of behavior was said to be necessary to decorum but not to the eucharistic miracle or to generating grace; see e.g. Landgraf, *Dogmengeschichte*, vol. 3, pt. 1, pp. 134 (Courson), 162 ff. (Uguccio and the Chanter). But in the *Summa* Peter does requires the "mistica benedictio"; E. Dumoutet, "La théologie de l'Eucharistie à la fin du XII siècle. Le témoignage de Pierre le Chantre d'après la 'Summa de Sacramentis'," *Archives d'Histoire doctrinal et littéraire du moyen age* 18–20 (1943–45): 256. On the importance Peter attached to the priest crossing the bread and wine, see further below. If done by a behavioral scientist, a study of the behavioral requisites of consecration would reward attention, since from a practical point of view good behavior must have been of quintessential importance to superiors.

25. The radical pole of the argument came from Abelard: no act is intrinsically moral; only intention bestows that quality; the opposite pole is that considered objectively, certain actions had intrinsic morality and others intrinsic immorality; see the proponents in O. Lottin, *Psychologie et morale aux XII* et *XIII* *siècles*, 6 vols. (Louvain, 1942–60), 2: 421–30; 3: 309–32; see also my later study of certain prayer postures. But my interest is where, between domestic prayers and the consecration, and from the lay child to the priest, *intentio mentis* or *cordis* was thought to lose its essentiality.

26. The Chanter's collected *questiones* on intention in his *Summa* do not consider the problems that interest us; Dugauquier, *Summa*, III, pt. 2 b, pp. 529–67. See, however, elswhere in the *Summa*: "dummodo hoc agendi serio habeat intentionem" as a prerequisite of the eucharistic miracle; cited in Dumoutet, "Théologie," p. 255. On this equivocation, see Renwart, "Intention," pp. 818 f.

27. Contemporary theologians also recommended repetition, sometimes by the same, sometimes by another celebrant, in certain unforeseen emergencies; see V. Kennedy, "The Moment of Consecration and the Elevation of the Host," *Medieval Studies* 6 (1944): pp. 125, 134, 142 (Peter). Peter also recommended repetition of sacramental words

in his *Summa*, "si forte omissa essent"; cited in Landgraf, *Dogmengeschichte*, vol. 3, pt. 1. p. 163.

28. We are assuming of course that some of the faithful, for example the *potentes* or assisting clerics who did enter the choir area, could have seen or heard this eucharistic verbal performance, and thus been aware; on the elevations of the host for the faithful that increasingly marked the points of the eucharistic ceremony, see Kennedy, "Moment of Consecration." The phenomenon of anxious faithful fearing that because of faulty performances by their ministers they might not receive God but just bread and wine, or not receive other sacraments, and thus not be sure of their spiritual health, has gotten insufficient attention; see for leads Renwart, "L'Intention," pp. 474; "Intention," pp. 803, 806; Bouësse, "Intention," pp. 1073 f.

29. On the "significatione istius pronominis 'hoc'," however, see k: 27va. In his *Summa*, Peter made a distinction between the words necessary to effecting the eucharistic miracle and preparatory ones, yet recommended repeating either if omitted; cited in Landgraf, *Dogmengeschichte*, vol. 3, pt. 1, pp. 162 f.

30. See a critique of the concept of religions of the book in R. Trexler, "Historiography Sacred or Profane? Reverence and Profanity in the Study of Early Modern Religion," in K. von Greyerz (ed.), *Religion and Society in Early Modern Europe, 1500–1800* (London, 1984), pp. 245–69.

31. For general literature, see D. Morris *Gestures. Their Origin and Distribution* (New York, 1979), which includes distribution maps of 20 key gestures. The modern scientific literature on reverential postures and gestures, including prayer, is scant; see however, the work of M. Argyle, a scholar who entered this field from the study of religious behavior; *The Social Psychology of Religion* (London, 1975); *Bodily Communication* (London, 1975). See also the recent work of Schmitt, cited at nn. 11, 33, 36. Solid foundations for the study of corporal prayer were laid by L. Gougaud, "Attitudes of Prayer," in his *Devotional and Ascetic Practices in the Middle Ages* (London, 1927); P. Browe, "L'Attegiamento del Corpo durante la Messa," *Ephemerides Liturgicae* 50 (1936): 402–14. T. Ohm, *Die Gebetsgebärden der Völker und das Christentum* (Leiden, 1948), with the older literature. On Cistercian sign language, apparently only taught through written, not figured, descriptions, see the invaluable work of G. Van Rijnberk, *Le langage par signes chez les moines* (Amsterdam, 1954). A good specific study is by G. Ladner, "The Gestures of Prayer in Papal Iconography of the Thirteenth and Early Fourteenth Century," in *Didascaliae. Studies in Honor of A. M. Albareda*, ed. S. Prete (New York, 1961), pp. 245–75. Recent conventional scholarship on the subject is in *Gestes et paroles dans les diverses familles liturgiques* (Rome, 1978); none of the collected papers in *La prière* (cited above, n. 17), deal with the body.

32. K: 28ra; see n. 24 above.

33. Hugh's work is in PL, 176, cc. 925–52; on it, and on other pre-Cantor devotional tracts, see C. Walker Bynum, *Docere Verbo et Exemplo. An Aspect of Twelfth-Century Spirituality* (Cambridge, Mass., 1979), pp. 10 and seq.; J.-C. Schmitt, "Le geste, la cathedrale et le roi," *L'Arc* 72 (1978): 9–12.

34. Baldwin, *Masters* 1: 6.

35. For example, he combined the Vulgate and *Vetus latina* version of the psalms to produce documentation; "Legitimizing," p. 101.

36. J.-C. Schmitt, "'Gestus'–'Gesticulatio'. Contribution à l'étude du vocabulaire latin médiéval des gestes," in *La Lexicographie du latin médiéval et ses rapports avec les recherches actuelle sur la civilisation du moyen-age* (Paris, 1981), pp. 377–90. In path-finding research, M. Franko found that neither late-medieval and early modern manners books nor dance manuals give attention to the dynamics of individual body movement; "Renaissance Conduct Literature and the Basse Dance: the Kinesis of *Bonne Grace*," in

Persons in Groups. Social Behavior as Identity Formation in Medieval and Renaissance Europe, ed. R. Trexler (Binghamton, 1985), pp. 55–66.

37. On such frozen figures, see recently C. Davidson, "The Visual Arts and Drama, with Special Emphasis on the Lazarus Plays," in *Le théâtre au moyen âge,* ed. G. Muller (Paris, 1981), pp. 45–59. An example of the stigmatized Francis is in Trexler, "We Think, They Act. Clerical Readings of Missionary Theatre in Sixteenth-Century Mexico," in S. Kaplan (ed.), *Understanding Popular Culture: Europe from the Middle Ages to the Nineteenth Century* (Berlin, 1984), p. 195.

38. However, Peter's reference in these lines to the application of skin oils is interesting; on liturgical theatre, see O. Hardison, *Christian Rite and Christian Drama in the Middle Ages* (Baltimore, 1965).

39. The Conversion of Paul occasionally shows this stance in Carolingian illustrations; J. Gaehde, "The Turonian Sources of the Bible of S. Paolo Fuori Le Mura in Rome," *Frühmittelalterliche Studien* 5 (1971): pl. 91.

40. On the sitting posture of judges, see H. Martin, "Les enseignements des miniatures. Attitude royale," *Gazette des Beaux Arts,* ser. 4, 9 (1913): 173–88. Note that the discussion has to do with the chairs available to canons and monks; there were no chairs for the average visitor in medieval churches.

41. "Nec illud est omnino reprehensibile: cum enim sedentes essent Apostoli, receperunt Spiritum Sanctum. . . . Non igitur abominatur Spiritus Sanctus semper sedentes in orando"; *Opera de Vita Regulari* 2 (Rome, 1888–89): 168. Interestingly, Humbert cited biblical authority for his view. See further Jungmann, *Missarum* 1: 315 f.

42. For the practice of translating certain behaviors into equivalent insulting verbal prayer, see further k: 1va, 3va.

43. W. Christian, Jr., "Provoked Religious Weeping in Early Modern Spain," in J. Davis (ed.), *Religious Organization and Religious Experience* (London, 1982), pp. 97–110. Peter tends to make all but weeping the result of conscious decisions; see e.g. his discussion of breast-beating in k: 2va, 5ra.

44. Early modern examples of this important means of legitimizing postures or proving saintliness are in Trexler, "Alla destra di Dio. Organizzazione della Vita attraverso i Santi Morti in Nuova Spagna," *Quaderni Storici,* no. 50 (1982), p. 500. Peter referred to new prayers springing up to prove that the power of prayers did not reside in the words themselves; Dugauquier, *Summa,* vol. 3, pt. 2 b, p. 467.

45. H. Leclercq, "Genuflexion," *Dictionnaire d'archéologie chrétienne et de liturgie* 6, pt. 1 (Paris, 1924), cc. 1019 f. Further J. Jungmann, *Missarum Sollemnia,* 2 vols. (Vienna, 1952), 1: 314 f.

46. Cf. *ibid.,* 1: 314, 471–76; Humbert of Romans, *Opera,* p. 163.

47. On Peter of Roissy's prayers at communion at this time, see V. Kennedy, "The Handbook of Master Peter Chancellor of Chartres," *Medieval Studies* 5 (1943): 8 f.; and esp. his "Moment of Consecration," p. 149, for a reference to one he said was composed by Peter the Chanter.

48. Notoriously, the French Crusaders resisted the deep reverences practiced at Constantinople. On twelfth-century prostration in civil and ecclesiastical life, see G. Koziol, "Law, Lordship, and Ritual: Political Order in the Diocese of Noyon (1000–1150)," (diss., Stanford Univ., 1982), pp. 90–102.

49. Trexler, *Public Life,* index "punishments, criminal" gives several examples of riding on an ass, crucifixion, etc. See the pictures of penitents with hands tied behind their backs in J. Martin, *The Illustration of the Heavenly Ladder of John Climacus* (Princeton, 1954), figs. 84, 249. Note the case above, where "genuflection" was resisted because it reminded one of Jesus' humiliation.

50. Commentary on Mt. 11, in turn interestingly glossed by Francesco da Barberino; see Trexler, *Public Life*, pp. 107f.

51. On norms of decorum as a traditional charge of the intelligentsia, see Trexler, "Historiography." Sixteenth-century clerics characterized their status as "the devout ones"; R. Trexler, "Aztec Priests for Christian Altars. The Theory and Practice of Reverence in New Spain," in *Scienze, Credenze Occulte, Livelli di Cultura* (Florence, 1982), p. 190.

52. On Peter's opposition, see Baldwin, *Masters* 2: 65. Smalley emphasized Hugh of St. Victor's visual imagination; *Study*, pp. 95 f.

53. Considering the importance of the subject to the Chanter, it is noteworthy that he does *not* say the pictures will help *memory*; on that subject, see the marvelous text of Richard de Fournivall (1246–50), reproduced in V. Kolve, *Chaucer and the Imagery of Narrative* (Stanford, 1984), pp. 25 f.

54. See Trexler, "Historiography," for a discussion of such polarities.

55. See the marvelous quote at the following note. Hugh of St. Victor regularly referred to himself as an artist; Smalley, *Study*, p. 96.

56. " 'In vicium ducunt culpe, fuga, si caret arte.' 'Si latet ars prodest: affert deprensa pudorem.' 'Arte facis si non late, nec idem facis arte.' Verborum sensus pateat: dum verba coloras — nec nimium obscurus sis —, dum brevis esse laboras nec nimium taceas nec verba superflua dicas." For "In vitium . . . caret arte," see Horace's *Art of Poetry*, and for "Si latet . . . pudorem," see Ovid's *Art of Love*; cited in Walther, *Proverbia*, reg. 12151, 28565. The Loeb translation of what comes right before the quote of Ovid used by Peter clarifies the context: "Only while so talking take care not to show you are feigning, nor let your looks undo your words"; further on Peter's view of deceit in Smalley, *Study*, p. 212. It goes without saying that Peter's recognition here that "coloring" is essential conflicts with his previous denunciation of poets, painters, and academic enemies. It is indeed the point of my discourse that intellectual organization forces such polarizations.

57. See above.

58. In a work in preparation, I will show how preachers encouraged emulation of the sculpted and painted reverences of the Magi; Peter pointed to sculptures of hell to teach its pains; DVV, 361.

59. Most recently P. Brown, "The Saint as Exemplar in Late Antiquity," in Trexler, *Persons in Groups*, pp. 183–94.

60. Schmitt, "Between Text and Image."

61. See the references on technology above, at n. 10.

62. I could find no evidence that any of this writing around the pictures was done after the pictures.

63. G. Duby, "The Nobility in Eleventh- and Twelfth Century Mâconnais," in F. Cheyette (ed.), *Lordship and Community in Medieval Europe* (New York, 1968), pp. 137–55; Trexler, *Public Life*, pp. 388 ff.

64. Monastic oblates were tonsured when they were offered; A. Michel, "Tonsure," *Dictionnaire de Théologie Catholique* vol. 15, pt. 1 (Paris, 1946), c. 1229.

65. Peter discussed them; Dugauquier, *Summa*, vol. 3, pt. 2 b, pp. 770 f. General information on early confraternal practices, including the sparse data on clothing, is in G. Meersseman, *Ordo fraternitatis. Confraternite e pietà dei laici nel medioevo* 1 (Rome, 1977).

66. Recall that Peter describes purely physical postures. Thus it could be argued that from the start illustrations of clothed figures could not show Peter's postures as he scrupulously defined them.

67. On older boys teaching younger ones, see the analysis, especially of a text of Walafrid Strabo, in P. Quinn, "Benedictine Child Oblation. A Behavioral Study," (diss.: State University of New York at Binghamton, 1985).

68. "Sed inter istas privatas sunt quaedam quae fiunt a quibusdam saecularibus, sed a religione non approbantur, ut sunt prostrationes cum extensione brachiorum in modum crucis, et cum osculo terrae: quia non sunt decentes, et quia etiam indiscrete gravant corpus interdum ex terrae frigiditate"; *Opera* 2: 167.

69. See the reactionary views of S. Antonino in C. Gilbert, "The Archbishop on the Painters of Florence, 1450," *Art Bulletin* 41 (1959): 75–87.

70. Note also fig. 1 of Prague. An alternate reading of such faces turned toward the viewer is that they were turned away from God for fear (848–50). Yet in that case, they should have been turned away from the viewer as well, for humility.

71. While the cataloguers make no such suggestion, R. Bruck states that one of the Leipzig mss. described below ("pe") is French; *Die Malereien in den Handschriften des Königreichs Sachsen* (Dresden, 1906), p. 95. Even if, as seems unlikely, it was done by a Frenchman, it descends from two texts of Austrian provenance; see below. For the locations, see Baldwin, *Masters* 2: 250. I established through correspondence with the relevant depositories that none of the mss. of the "Verbum Abbreviatum" that Baldwin did not consult (*Masters* 2: 255) contains either the explicit *premium perfectorum*, the pictures, or places for pictures.

72. A half-folio fragment of an apparently unknown Crusade text used to protect the front of the codex has Barbarossa (d. 1190) dead but Constantinople still in the hands of the Greeks, as it was till 1204. My thanks to Donald Queller for advising me on this text.

73. P. Lehmann, "Mitteilungen aus Handschriften II," *Sitzungsberichte der Bayerischen Akademie der Wissenschaften, Philosophisch-historische Abteilung* (1930), *Heft* 2, pp. 5 f.

74. I now prefer the Pegau attribution to the one to the church of St. Thomas in Leipzig, as speculated by R. Helssig (ed.), *Katalog der Lateinischen und Deutschen Handschriften der Universitäts-Bibliothek zu Leipzig* 1 (Leipzig, 1926–35): 675, and assumed by me in my "Legitimating." On the scriptoria, see S. Dupont, "Anatomy of a Scriptorium: the Origins and Early Development of a Scriptorium at the Cistercian Abbey Altzelle (ca. 1190–1215)," (diss.: Johns Hopkins Univ., 1979), esp. pp. 399 f. The same author also writes me that this 432 ms. is the same ms. as the Leipzig Paulina ms. listed by Baldwin among his unconsulted mss.; *Masters* 2: 255.

75. Helssig, *Katalog*, p. 674; Bruck, *Malereien*, p. 95.

76. Note at the end of n. 175 in the inventory of the *fondo Miscellanea Codici (vecchio ordinamento)*, preserved in the *Archivio di Stato, Venezia*, and kindly communicated to me by its director, Maria Francesca Tiepolo.

77. G. Abate and G. Luisetto (eds.), *I Codici e Manoscritti della Biblioteca Antoniana di Padova* 2 (Vicenza, 1975): 551 f.

78. Cf. *Recueil des Historiens des Croisades* vol. 1, pt. 2 (Paris, 1844), pp. 1109–13, 1091–94.

79. William of Tyre, *A History of Deeds Done Beyond the Sea*, eds. E. Babcock and A. Kay (New York, 1943): 1: 41; "William of Tyre," *Encyclopedia Britannica*, 11th ed., 28 (1911): 677.

80. H. Mayer, "Zum Tode Wilhelms von Tyrus," *Archiv für Diplomatik* 5–6 (1959–60): 186.

81. On f. 27r at the roman numeral xlii one reads in the margin: "supra xxxiiii et cetera," the relevant material in fact being there, on f. 20vb. The first section of these paragraph numbers goes from xxvii on f. 17r, near the beginning of bk. 4, to lii on f. 35v, shortly after the beginning of bk. 7. It resumes shortly after the description of the 7 prayer modes with lxxxiiii on f. 52r, and ends with cxxiii on f. 74r, after the beginning of the final tractate on the mass. Several of these numbers have been crossed out,

and several others are skipped, but the paragraph sequence within the two ranges, and even between them, can be figured out. I had no such luck discovering an order for the missing numbers i–xxvi that would bring me to the first section of roman numerals. Presumably a list of the paragraphs in roman characters existed from which our numerator worked.

82. A new partial index in a later hand is found on ff. 78rv, and includes rubrics up to f. 57 of the text.

83. Abate and Luisetto, *Codici* 2: 551.

84. *Masters* 2: 254. Indeed, in a personal communication, the paleographer F. Gasparri hypothesizes that both the *De penitentia* and the William of Tyre fragments of the Paduan ms. were written by a southern French scribe. She excludes a Parisian origin. My thanks to her for her informed opinion.

85. See the account in a letter of Innocent III in PL, 214, cc. 12 f.; Baldwin, *Masters* 1: 9; 2: 4, n. 55. Note that Emperor Henry VI came to Italy from Germany in the summer of 1196, dying in the south of Italy in Sept. of the following year. But I had no success finding Peter in the imperial entourage. Baldwin takes Peter's detailed description in the DVV of the Third Council of the Lateran (1179) as possible evidence he had been at Rome before; *Masters* 1: 9. Our author's only reference to this Council "cum trecentis episcopis" in the present work (k: 6ra), a formulation not found in DVV, is inconclusive on this score.

86. It is possible but improbable that this passage points instead to a non-French author bringing news home from Paris: there is no further evidence for such a view and much for Peter's Parisian ambience.

87. "Werke aus der engeren Schule des Petrus Cantor," *Gregorianum* 21 (1940): 50–55.

88. The Paduan cataloguers missed, but the Klosterneuburg and Zwettl cataloguers caught what might seem an errant spelling; *Catalog of Manuscripts in Stift Klosterneuburg, Austria*, 3: 493 (cod. 572.1), made available to me by the Monastic Film Project; the edition of the new catalogue has not reached our codex: A. Haidinger (ed.), *Katalog der Handschriften des Augustiner Chorherrenstiftes Klosterneuburg* (Vienna, 1983–). For Zwettl, see *Die Handschriften-Verzeichnisse der Cistercienser-Stifte* 1 (Vienna, 1891): 328 (cod. 71), (Zwettl catalogue by S. Rössler). Yet in pa (64r), cf. "pariēsis" to "elemoīa," where the "s" is also missing, but "elemosina" is obviously intended. In what follows, I am obviously more interested in the consistency of the transcription "pariēsis" in these three mss. than in its correctness or incorrectness.

89. The expression "facing toward Jerusalem" (Lk. 9.51) means doing penance; cf. PL, 205, cc. 314–27; pa: 35rb, 39va; k: 6vb, 11vb–12ra. See below, where fasting, and k: 6vb, where magnanimous almsgiving, that is, two of the three parts of penance, are "most potent parts of penance" or of "turning toward Jerusalem." Thus a viaticum of a person turned toward Jerusalem was a penitential guide; this title is essentially identical to the usual *De penitentia*. Curiously, the *Catalogue of Additions to the Manuscripts in the British Museum, 1854–60*, p. 4 (ms. 19,767), gives the incipit in quotes, but then adds: "sive, Verbum abbreviatum de vitiis et virtutibus." In correspondence, Ms. Patricia Basing of that Library assures me that a cataloguer added these words; they are not in the manuscript.

90. Baldwin, *Masters* 1: 6; 2: 3, n. 28; see also Landgraf, "Werke," p. 48. I assume the correct translation of Venice's "cantoris" is "the" rather than "a" chanter because of Venice's explicit identification of Peter as of Paris.

91. Note that these cross-references amount to authorial abridgement; Landgraf, who remained unaware of them, thought that our work came from someone else's *expansion* of the DVV. As to the relation of the long and short versions of the DVV, Baldwin,

Masters 2: 256–65, decided for abridgement of the long rather than expansion of the short version.

92. In a personal communication, J. Baldwin hypothesized that this might refer to William of Auxerre's *Summa aurea super quatuor libros sententiarum*. If so, this particular text post-dates Peter's death even if it is made to come from Peter's heart and mouth. For William's work was written between 1215 and 1220.

93. Cf. the former text to pa: 23ra (paragraph: "De bona violentia"); a fulfillment of the latter "God-willing" is not found in our work. For Peter's attacks on lucre-oriented doctors and lawyers, see Baldwin, *Masters* 1: 85 f.

94. An example of Peter in his sacramental *Summa* referring to an earlier work is in Baldwin, *Masters* 2: 261. The argument of Landgraf that remains significant is that in our work Christian authorities are not cited as they are in Peter's DVV; *ibid.*, p. 55. In comparison to the DVV, Peter's Christian sources in the *De penitentia* seem to me rarely if ever to include the ordinary gloss, commonly cited in DVV, and to cite the Fathers as found in Gratian's Decretals and wisdom literature ("ut ait sapiens") much more often here than in the DVV.

95. K: 1ra, 11va; pa: 34rb. I found no significant variation in the author's use of pre-Christian sources here and in the DVV, on which see E. Matthews Sanford, "The *Verbum Abbreviatum* of Petrus Cantor," *Transactions and Proceedings of the American Philological Association* 74 (1943): 33–48. On the liberal arts and classical sources, see Baldwin, *Masters* 1: 77 ff., 315 f.; 2: 53, n. 8, and 55, nn. 95–100.

96. The first phrase comes from Gregory, and is in the DVV's introduction, p. 205; Baldwin, *Masters* 1: 24; 2: 15. Also Smalley, *Study*, p. 208. For its use by a student of Peter's, see V. Kennedy, "Robert of Courson on Penance," *Medieval Studies* 7 (1945): 294.

97. Landgraf was unaware of the short version of our work; he knew only the Leipzig mss. and reached his conclusion that the latter were elaborations by comparing certain paragraphs of the Pegau ms. with DVV. But a comparison of two early paragraphs of the Pegau text published by Landgraf with the other manuscripts of the *De penitentia* reveals buildups or reductions similar to those in our prayer book. Thus the pe text on pp. 51 f. of his "Werke" has a sentence (lines 6–9, p. 52) that is not found in k (f. 1rb) and was probably added by pe. The text of pe on Landgraf's pp. 52 f, on the other hand, is identical to k, but not to pa: the first two sections of pe that Landgraf did not find in DVV are also not in pa (f. 6vb), but the third text he did not find in DVV *is* in pa (f. 7ra).

98. "Werke," pp. 48 f.

99. See above, at n. 91; also k: 15va and pa: 40vb: "misericordia, que est idem significatione cum elemosina et caritate." This passage says that many fast and pray without meaning it, but no one does "charity" without merit; a later passage (k: 24ra) says that one cannot be saved without exercising the "reales horas," even if one fasted for a century and prayed daily. Thus Peter's understanding of this book on real prayer as treating the last of the parts of prayer is evident. Near the end of the whole work (k: 31ra), one reads: "circa opera caritatis, id est, misericordie, hoc est, reales horas."

100. DVV has sequential chapters on several of the corporal works of mercy; this penitential work does not.

101. Cf. chs. 28–30 (DVV, 104–18) to pa: 72rb–73va.

102. Z: 39rb; k: 27r ("ducalis" for vocalis); pr: 92vb; v; pa: 69rab. O: 209v and m: 164rb read: "Premisso tractatu de oratione vocali et reali, consequenter agendum est de sacramento altaris. Verumtamen in primis sciendum quod multiplici est causa. . . ."

103. K: 26ra, 29ra; see a cross-reference to bk. 6 of the long version in Landgraf, "Werke," p. 50. On the other hand, the prayer book does have two "God-willings" or

augurs that the author will write more on a particular subject further below; see above, n. 94. Both of these are only in the long version, and the latter refers to real prayer, which Peter obviously did then write on.

104. The folio also is the first of a new quire; the "blank" one opposite, f. 42v, actually now has an unrelated note of a later writer listing the 4 virtues one should possess before receiving the eucharist.

105. Jungmann, *Missarum* 1: 162, 595 f; 2: 264 f; A. Mullahy, "Liturgical Gestures," *New Catholic Encyclopedia* 8 (New York, 1967): 895; T. Klauser, *The Western Liturgy Today* (Westminster, Md., 1963), p. 27; Browe, "L'Attegiamento," pp. 405f.

106. *Opera*, p. 165, and generally pp. 160–71.

107. Comparing pa to v, one find that pa: 36vb comes right up to the beginning of our edited genuflection texts, which are absent. Pa continues with our *De causis quare penitentia non debet deferri* up to 38ra, where after describing the multiple penalties of evil also in v and k, it breaks again and lacks the three species of penance, the antidotes to vices, our paragraph *De genuis* and two following, to rejoin Venice at that point.

108. *Masters* 2: 258.

109. See above, n. 101.

110. It needs a separate edition before it can be fruitfully exploited and compared to the Chanter's texts in Dugauquier, *Summa*, vol 1. The teachings of this *Summa* on the eucharist have been analyzed in Dumoutet, "Théologie," pp. 181–262; and one aspect of his teaching is reviewed in Kennedy, "Moment of Consecration," pp. 139–44.

111. K begins bk. 7, in fact, with one of the paragraphs (on priests selling masses) that strongly evokes a chapter (28) in DVV.

112. The inserted chapter deals with the Eucharist. K places it in a context of mass and eucharist, but pa has it in the midst of more general declamations against bad priests, so that it later has to return to the subject of the mass and eucharist.

113. The various ways such compilations might have occurred are examined in Baldwin, *Masters* 2: 241–65. Note esp. 244 for evidence that in assembling his sacramental summa, at the point of his treatise on penance (the subject of our work), Peter may have become less fully involved in editing his students' records of his lectures than he had been for previous sections.

114. Cf. the first z insert (7ra) to k: 3vb and to pr: 41va. The 2nd and 3rd are lines 410–15 and 497–507 of this edition.

115. The marginalia are at k: 6ra, 6vb, 8ra, 9va and 11rb.

116. For example, the modes of prayer are not mentioned in the *De vitiis*. Conversely, certain texts from the *De vitiis* are found in the *De oratione*. See the apparatus of variants, lines 1187–89 and 1219–22.

117. I compared the unpublished long version of the *De vitiis* with our *De penitentia* for leads, without results. I especially studied the sections on prayer in the unpublished long version of the *De vitiis* to the same end, and with as little issue. In fact, most of the sections on prayer there are in the published short version. A more serious chronological study would include, of course, other penitential works and those on prayer written contemporarily; for them, see the information in V. Kennedy, "The Date of the Parisian Decree on the Elevation of the Host," *Medieval Studies* 8 (1946): 89 (Robert of Flamborough), 94 (Peter of Roissy); and Kennedy's "Robert Courson on Penance."

118. See above, at nn. 111–12.

119. *Opera* 2: 165.

120. In all five of these manuscripts lines 1227–32 and 1245–54 are missing, though Ottobeuren introduced and Munich copied a new text into the former area.

121. E.g. 409–13 and 461–63 are in v and pa, but not in o and m; 560–603 and 678–83 are in o and m, but not v and pa. See the apparatus for other examples.

122. Significantly, the first of the three texts, found only in the idiosyncratic o/m tradition, was clearly written after the section on the modes of prayer in the present work, since it treats of them. Note that o and m have both texts that v and pa have, and that none of the three is found only in v and pa. This is another indication of the precedence of the two Italian mss. I have been unable to find any of the three texts in the long or short versions of DVV, so the origins of at least the latter two texts remain unknown.

123. See the self-reference (211–14) discussed above.

124. See the self-references (2110) discussed above. For doubtful first person usages in Peter's *Summa*, see Dugauquier, *Summa*, vol. 3, pt. 1, pp. 345f.

125. On whose use of Peter's work, see Baldwin, *Masters*, passim.

126. See nn. 39, 40, 128 for a few of the illustrated works I consulted. The earliest illustrated mss. of the Sachsenspiegel is too late to be relevant; K. von Amira, "Die Genealogie der Bilderhandschriften des Sachsenspiegels," *Abhandlungen der königlichen bayerischen Akademie der Wissenschaften*, Cl. I, vol. 32, pt. 2 (1902), p. 327. Model books would not seem to have been relevant for our texts; on them, see R. Scheller, *A Survey of Medieval Model Books* (Haarlem, 1963).

127. The same "awkward" or surrendering figure is found in the prayer figures of St. Dominick, but at least in that case, the supplicant stares at an altar, which is not in Ottobeuren; see Schmitt, "Between Text and Image," p. 160, fig. 11.

128. The closest to such a rectangular figure I found is a *kneeling* obedient thief brought to my attention by Penelope Mayo: Martin, *Heavenly Ladder*, p. xxii, fig. 79.

129. O: 216r.

Part Two
The Pictures

Venice

Padua

Zwettl

Klosterneuburg

Pegau

Altzella [missing]

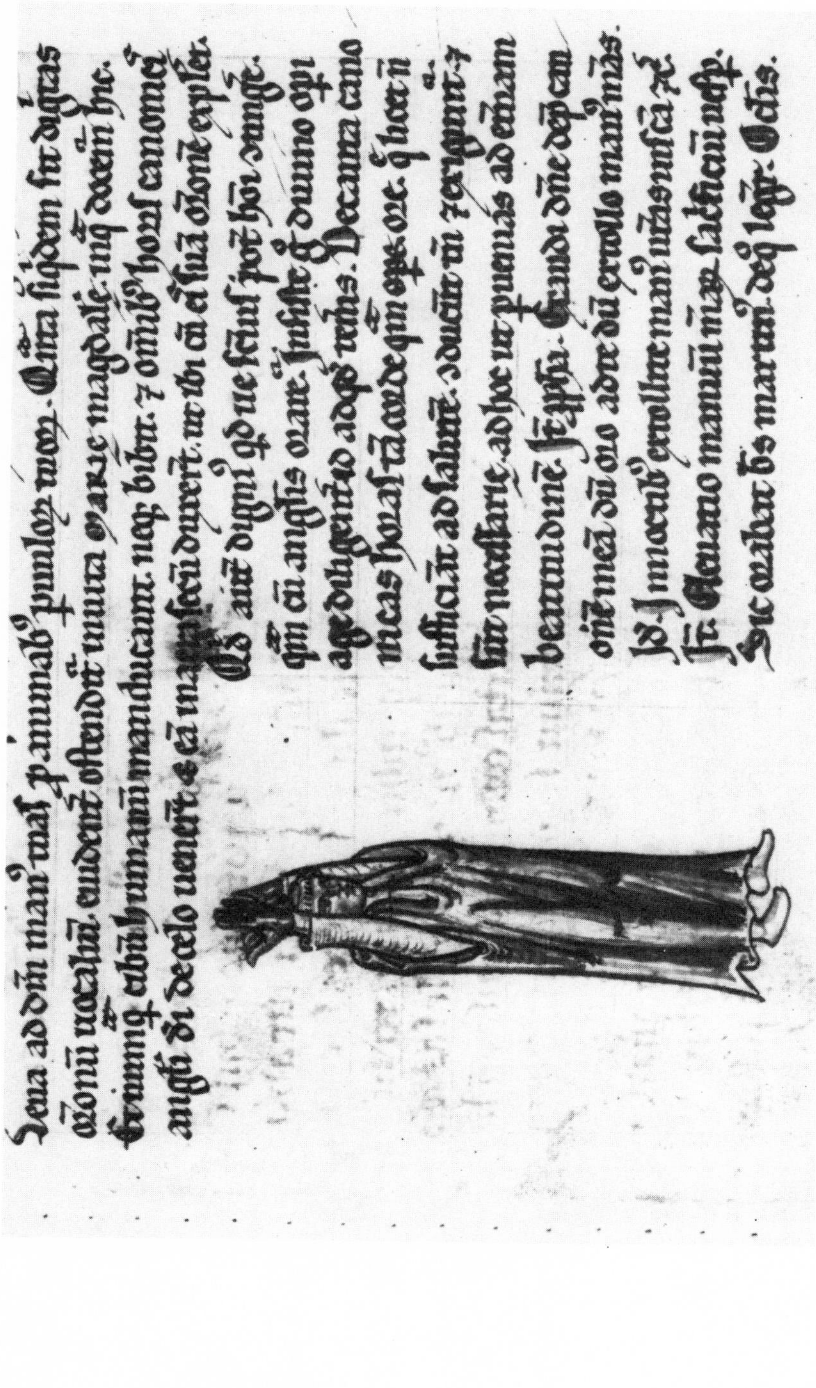

Ottobeuren, fig. 1

ac manib° in celum semp intent̄
ē figura octis subiecta euidēt ×

Sc ds modū
Suluf erpa
eruas. Ṽn apl
meas. It alibi
mea sic tū sū.
meāe. sal; exter
tuaf sm̄do spr̄
filiū uidue. Qd
hia. Erpandit se
clamaurup ad t
piū hui̅ musc̄
or demonstratiua. ❧emor. q̄n

fig. 3   *Ottobeuren*   *fig. 2*

Prague

Venice

Padua

Zwettl

Klosterneuburg

Pegau

Altzella

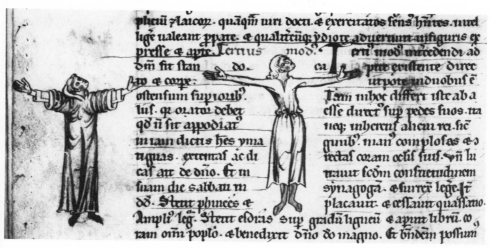

fig. 2 — *Ottobeuren* — *fig. 1*

Prague

dict · Et maledictu postu
ni maledice. Quo tn h fiat·
figa demostrat ·

Quar sit stan dui oi oi
Quo tde sit orare ꝶ pug
re euronu ostedit · Est au
sede pausantiu · seu uiorica

Venice

Padua

Di
fta
vo.
ratio
uobi;
i ili
b aliis
ratio
suos.
us ·
ra
s ma
us
s cori
ur
s o

Quar sit stand ioiu
oratioe
Quo tde sit orare ꝶ pu
gre euronu ostendit· Est
au sede pausantiu· seu iu
dicatiu· Stare u e pugn

Zwettl

Klosterneuburg

Pegau

Altzella

Prague

Ottobeuren

vuj·

ī tīa dūe axinos pedū cuie
lox· o.ð aū ē vm̄n· q̄ līf illud
fiar· p̄sens ymago vocer.

Ɒ̄uuū oxoūus.

Ɒ̄uū̄ n̄epe m̄os obsecratū
ē iste· uol̄ qn̄ ħo pieat sepla
nū ī tīa sup̄ fan̄e sūa· vī
c̄elo· ds appiel esto m̄i pec
tōn· ꝫ ego sū q̄ pectauū· aūꝗ
iniꝗ egī ꝗ om̄em uisū̄ tīa
tuā· ꝫ īsū̄ uigū uideat
anuūue cū p̄multudine

Venice

Padua

Ɒ̄ð quīto m̄ c̄oxtaōī
Q̄uīnus n̄epe m̄dus ob
ceau dī ē istr· uuol̄ qn̄ ħo
pieat se plm̄ū ī tīa sup̄ fa
cīe sūa· diceudo· ds p̄piel
esto m̄i pectōn· ꝫ ego sum

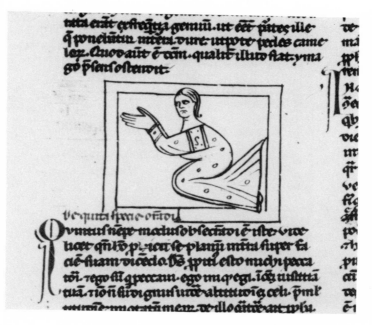

Zwettl

Klosterneuburg

Pegau

Altzella

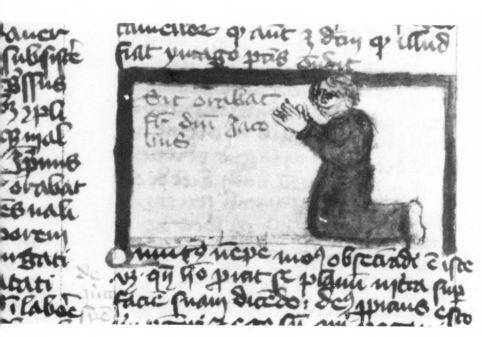

Ottobeuren

Prague

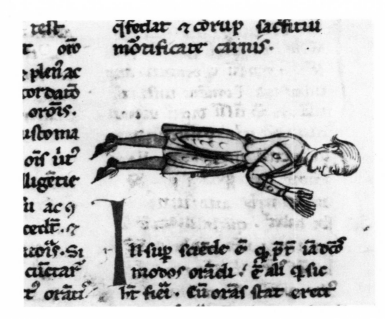

Venice

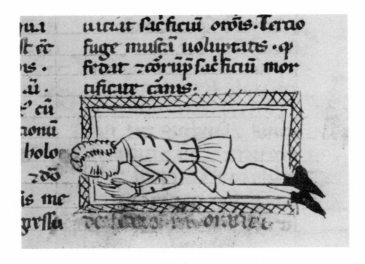

Padua

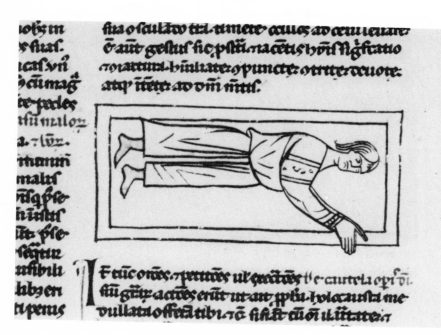

Zwettl

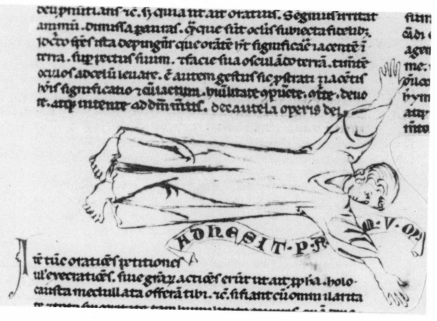

Klosterneuburg

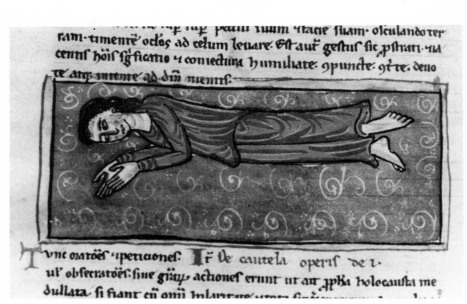

...... up sup peali iuum state suam· osculando ter
ram· timente octos ad celum leuare· Est aut gestus sic pstrati ·iu
centis hois sgficatio ·i coniectura humiliate· ·puncte· ·gt· te· deuo
te atqʒ intente ad dm mentis·

Tunc oratões ·ipeticaones· Ir ve cautela operis· de ·i·
ul· obsecratões· siue grarz· actiones erunt ut an ipKa holocausta me
dullata si fiant cu omi inlurture ....

Pegau

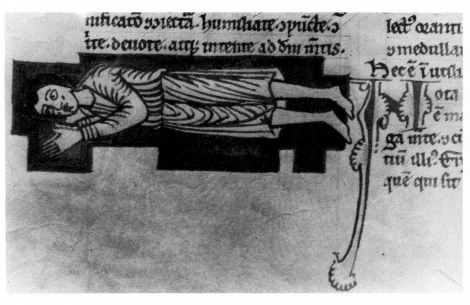

nificato ·ssi ecta· humiliate ·spucte· ·s
ite· deuote· atqʒ intente ad dm mtis·

lect oranti
ʒ medullan
Hece intuitu
Nota
tʒ ma
ga inte· ʒ ci
tu illi· Ei
quē qui sit

Altzella

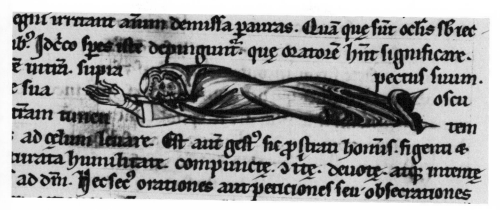

egni irritant alium demissa paucas. Qua que sur octis sb rec
ib? Jdcco spes iste depingunt. que oratore hr significare.
e uiriä. supra ... pectus suum.
e sua ... oscu
nam tunen ... ten
ad celum leuare. Est aut gest? sic p stran horuis. figenti e
aurata humilitate. compuncte. s rc. deuote. atq menne
ad dm. Hec sec? orationes aur peticiones seu obsecrationes

Ottobeuren

Prague

Venice

Padua

Zwettl

Klosterneuburg

Item nota qg̃. iṗ doc̃e difficilem Ve̅ ·vii· modo nol. modum orandi· alium a predictis· ut in exposit̃oe parabole illius·Simile factum e̅ regnum cel̃oꝛp ho̅i regi ꝝc̅· ubi ait de quadam sorore

Pegau

Altzella

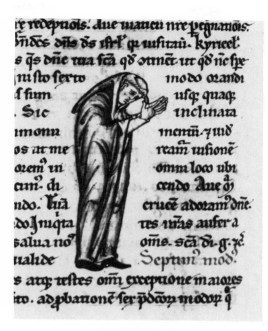

Ottobeuren

Prague

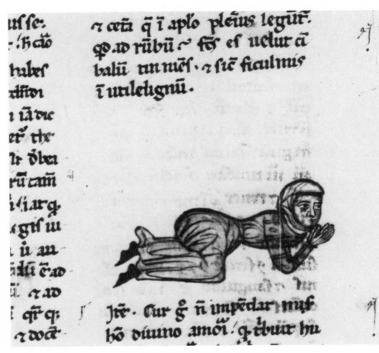

Venice

Padua

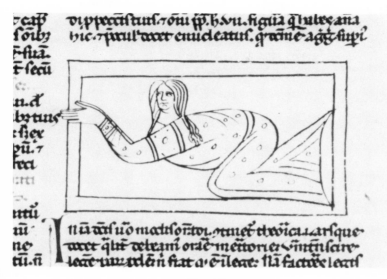

Zwettl

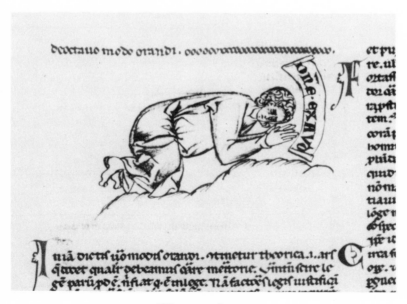

Klosterneuburg

mortua testabat. ч ita habes. vii. utiles modos intcedendi p petis
tuis romu pplop. hec. vii. figura qua habes antea. яp oculis docet
enucleati. quod dictum ē a gg supnis.

Pegau

bes antea. яp octis docet enucleat? qd
dicti ē a gregorio supi?

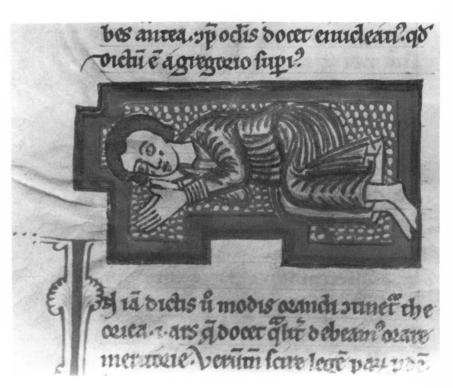

Altzella

osulendo infirmis. quib⁹ cibis possint
af in bo futuro. ūmo pmias̃ eg̃ũ moɹi.
vgart.   Hec
luf. do   cet
goɹi o   su
pnam   sci
s obest   se
i mai⁹ donũ scientie ibi transgressoɹ ma
bes theologye. ꝶ nosti oms̃ reg̃tas nuris.
s. ꝶ cēta. que in apto pleni legunt. Q̃d
sonans aut cymbalum tinniens. ꝶ sic

Ottobeuren

Prague

Part Three
The Edition

Introduction to the Texts

The edition begins with the concluding lines of book 4 of the long version (1–264). Though not found in the short version, the text is significant because it characterizes the author and the work as a whole.

Most of the edition (lines 265–2309) is made up of the book called *De oratione et speciebus illius*, taken from the work of Peter the Chanter that we have entitled *De penitentia et partibus eius*. *De oratione* forms book 8 of the short version and book 5 of the long version of this work. To this book is appended (2310–11) the incipit of the following book, respectively book 9 or 6.

The edition concludes (2312–64) with texts on "genuflexion" taken from an earlier part of the *De penitentia*.

Generally, this edition renders the foliation and text of the Klosterneuburg manuscript of the *De penitentia*. This text was chosen because it is centrally located among the five manuscripts of the long version of this work. Still being developed in Zwettl, the work's rubrication is largely complete in the Klosterneuburg manuscript. The preponderence of the text that appears in the Altzella and Pegau manuscripts, the longest version of the long version and the last manuscripts from a textual point of view, is already in Klosterneuburg.

Klosterneuburg was collated with the eight other extant texts of the work. In what follows, I list all the manuscripts: the letter(s) I use to identify each of them in the study and apparatus, their shelf numbers and the folio numbers of the *De penitentia*, catalogue descriptions, reference to Baldwin when he describes a manuscript as a "reorganized abridgment" of DVV (*Masters*, II, 253 f.), and other miscellaneous information. All but the Prague manuscripts are vellum.

A(ltzella) = manuscript Leipzig Univ. Library, n. 433. Ff. i-ra–cvi-ra. 13th century. See R. Helssig (ed.), *Katalog der Lateinischen und Deutschen Handschriften der Universitäts-Bibliothek zu Leipzig*, I (Leipzig, 1926–35), pp. 676 f., and Baldwin.

K(losterneuburg) = manuscript *Stift* Klosterneuburg, n. 572. Ff. 1ra–32ra. 13th–14th centuries. See the ms. *Catalogue of Manuscripts in Stift Klosterneuburg, Austria*, III, p. 493. A copy of this catalogue is at the Monastic Film Project Library, St. John's Univ., Collegeville, Minnesota. See the forthcoming entry in A. Haidinger's *Katalog der Handschriften des Augustiner Chorherrenstiftes Klosterneuburg* (Vienna, 1983–), and Baldwin.

M(unich) = manuscript of the Bavarian State Library (Munich), n. 17458. Ff. 105ra–171vb. 15th century. See *Catalogus codicum Latinorum Bibliothecae Regiae Monachensis* IV, pt. 3 (Munich, 1873), p. 99, and Baldwin.

O(ttobeuren) = Additional manuscript of the British Library, n. 19,767. Ff. 153r–216r. 1227–1246. See *Catalogue of Additions to the Manuscripts in the British Museum, 1854–60*, p. 4. See further P. Lehmann, "Mitteilungen aus Handschriften II," *Sitzungsberichte der Bayerischen Akademie der Wissenschaften, Philosophisch-historische Abteilung* (1930), *Heft* 2, pp. 5 f., and Baldwin.

Pa(dua) = ms. of the Antonine Library, Padua, n. 532, scaff. XXII. Ff. 1ra–78vb. 13th century. See G. Abate and G. Luisetto (eds.), *I Codici e Manoscritti della Biblioteca Antoniana di Padova*, II (Vicenza, 1975), pp. 551 f., and Baldwin.

Pe(gau) = ms. Leipzig Univ. Library, n. 432. Ff. 9r–127v. 13th century. See Helssig, *Katalog*, pp. 674 ff. See further A. Landgraf, "Werke aus der engeren Schule des Petrus Cantor," *Gregorianum* XXI (1940), pp. 46–55, and Baldwin. Some of the illustrations have been reproduced in R. Bruck, *Die Malereien in den Handschriften des Königreichs Sachsen* (Dresden, 1906).

Pr(ague) = manuscript in paper of the Prague University Library, Latin ms. n. 1518. Ff. 36ra–100rb. 15th century. See *Catalogus codicum manu scriptorum latinorum qui in C. P. Biblioteca publica atque universitatis Pragensis . . .*, I (Prague, 1905), p. 558.

V(enice) = Venetian State Archives, S. Maria della Misericordia in Valverde, b. 1. Unpaginated. 13th century. See there the manuscript inventories: 1) of the *fondo Miscellanea Codici (vecchio ordinamento)*, n. 175; 2) of the manuscripts earlier on display in the Sala Regina Margherita. The illuminations in this manuscript have been reproduced by P. G. Molmenti, *La Storia di Venezia nella Vita Privata*, I (Trieste, 1973), p. 124, and by R. Trexler, *Public Life in Renaissance Florence* (New York, 1980), p. 23.

Z(wettl) = manuscript of Stift Zwettl, n. 71. Ff. 4ra–45vb. 13th century. See *Die Handschriften Verzeichnisse der Cistercienser-Stifte*, I (Vienna, 1891): S. Rössler (ed.), *Verzeichniss der Handschriften der Bibliothek des Stiftes Zwettl*, pp. 327 f., and Baldwin.

Reading the Edition

Typeface distinguishes the long version of 7 books (a, k, pe, pr, z), from the short version of 10 (o, m) or 9 (v, pa) books. Italics indicate texts that are found in both versions, except where they are used to identify legal and biblical titles. Roman type designates texts found only in the long version. The majuscule type on lines 454, 508, 524, 628, 693, 764 and 775 shows the words on the scrolls of the Klosterneuburg prayer figures.

Angle brackets enclose significant titles and texts that are not found in the basic long and short versions. The apparatus of variants states which manuscripts have these bracketed texts. A few of these texts are found only in the short version, while others are additions made by a and pe to the basic long version.

Reading the Apparatuses

1. The apparatus of variants. Each entry begins by identifying the inclusive line numbers of a variant, and then lists the manuscripts containing the variant. The first text word(s) given is the last in the edition before the variant begins, and the last word(s) given is the first in the edition after the variant ends. Ellipses (. . .) within variants indicate that the words between those on either side follow the language in the main text.

2. The apparatus of authorities. If no reference is given for an authority cited by the author, I was unable to verify the quotation. For the biblical, legal, and other bibliographic conventions, see the list of abbreviations at the beginning of this work.

Editorial Principles

The text before the reader is, in general, a scribal version of the Klosterneuburg manuscript. Therefore it contains many errors and inconsistencies. In preparing this edition, I did not intend to correct this or any other scribe's Latin. Only in those few cases where the Klosterneuburg scribe erred in such a way as to compromise meaning did I use the better reading of another manuscript (where one was available), and consign Klosterneuburg's reading to the apparatus of variants.

There are certain passages in the edition that are found only in the short version manuscripts, and thus not in Klosterneuburg. The Venetian text is before the reader for those passages; variants from it are in the apparatus of variants. There is one case where only Ottobeuren and Munich had a substantial text. The Ottobeuren text is before the reader, with the Munich variants in the apparatus. Finally, for the additions to the Klosterneuburg text of the Leipzig manuscripts, I edited Pegau and give Altzella variations in the apparatus.

What follows is not a critical edition of any text or combination of texts. First there is the matter of quotations. Peter often cites them wrongly, and only rarely identifies them with quotation marks. Whenever I could verify a quote (as shown in the apparatus of authorities), I introduced quotation marks as appropriate, though I kept the author's often imperfect text. When I could not verify one of Peter's quotes, I used quotation marks sparingly, as they seemed called for by Peter's text. They may be imperfectly placed.

Far more important, I recorded only a fraction of all variants: those that were necessary to establish relations between sets of manuscripts. I did not intend to study variants closely enough to establish a proper stem that would link the source manuscripts, let alone all the manuscripts, to each other. I have been especially careful to identify all external variants such as titles, incipits and explicits, and the table of incipits and explicits in my study offers a sure guide, I hope, for the further study of the *De penitentia* as a whole. Yet the extensive apparatus of variants for the book *De Oratione* does repeatedly record cases where identical prose was shared by pairs of manuscripts. These variants indubitably establish the relations between sets of manuscripts, as was my intention.

This apparatus omits, therefore, variants that in my judgment would not have yielded information on the source of the text in question or on one manuscript's relation to another. With a few significant exceptions almost all spelling variations went unrecorded. Indeed, without listing variants, I standardized the spelling of the letters c / t and n / m (e.g. iuditium = iudicium, inmaculata = immaculata, etc.) at those places where the reading is usually uncertain. I also do not list the following variants: all but significant word (not phrase) inversions; common synonyms (e.g. supra/super; nam/quoniam; ait/dicit, etc.); deletions or additions of optional words like "item" or "enim"; small variations in citing the Bible or decretals. A work whose primary purpose was to understand the text tradition definitively would, of course, have tracked precisely such variants, not only in the *De oratione*, but in the *De penitentia* as a whole. Perhaps another scholar will take on this task once it is certain that all the manuscripts of this work have been located.

The Texts

Commendatio istius operis

Toto igitur mentis desiderio, diligens lector, hoc nostrum opusculum
amplectere, in quo est regula iuste, sancte, et pie vivendi, et ars bene
recteque operandi. Hic vero natat elephans et pedibus siccis pertransit
agnus. Hic sunt fructus totius sacre pagine. Hic namque reperitur unde
sapientes exerceantur atque in quo simplices instruuntur. Hic liber est
apotheca spiritus sancti nec non paradisus omnium deliciarum. In hoc
utique opere, quilibet sexus, omnis etas admonetur. Nec homo alicuius
10   conditionis |16vb| ab eadem norma excluditur. Immo, universi exor-
tantur sic conversari in medio prave et perverse nationis, quatenus ad
celestem mansionem valeant pervenire.

De tribus mortuis

Prelibata vero per dei gratiam conferentur universis qui de numero
non sunt illorum mortuorum, de quibus ait Augustinus. Bene intel-
ligimus tres illos mortuos, quos in corporibus suscitavit deus, aliquid
significare et figurare de resurrectione animarum que fit per fidem.
Resuscitavit enim filiam archisinagogi adhuc in domo iacentem. Resuscitavit sane filium vidue extra portam civitatis elatum. Resuscitavit
20   porro Lazarum sepultum quatriduanum. Intueatur quisque animam
suam quia si peccat moritur. Peccatum autem mors anime est, quod
fit dilectatione et cogitatione. Idem mors est intus quando malum ex-
cogitatum nondum processit in actum, talem utique animam se resu-
scitare significans dominus resuscitavit illam puellam que nondum erat
foras elata, sed in domo mortua iacebat. Si autem non solum male
delectationi consensisti, sed etiam ipsum malum fecisti, quasi mortuum

extra portam extulisti; si peccasti, peniteat te ut resuscitet te dominus
et reddet te matri tue ecclesie. Tertius mortuus est Lazarus, qui signi-
ficatur mala consuetudine, que est immane genus mortis. Idem Augustinus ait: "Aliud est non peccare et aliud est peccandi consuetudinem   30
facere." Si peccat et continuo corrigitur, cito reviviscit consuetudine,
non est sepultus. Qui enim peccare consuevit, est quasi sepultus. Iamdicti quoque mortui significantur istis versibus: "Mens mala, mors intus;
malus actus, mors foris, usus. Tumba ista notant." Item Augustinus:

⟨Non prodesse malos   "Non itaque illi quos monemus agere penitentiam
   socios habere   querant sibi comites ad supplicia. Nec gaudeant,
    penarum⟩   quoniam plures inveniunt sibi similes. Nam non
                       minus propterea ardebunt quia cum multis puni-
entur." Neque confert eis quicquam ad pene mitigitionem, quod dicitur solatium est miseris socios habere penarum, similes aliorum respice   40
casus mitius ista ferens. Noli ergo emulari inter malignantes, sane
qui malignantur exterminabuntur. Non capere exemplum, sed dare,
dignus eras. Imitare igitur Christum, qui est via sine errore, veritas
absque falsitate, et vita sine fine. Idem autem Christus est via in exemplo, veritas in promisso, vita enim in premio.

De laude huius libelli

Numquam porro, karissime, hic liber de manu tua cadat, quem pre
oculis habes. Nam hic quanto in superficie videtur apertior, tanto
altitudine misteriorum est profundior. In eodem utique est lac puerorum et cibus fortiorum;scriptura enim sacra est solidus cibus pruden-   50
tium, qui diu debet masticari antequam incorporetur. Est quoque
scriptura sacra suavis et dulcis potus simplicium, qui leviter haurietur.
Si enim esset theologia tantum cibum, terreret idiotas; si vero esset solummodo potus contemneretur a peritis. Eapropter illa cibus et potus
est, id est, fortis et levis, ut fatiget validos et reficiat imbecilles; pascit
enim manifestis, exercet obscuris. Omnis utique splendor rethorice,
eloquentie, cuncti modi poetice locutionis: quelibet varietas decore
pronuntiationis a divinis scripturis sumpsit exordium. Item Ambrosius:
"Quicquid alibi queritur, hic perfecte invenitur." Noli ergo querere
aurum in luto, id est, sapientiam superne scientie aut rationem ter-   60
rene creature in libris ethnicorum et gentilium, sed require illa in
theologia, cuius radices sunt in coelo, quamobrem fructus illius arboris
non facile, immo difficulter carpuntur. Est namque admodum difficile
scripturas sacras perfecte intelligere et ad unguem illas exponere. Item
in hoc opere ad salutem consulitur universis. Hic est quod omni etati

congruat, ibidem est quod cuilibet professioni expediat. In eodem
namque reperitur quod omni sexui conveniat. ⟨Hic habentur prohibi-
tiones que summopere sunt fugiende, quoniam cum eis non est salus.⟩
Ibi leguntur precepta que faciamus. Hic sane intelliguntur premia que
70   speremus; ibi profecto nec pastoribus desunt alimenta nec ovibus pa-
bula. Hic denique est visio que per litteram doceat ad scientiam. In
eodem porro est promissio que trahat per gratiam et deducat ad gloriam; ibi prorsus sic exuberat copia spiritualis celestium deliciarum, ut
ibi habundet quod perfectus comedat et etiam quod parvulus sugat.
Hic est utique lactens potus quo tenera fidelium nutriatur infantia, et
solidus cibus quo robusta perfectorum sancte virtutis recipiat incre-
menta. Denique si est tibi cor, carneum, et ingenium laudabile ac
docile, et si es tenacis memorie et non labilis ubique, invenies quod
possis discere atque melior effici et semper proficere. Utilius autem est
80   aliena verecunde addiscere quam tua impudenter ingerere.

Contra avaritiam

Item Ambrosius: "Aurum ecclesia habet, non ut servet, sed ut eroget,
et ut pauperibus subveniat in necessitatibus. Quid est opus custodire
que nichil adiuvat?" Idem in causa XII, questione II: "Nonne dicturus
est dominus: 'Cur passus es tot inopes fame mori?' Et certe habebas
aurum, unde ministrares alimoniam. Cur tot captivi in |17ra| com-
mertium ducti, nec redempti ab aliquo, sed ab hoste occisi sunt?
Melius fuerat, ut vasa viventium servares, quam metallorum." Solvendo
respondens: "Ne templo dei ornatus deesset timui? Dicet tibi deus:
90   'Aurum sacramenta non querunt, neque auro placent que auro non
emuntur.' Ornatus sacramentorum, redemptio est captivorum. Et vere
illa sunt pretiosa vasa, que redimunt animas a morte. Ille verus est
thesaurus dei, qui operatur, quod sanguis eius est operatus." Item
Ieronimus in eadem causa, questione II: "Gloria est episcopi pauperibus providere. Ignominia sacerdotis est, propriis studere divitiis. Natus
in paupere domo et in tugurio rusticano qui vix milio et cibario vel
eribario pane rugientem ventrem poterat saturare, nunc similam et
mella fastidio." Item: "Nunc vero cum paupertatem domus sue pauper
dominus dedicavit; portemus crucem et divitias lutum putemus." Ex
100 ecclesiarum vero bonis aliquid subtrahere "superat omnium predonum
crudelitatem." Idem ibidem: "Nos subfarcinati auro Christum pau-
perem sequimur, et sub pretextu alimonie pristinis opibus incubantes,
quomodo possumus aliena fideliter distribuere, qui nostra timide re-
servamus? Plenus autem venter facile de ieiuniis disputat."

De distractione rerum ecclesiarum

Item nota istos casus in quibus pecunia et res ecclesie debent vendi,
scilicet, in sustentatione et alimonia pauperum et in redemptione captivorum et in structione ecclesiarum et cimiterii ampliatione et sepul-
crorum edificatione. Hec probantur quod illum capitulum suprapo-
situm, scilicet, *Aurum habet ecclesia*, etc. Sunt etiam alii casus quando   110
bona ecclesie et hospitalis sunt distrahenda et alienanda, videlicet, ne
miserabiles persone, ut sunt paupercule mulieres, prostent et forni-
centur nimia paupertate. Tenentur autem omnes divites, et precipue
clerici et hospitalarii, puellas, virgines, et iuvenculas viduas et pau-
perimas dotare et nuptui tradere. Ille vero que sunt anus et decrepite
sustentari debent a predictis. Unde Ieronimus ait: "Ille muliercule ecclesie pascantur elemosinis, et ille tantum accipiant pauperum cibos
que iam laborare non possunt." Item: "Sicut verum est, te tot interfe-
cisse quot pascere potuisti et non pavisti, ita verissimum est, te pro
tot peccatis debere puniri quot miserabiles persone in edidia et penuria   120
commiserunt quas iuvare debuisti et noluisti. Verumtamen ad quid
non mortalia pectora cogit auri sacra fames, hoc est execrabilis."
Item: "Toto orbe terrarum acersitur quo gens queque perit." "Fecunda virorum paupertas ⟨fugitur." Quoniam ut ait poeta: "Non habet
unde suum paupertas⟩ pascat amorem, non tamen est tanti pauper ut
esse velim." Hec utique plurimum est diligenda bonis. Est autem custos virtutum paupertas.

De his que multum nocent hominibus

Econtrario pecunia est unum illorum que vitiant hominem et pervertunt. Sunt vero tria que impediunt hominem benefacere. Hinc sapiens: 130
"Plurima cum soleant hominum corrumpere mores, fortius enervant
femina, sensus, honor, inter que appetitus honoris est peius." Unde
legitur: "Infelix quem, nec res nec femina vincere possunt, subiungit
ambitio," etc. Sit ergo in voto tuo, karissime, iamdicta, omni nisu et
toto conamine, fugere tamquam pestifera, et saluti contraria, que
quoniam sepe et sepius confutata et reprobata in presentiarum sunt
pretermitenda. Sunt enim timenda et etiam cavenda ⟨viro dei themata
atque problemata⟩ sive colores atque ornatus verborum et rhetorice.
Nec est siquidem curandum de dialetica et cornutis sophismatibus atque de insolubilibus questionibus dialectice. Nichilominus contemp-   140
nere debet scemata et thropos gramatice, qui vult imitari sanctam
simplicitatem et veritatem Christi, qui est duplicitatis aspernator et

simplicitatis amator. Nimia porro subtilitas trivii immense stoliditati
operatur. Quid namque est subtilius acutiusve Aristotele? Nil tamen
est vilius et magis inutile. Subtilitates etiam in humano iure sunt per-
niciose. Itaque, karissime, ut ea que in hoc libello et in aliis libris continentur, firmiter menti tue inhereant, utere istis versibus cuiusdam

De clavibus   sapientis: "Clavis prima datur si lectio continuatur.
scientie   'Mente tua funde quicquid legis'; ecce secunda. Ter-
150   tia: 'Que sequitur stipulando, frequenter additur.'
Pandit quarta: 'Fores rabi sint semper honores'; quinta: 'Caducarum
despectus divitiarum.'" Si vero quinque claves sapientie, que prefatis
versibus denotantur, fuerint in corde tuo, continue maximum consequeris scientie profectum atque immensam commoditatem vite, que
nunc est eventure, percipies. Insiste igitur huic operi, in quo est copiosa materia publice predicationis, nec non et spiritualis exortationis
atque private ammonitionis. Ceterum si aliquid minus caute impro-
vide et non ad unguem dictum est aut dicetur, ne turbetur caritas
vestra. Quoniam ut ait Oratius: "Fas est operum longo obrepere
160   sompno." Et etiam: "Quandoque bonus dormitat Homerus." Item
apostolus: "Si dixerimus quia peccatum non habemus, nosmet sedu-
cimus, et veritas in nobis non est." "In multis offendimus omnes."
"Non enim omnia possumus omnes." "Nec cuivis homini contingit adire
Corinthum." Item in nullo peccare et omnium |17ʳᵇ| habere memori-
am potius est divinitatis quam humanitatis. Neque omnium eorum
que ab antiquis tradita sunt ratio reddi potest. Similiter est valde
arduum et admodum difficile perfecte aliquid corrigere. Unde sapiens:
"Non tamen emendo, labor hic quam scribere maior." Hoc autem relinquimus diligentie prudentis et providi lectoris, cuius est minus
170   dicta supplere, errores corrigere, et superflua resecare, subobscura
et difficilia enucleare. Ad hoc utique sunt terenda magistrorum limina ut ea ibi, dente disputationis, adterantur et multa inquisitione in
scolis exponantur. Ammonitoria vero quoniam per se patent, seorsum
et in loco privato legantur. Item propheta: "Imperfectum meum vi-
derunt oculi tui," etc. Ergo si quod medicorum est promittunt medici,
tractant fabrilia fabri. Quam scit quisque, libens censebo exerceat
artem.

Quod vitietur utile per inutile

Item nota quod tam hore reales quam vocales inficiuntur et corrum-
180   puntur. Reales utique hore frivole fiunt et evanescuntur multipliciter,
verbi gratia, quotiens autem fiunt spe retributionis terrene bona, seu

pro vanagloria, vel aliquo indebito modo, perperam et male aguntur.
Qualiter vero vocales hore depereant et nichil valeant, infra decli-
nabitur ubi tractabitur de vitiis earum, confutando ea et reprobando.
Nunc autem restat videre quomodo utile vitiatur per inutile. Hinc
Augustinus ait in IX distinctione decretorum, *Si ad scripturas sacras
fuerint admissa vel officiosa mendacia, quid in eis remanebit auctoritatis*, etc.

De eodem

Item Ambrosius in tertia causa, questione IX decretorum: "Pura et
simplex testimonii series intimanda est. Plerumque testis, dum ad   190
seriem gestorum aliquid de suo adicit, totam testimoni fidem partis
mendacio decolorat." Item de consecratione, distinctione III, Martinus
⟨Item de   papa: "Non licet quinta feria ferias novissime septimane
eodem⟩   ieiunium solvere et omnem exonerare quadragesimam,
                 sed sincere astinentes totam quadragesimam perexire."
Item ibidem legitur: "Non oportet in quadragesima, quinta feria ultime ebdomade ieiunium dissolvere, et tota quadragesima inhonorare,
sed per totos dies est necesse et ieiunare et escis abstinentie convenien-
tibus, id est aridioribus, uti." Item apostolus: "Modicum fermentum
totam massam corrumpit."   200

De dictorum et dicendorum effectu

Noli ergo, karissime, iamdicta negligere et contempnere tamquam sint
nichili et inepta, sed amplectere memorata, utpote salutifera et pleni-
tudine omnis gratie referta. Prelibata vero et etiam dicenda, et quilibet sermo divinus, habent se more aromatum que quanto subtilius,
quasi terendo et cernendo discutiuntur, tanto maiorem sue interne virtutis fragrantiam emittunt. Sunt autem in prefatis et memorandis an-
tidota et validissima medicamenta contra universa vitia et peccata et
fomenta cunctarum virtutum, si vigilanti mentis oculo intueantur. Est
quoque materia in hoc nostro opere amonendi, exortandi, predicandi,   210
instruendi docendique singulos et universos fertilis et copiosa. ⟨Item
hoc opus precellit cunctis, eminet universis, antecedit cuncta ethnicorum dicta, et supergraditur universa paganorum volumina ornatu
verborum et utilitate sententie et pondere sententiarum.⟩

De eodem

Declina ergo summopere curiositatem astronomie, que contemplatur
vagos discursus planetarum, motumve firmamenti atque revolutionem
orbis terrarum de zodiaco et emisperio superiori et inferiori, atque de

orizonte disceptando. Neque emuleris stoliditatem geometrie, que
220 perperam tempus consumit in lineis et superficiebus et quomodo quilibet triangulus habet tres angulos, equales duobus rectis. Nec vaces
musice, que frustra laborat circa proportiones sexqualteram et sexqui-
terciam et hemioliam. Fugies quoque arismeticam, que non multum
commode tractat de numeris paribus et imparibus. Expedit autem
prepropero gressu ad eternam patriam suspiranti, omittere quadrivium, in quo, licet sit magna subtilitas, est ibi tamen modica utilitas.
Ideo dic: "Linguo coas ranis, cras corvis vanaque vanis; Ad logicam
pergo, que mortis non timet ergo."

Contra eos qui non intrant ecclesiam per hostium

230 Item sciendum est, hoc esse valde timendum quod legitur in primo
libro regum, scilicet, quod capta arca domini a Philisteis in bello,
"statuerunt eam iusta Dagon. Cumque surrexissent diluculo Azocii
altera die . . . invenerunt Dagon iacentem pronum in terra super faciem suam coram arca domini. Caput autem Dagon et due palme
manuum eius abscise erant. Porro Dagon truncus solus remanserat."
Ad idem utique facit, hoc legitur in libro Paralipomenon, id est, repe-
titionum, in quo docetur istud: "Tetendit sane Oza manum suam, ut
sustentaret arcam, bos quippe lasciviens paululum inclinaverat illam.
Iratus est itaque dominus contra Ozam et percussit eum, eo quod
240 tetigisset arcam. Et mortuus est ibi coram domino." Tecta siquidem
sunt omnia dicta, karissime, et referta magnis misteriis et gravida
pluribus sacramentis atque plena fortissimis questionibus.

De eodem

Potest equidem per arcam intelligi ecclesia, per Dagon et Ozam significantur universi qui non intrant ecclesiam per hostium, id est, Chris-
tum. Est autem humilis ianua Christus dominus, qui vero se |17va|
non humiliat sed extollit, per maceriam vult ascendere. Et ideo non
valet sano capite, hoc est bona conscientia, dei ecclesiam intrare.
Tales denique sunt cuncti simoniaci atque chorite, nec non et greziti,
250 quorum omnium vera et sola penitentia est hec: ecclesie et spiritualis
beneficii abrenuntiatio. Item si Philistei graviter puniti sunt, ut ait
Samuel in primo libro Regum, quia posuerunt arcam domini iuxta
Dagon, multo itaque fortius illi punientur qui proponunt Dagon, id
est, idolum surdum et mutum arche, hoc est, personam despicabilem
vultu, veste sordidam, crine deformem, inutilem, et abiectam, caren-
tem vita et scientia et facundia preficiunt ecclesie, que deberet com-

mitti viris litteratis, honestis, castis, sobriis, temperatis. Tales vero in
dei ecclesia instituantur qui sint misericordes, pudici, in lege dei in-
structi, in sensibus scripturarum acuti, in domatibus litterarum exer-
citi. Isti autem tenentur excutere manus suas ab omni munere, que   260
sunt occasio multorum malorum et omnium criminum. Inter cetera
siquidem, karissime, hoc summopere tibi est observandum quod docet
sapiens, "ut primum medio, medium quoque et consonet immo."

Explicit liber iiii

Incipit Liber V Cantoris Parisiensis
De oratione et speciebus illius

*Conforta me rex sanctorum principatum tenens, et da mihi sermonem rectum, qui
sit mihi et omnibus expediens. Nam ut apostolus ait: "Omnibus tam sapientibus
quam insipientibus debitor sum." Idcirco ut ab hac obligatione commode possimus
absolvi, illius prius implorandum est auxilium, sine quo nullum recte fundatur*   270
*exordium, quatenus dignetur dirigere opus nostrum in via salutis eterne. In primis
ergo sciendum est, quod oratio valde neccessaria est vere penitenti, unde dignum
duximus post tractatum penitentie et ieiunii agere de oratione, que est unum alarum
eius. Omnis enim qui meritorie penitet tenetur habere hunc triplicem funiculum,
qui difficulter solvitur, videlicet ieiunium, elemosinam, et orationem, de qua est
hic agendum, aliis duobus omissis, quoniam alias dictum est de illis. Unde in
primis videndum est quid sit oratio, secundo quot sint eius species, tertio qualiter
subdividantur partes sive species orationis in diversos modos orandi. Quarto illa
breviter sunt tangenda que in omni negotio ad hoc, ut rite et perfecte perficiatur,
sunt necessaria.*   280

De hiis que exiguntur adesse rei

*Sunt autem multa. Primum quorum est materia, de qua res illa est facienda. Et
hoc est evidens cum ferro, quod est materia cultelli, similiter in ligno, quod est
materia preiacens domus, et in multis aliis. Nullum enim materiatum possit fieri
sine materia preiacenti. Secundum est artifex. Tertium est scientia eius. Quartum
est voluntas illius. Quintum vero est facultas sive possibilitas eius seu potentia
operandi. In hac quinta specie comprehenduntur naturalia instrumenta, ut sunt
pedes et manus et alia membra hominis. Sunt enim lingua et dentes instrumenta
loquendi, et oculi videndi, et aures audiendi et os gustandi, nares odorandi. Sunt*

290 *etiam instrumenta artificialia, quibus cooperantibus homines colunt terram, ut-*
pote sunt ferramenta varia et diversa. Sextum est qualitas vel modus faciendi. Sep-
timum est quantitas. Octavum est ad quid illud fiat.

De eodem

Videntur tamen hee tres species ultime contineri sub tertia specie. Nam qui habet
scientiam aliquid operandi, oportet eum scire qualiter illum sit agendum, et quan-
tum in eo negotio sit procedendum, et que commoditas seu utilitas ex tali negotio
consequatur. Quicumque sane caret aliquo predictorum reputet se insufficientem
et imperfectum ad opus inceptum exequendum et consummandum. Iamdicta seu
prelibata omnia satis eleganter et commode operi nostro conveniunt, si diligenter
300 *singula considerentur. Materia orationis sunt littere et sillabe, dictiones et ora-*
tiones. Artifex est orator, cui necessaria est scientia, que instruat eum esse oran-
dum aliquo septem dicendorum modorum. Eadem docet quantum deus sit orandus.
Est deus laudandus omni tempore. Ipsa eadem amoneat quare deus sit invo-
candus et diligendus. Ideo est colendus quatenus in suo regno nos collocare digne-
tur. Potest igitur constare lector, tibi karissime, quid primo et secundo et ultimo
ex prefatis expediat. In primis ergo scis quod teneris orare et laudare et benedicere
deum. Hoc est quasi materia et propositum negotii tui. Secundo oportet te scire
qualitatem seu autenticos modos orandi, qui dicentur inferius. Tertio necesse est
considerare qualiter illud est agendum. Quarto expedit tibi animadvertere ad quid
310 *laboras, et quod sit premium tui certaminis.*

Cito esse ad propositum perveniendum

Veruntamen ne in prefacione seu exordio imperitorum more videamur effluere et
abundare et in ipsa materia subcingi et quasi deficere, admodum extravagantia
et quasi incidentia pretermittamus. Dum enim temporibus et figuris atque
casibus inseruit oratio, quod brevi poterat indicare, sermone longo verborum ambitu circumacta vix eorum explicat sententiam et auctoris
intentionem. Eatenus |17vb| sunt omittenda verba humane sapientie
persuasibilia et colores rethorum et sophismata dialecticorum, nec non
et barbarissmum ac solocissmum gramatice inherentes atque emu-
320 lantes. Solummodo sanctam simplicitatem theologie *ad rem est properan-*
dum, ne nobis obiciatur illud Horatii: "Sed nunc non erat his locus et fortasse
cupresum scis simulare."

De oratione

Est autem oratio dei benivolentie captatio. Item Cassiodorus: "Est autem oratio
oris ratio, frequens deprecatio et assidua supplicatio, que ab imo pec-
toris archano procedit" cum pietate et devotione. *Effectus vero orationis*

est domini misericordem et propitium nobis efficere." Item: "Orare siquidem est
vota deo reddere." Item propheta: "In me sunt deus vota que reddam
laudationes tibi." Item nota quod in dictis verbis David argumentum
habes quod in homine est unde potest deum laudare. In alio psalmo   330
invenitur: "Reddam tibi vota mea que distinxerunt labia mea." Hoc
est distincte et aperte: "Proferam laudes tuas que sunt vota mea." Volun-
tate et intentione mentis et cordis est deus laudandus et invocandus
precipue ac principaliter. Hinc propheta: "Omnis gloria eius filie regis
ab intus." Intrinsecus autem et cum mente et conscientia teneris exorare deum ut potius intriseca sit, id est, in corde quam in ore oratio.
Unde sapiens: "Nec te quesieris extra." Hoc est, non coneris magis
placere hominibus quam deo, sed potius dic cum apostolo: "Michi autem
pro minimo est an a vobis iudicer, an ab humano die," ab illis qui
querunt laudem hominum et non dei. *Item inter opera virtutum maximum*   340
et potissimum est orare frequenter, et assiduum esse in oratione. Precipue convenit
faciei tendentis in Ierusalem, nam ut ait Augustinus: "Vage mentis et instabilis
est non posse diutius in oratione consistere." Item idem: Duo sunt opera excel-
Quod sit melius *lentissima et specialia viri viventis religiose et maxime*
orare quam legere *claustralium, scilicet legere et orare, quorum utrumque, si*
fieri potest, bonum est. Ceterum si non, melius et utilius
est orare, quod patet ex verbis domini, qui ait: "Hoc genus demonii non eici-
tur nisi in oratione et ieiunio," id est, in abstinentia a malo et devotione orationis,
que nutrit animum in bonum. Amplius idem: "Qui orat loquitur cum deo," id
est, dicit deo vel petit quod vult ab eo. ⟨Immo, ut minus proprie lo-   350
quamur, et salva pace domini, homo dum orat est quasi maior domino. Nam homo dum dicit orando: "Miserere mei deus," "Domine exaudi orationem meam," et similia, est tunc quasi maior deo. Maioris
est utique imperare, et minoris obedire, secundum verborum pro-
prietatem. Sicut homo, qui nichil est respectu creatoris, imperat deo
cum ait: "Erue a framea, deus, animam meam," et "Doce me facere
voluntatem tuam." Item idem reperies in multis auctoritatibus. Et ita
homo quodammodo prefertur deo quando orat.⟩ *"Qui legit, deus cum eo*
loquitur," hoc est, deus docet eum quid sit agendum et quod vitandum.
Orationibus namque a peccatis mundanis lectoribus instruimur. Item   360
Ieronimus: "Sicut autem milites ad bellum inermes exire non convenit, ita cuilibet homini procedere vel aliquid agere sine oratione minime expedit." Item sciendum est quod sunt V fines quibus homines
legunt. Aliquis vero legit tantum ut sciat, et hoc est superbie. Alius
enim legit ut sciatur, quod est vaneglorie. Tertius quoque legit ut
lucretur, et hoc est avaricie; quartus ut edificetur, quod est prudentie.

Quintus etiam legit ut edificet, et hec meta est caritatis. Item sapiens:
"Tertius modus legendi est pessimus, avaritia utique et amor carnalis
et timor." Plerumque sensus hebetant humanos et pervertunt oppini-
370   ones, ut questum putent pietatem, et pecuniam quasi mercede prudentie.

De hiis que impediunt sapientem

Item nota quod hec faciunt intelligentiam dei et sacre scripture,
quorum unum est vacatio. Unde illud: "Vacate et videte quoniam ego
sum dominus." Et alibi: "In tempore ocii tui describe tibi sapientiam
et si minoraberis actu precipiens illam." Secundum est munditia vite,
hinc sapiens: "In malivolam animam non intrabit sapientia." Tertium
est humilitas, unde illud: "Valles habundabunt frumento." Quartum
est mansuetudo, hinc Iacob: "Cum mansuetudine suscipite insitum
380   verbum , quod potest salvare animas vestras." Quintum est sollicitudo,
unde sapiens: "Beatus qui vigilat ad fores meas et observat ad postes
hostii mei." Item sapiens: "Carmina secessum scribentis et otia querunt." *Plerumque autem multus pulvis et maxima vanitas inheret lectori. Item
licet dicatur quod omne bonum opus est oratio, secundum quod dicitur non desinet
orare qui non cessat benefacere, hinc tamen inspecificatur et restringet. Hoc nomen
oratio ut dicatur et ponatur pro affectu animi aut motu in deum, qui impigritetur
quandoque prorumpit in voce, de qua David ait: "Pro eo ut me diligeret, detrahe-
bat mihi. Ego autem orabam." Quasi dicat propheta: "In omni tribulatione mea
confugi ad orationem." Hoc est armatura, qua omnis homo potest resistere cuilibet*
390   *temptationi et adversitati. Ista enim Martinus armatus omne nocumentum fugie-
bat, ad hanc ut ad solita arma confugit vir dei. Martinus denique,⟨qui visu,
auditu, et gestu iustus erat,⟩ cum domus arderet in qua molliorem et sua-
viorem solito lectulum habuerat, de qua, cum non posset exire, novissimo ad terram genibus est provolutus, et ita oratione sua deus igne extinxit.*

De speciebus orationis

*Nota quod orationum alia est vocalis et quedam est realis. Vocalis vero continet
vii horas canonicas quibus cotidie utitur sancta ecclesia, videlicet matutinum,
primam, tertiam, sextam, nonam, vesperas, et complectorium. Quicumque ergo
|18ra| velit iamdictas horas cantare vel etiam alias preces privatas deo fundere,*
400   *ad hoc ut ei placeat et sibi et aliis prosit, debet orare aliquo istorum modorum
qui statim dicentur. Sunt autem septem modi regulares et auctentici et meritorii
orandi quod probantur auctoritate sanctarum scriptarum, porro ut ait sapiens:
"Quicquid asseritur, nisi idoneis et legitimis testibus convincatur et probetur, eadem
namque facillitate repellitur qua astruitur."*

De primo modo orandi

Primus orandi modus est talis, videlicet brachia et ambas manus coniunctas et extensas supra caput tuum versus celum, inquantum prevales extendere. Ita dico non sedens neque iacens nec appodiatus, sed erectus, sursum toto corpore. Unde apostolus: "Volo ergo viros orare in omni loco, levantes manus puras sine ira et disceptatione." Item apostolus Timotheo sic docet esse orandum: "Obsecro ergo primum omnium fieri obsecrationes, orationes, postulationes, gratiarum actiones pro omnibus hominibus, pro regibus, et omnibus qui in sublimitate sunt constituti, ut quietam et tranquillam vitam agamus in omni pietate et castitate," etc. Talis siquidem oratio plurimum est utilis oranti, quoniam est admodum grata et accepta deo. *Similiter et mulieres idem agere debent. Hinc vero habens argumentum orandi non tantum in ecclesia sed etiam in domo, in via et agro, in foro et ubique. Idem argumentum invenis in propheta, qui ait: "In omni loco benedictionis tue, benedic, anima mea, dominum." Et hoc quidem verum est, quod in omni loco et tempore deum tenemur laudare et benedicere, et adorare, atque de collatis beneficiis ei grates referre. Verumtamen longe melius est in ecclesia orare ubi sunt reliquie sanctorum, si adest facultas intrandi eorum limina, et si possit fieri eque et comode.* Item Isaia propheta: "Et cum extenderitis manus vestras, avertam oculos meos a vobis. Et cum multiplicaveritis orationem, non exaudiam vos," etc. Item Ieremia propheta in Trenis: "Leva ad deum manus tuas pro animabus parvulorum tuorum," etc.

410

420

De orationis dignitate

Quanta siquidem sane sit dignitas orationum vocalium, evidenter ostenditur in vita Marie Magdalene, in qua docetur hoc: "Et numquam cibum humanum manducavit neque vinum bibit, et in omnibus horis canonicis angeli dei de celo venerunt, et eam in aere secum duxerunt, ut ibi cum eis suam orationem impleret." Quid autem dignius, quidve sanctius potest homini contingere quam cum angelis deum exorare? Insiste ergo operi divino, age diligenter id ad quod teneris, decanta ergo horas canonicas tam corde quam ore. Que, licet non sufficiant ad salutem eis qui habent facultatem agendi reales horas, conducunt tamen et exiguntur et sunt necessarie tibi ad hoc ut pervenias ad eternam beatitudinem.

430

De eodem

Item propheta ait: "Exaudi, domine, vocem deprecationis mee, dum oro ad te et dum extollo manus meas ad templum sanctum tuum." Hoc exemplum habetur in psalmo qui sic incipit: "Ad te domine clamavi, deus meus, ne sileas a me." Item idem David ait in hoc psalmo: "Ecce nunc benedicite dominum: in noctibus ex-

440

*tollite manus vestras in sancta et benedicite dominum." Idem etiam docet in hoc
quarto psalmo: "Domine clamavi ad te et exaudi me; intende voci mee dum cla-
mavero ad te. Elevatio manuum mearum sacrificium vespertinum." Sic autem
orabat beatus Martinus, de quo legitur oculis ac manibus in celum semper in-
tendens, invictum ab oratione spiritum non relaxabat.* Ideo enim cum oramus
tenemur stare ut in erectione corporum ostendamus quod in laude dei
debemus habere corda sursum erecta. Nam nisi mens consonet lingue,
certum est vocem cuiuslibet quantumlibet clamosam deo non posse

450 *placere. Ad hoc autem ut melius intelligatur quod dictum est, sequens figura
oculis subiecta evidenter ac manifeste demonstrabit.* Nec deus est nec homo,
presens quam cernis ymago. Sed deus est modo presens quem ymago
signat.

ELEVATIO MANUUM

De secundo modo orandi

*Secundus modus orandi debet fieri manibus et ulnis expansis ad modum atque
similitudinem crucis. Unde David ait in isto psalmo: "Domine, deus salutis mee,
in die clamavi et nocte coram te: Clamavi ad te, domine, tota die; expandi manus
meas ad te." Idem propheta testatur in alio psalmo qui sic inchoatur: "Domine,*

460 *exaudi orationem meam, auribus percipe obsecrationem meam in veritate tua. Ex-
audi me in tua iustitia." "Expandi manus meas ad te.* |18ʳᵇ| *Anima mea sicut
terra sine aqua tibi." Hoc modo oravit dominus pendens in cruce, scilicet extensis
ulnis cum dicebat: "Pater, in manus tuas comendo spiritum meum." Item Elias
sic oravit quando suscitavit filium vidue, quod habetur in libro regum, ubi Samuel
ait de Elia: "Expandit se atque missus est super puerum tribus vicibus, clamavit-
que ad deum. Et ait: 'Revertatur, oro domine deus meus, anima pueri huius in
viscera eius.'"*

Quod sit melius orare in loco sacro quam in alio

Item, nota quod licet ubique teneamur laudare et adorare deum, tamen

470 convenientius atque utilius sit in loco religioso et sacro. Hic est quod
ait propheta Ioel: "Inter vestibulum et altare plorabant sacerdotes,
ministri domini." Non enim dixit cachinnabantur neque ridebant, sed
subiunxit dolebant. Merentes autem et flentes deus exaudit et letificat,
atque magnificat. Nec dictum est a propheta quod fierent presbiteri
in foro aut in teatro vel in bivio sive in trivio seu quadruvio ubi est
concursus gentium, immo in loco sancto. In templo sane invenitur
dominus, quoniam ipse in sanctis habitat. Item notum sit caritati
vestre, diligens lector, parvitatem meam vidisse hominem indutum

loricam, in maximo frigore super nudo, dicentes totum psalterium, expansis brachiis stando, et erectus toto corpore, qui nullo vestimento   480
aut calciamento utebatur preter tunicam qua prelibata lorica tegebatur.
Idem autem homo dei nolebat uti igne vel palea, sed iacebat in solo
aut in simplici ligno et duro. Iamdictus quoque vir secunda et quarta
et sexta feriam non solvebat ieiunia, hoc est, non aliquo cibo corporali
reficiebatur. In prefato equidem viro, cuius copiam habui, et quem
viva voce sum allocutus, erant plura que sunt digna relatu. Et ideo
non sunt pretereunda sub silentio, que sunt hec, videlicet ille fuerat
scientia literarum eruditus atque honestate morum preditus, et in
cathedrali ecclesia intitulatus et institutus nec non nobili genere ortus,
plurimum bonis naturalibus et gratuitis adornatus—que ferine omnia   490
raro unquam conveniunt et religioni concordant—prelibatusque vir
modico tugurio erat contentus, in quo non ad tempus sed perpetuo
residebat inclusus. *Verumtamen quoniam doctrina demonstrata est efficacior
et levior quam intellectualis, ideo fiat imago que representat gestum orantis. Sunt
autem figure, picture, et imagines quasi libri simplicium atque laicorum, quia
quod viri scolastici, et exercitatos sensus habentes, intelligunt per scripturas, pro
parte et qualitercumque idiote animadvertunt in figuris expresse et aperte.* Item
nota quod vita clericorum est liber vulgi quos imitari volunt et maxime in malo. Est etiam liber clericorum sacra scriptura, unde legitur:
"Claude sermones et signa librum," quia pertransiunt plurimi et multi-   500
plex et maxima scientia. Est namque liber conscientie, de quo ait sapiens: 'Sedit vetustus dierum et libri aperti sunt coram eo." Est quoque
liber predestinationis. Hinc habetur: "Nomina eorum scripta sunt in
libro vite." Est preterea liber nature, scilicet celum et terram et invi-
sibilia dei. Hinc apostolus: "Per ea que facta sunt, intellectu, a crea-
tura mundi conspiciuntur." Isti vero libri communes sunt rerum
omnium.

EXPANDI

De tertia specie orandi

*Tertius autem modus intercedendi ad deum fit stando orante, existente directo toto   510
corpore, utpote in duobus est agendum superioribus. Tamen in hoc differt iste
modus ab aliis, quoniam in hoc tertio tenetur orator esse erectus super pedes suos
ita quod non sit adpodiatus neque inherens alicui rei, sicut in iamdictis—habens
manus complosas, et contiguas extensas ac directas coram oculis suis. Unde
Lucas ait de domino: "Et intravit secundum consuetudinem suam die sabbati in
sinagogam, et surrexit legere." Item Davit ait in psalmo CV: "Stetit Finees et*

exoravit, et cessavit quassatio." Amplius legitur: "Stetit Hesdra scriba super
gradum et aperuit librum coram omni populo, et benedixit domino deo magno."
Et benedictum possumus benedicere, et maledictum possumus maledicere. Quo
520 *hoc fiat, figura declarat.* Nam ut ait Gregorius: "Quod legentibus
scrip|18va|tura, hoc idiotis prestat pictura cernentibus, quoniam in ip-
sa ignorantes vident quod sequi debeant, in ea legunt qui litteras
nesciunt."

DEUS PROPITIUS ESTO

Non esse sedendum cum oramus

Quod idem sit orare et pugnare evidenter ostenditur. Est autem sedere pausantium
seu iudicantium, stare vero est pugnantium. Unde beatus Stephanus cum lapi-
daretur et certaret pro fide, vidit filium hominis stantem a dextris virtutis dei,
qui est cum sanctis in bello et non deserit eos in adversitate, sed liberat eos oculta
530 *et spirituali liberatione quedam, licet caro detur in manus impii. Hinc propheta:*
"Quoniam in me speravit, liberabo eum; protegam eum, quoniam cognovit nomen
meum," etc. Item Lucas ait de Christo: "Et factus est in agonia, prolixius orabat," etc.; agonia, id est, pugna. Ideo apostolus ait: "Omnis qui
in agone contendit," etc., id est, qui in bello pugnat. Nota quod dixit
prolixius, habens argumentum quod non parum, sed multum et diu
orando pugnabat, et pugnando orabat. Quod enim orando certaret
Christus, in eodem evangelio probatur, cum subditur: "Et factus est
sudor eius sicut gutte sanguinis decurrentis in terra." Et quia sudavit,
tunc laboravit. Ex hoc sequitur quod pugnabat orando et econverso;
540 non enim solent pausantes sudare sed laborantes. In predictis habes
argumentum contra pigros oratores, qui statim cum debent orare, incipiunt sedere vel appodiare, se huc aut illuc adquiescendum. Tales
pro vili re tota die laborarent in agro et pugnarent in foro, qui una
hora nolunt servire domino deo.

Quotiens est dicendum Pater Noster ab idiotis

Item, nota quod multi viri sancti, expletis canonicis horis, totum
psalterium stando sic dicebant. Plures vero qui litteras ignorabant in
recompensatione matutini centiens Pater Noster orando repetebant.
Unde consuetudo talis inolevit apud religiosos quod iniungunt idiotis
550 et inlitteratis certum numerum dicendi orationem dominicam pro
qualibet hora vocali seu canonica. Pro mattutinis autem sive loco
vigilarum conversis imperant prepositi, ut centiens Pater Noster dicant, et pro laudibus XXX, pro prima XX. Pro missa vero imponunt

laicis ecclesie doctores L Pater Noster. Hoc enim non ideo sit, karissime, ut credas totiens repetitam orationem dominicam equipollere misse; nullus enim numerus orationum ei digne conferatur. Sed eatenus illum est dictum qua habeant carentes scientiam litterarum aliquam compensationem et quasi consolationem loco misse, licet non usquequaque condignam. Simile vero habes in LXXXII distinctione decretorum, Capitulum *Presbiter si fornicationem*, etc., versus finem ubi legi-   560
tur: "Sane sciendum est, quia secundam feriam unum psalterium canendo, aut unum denarium pauperibus dando, si opus est, redimere poterit. Finitis autem VII annis, deinde usque ad finem X annos, VI feriam, nulla interveniente redemptione, observet in pane et aqua." Non est autem illa usquequaque digna recompensatio, scilicet pro psalterio dare denarium, sed est qualiscumque commutatio pene et penitentis satisfactio.

Quod sint agenda non zelo invidie, sed dei amore

Item quidam dampnis, alii verberibus castigantur. Nichil sane fiat nocendi cupiditate, sed omnia consulendi caritate. Nam et plectendo   570
et ignoscendo hoc solum bene agitur, ut vita hominum corrigatur, quoniam hoc eis prestatur ne Gehenne ignibus tradantur. Item pro tertia tenentur canere iamdicti decies Pater Noster. Similiter pro sextis et nonis, loco autem vesperarum XX, et totidem pro complectorio. Et non solum prefati debent sic deum laudare, sed omnes homines. *Ille sane qui orat pugnat contra diabolum. Idcirco maxima indiget cautela qui tam vallidum et adeo callidum hostem debet superare. Oratio siquidem clippeus est: ignita, iacula antiqui hostis repelluntur. Secundus hostis noster est mundus, qui incessanter naviculam Petri impugnat, marinis fluctibus quatitur, vertitur, vergitur, et undique quatitur sed non submergitur. Illa vero navis potest signifi-*   580
care ecclesiam vel quemlibet virum fidelem, cui invidetur et detrahitur a falsis

Non omne
pacem Christi
ad Belial

fratribus. Nam ut ait sapiens: "Impia pars hominum partim est infesta piorum." Confortamini ergo in domino viri sancti et in potentia virtutis eius. Quoniam si deus est nobiscum, quis contra nos? Non est enim consilium vel sapientia nec potentia neque prudentia contra deum. Huic secundo hosti opponitur |18vb| *largitas, que est medium viciorum utrumque redactum. Hic eque distat a duobus extremis, videlicet ab avaritia et prodigalitate. Tertius siquidem hostis est caro, cuius voluntas est reprimenda. Hinc Oratius: "Sperne voluptates; nocet empta dolore voluptas." Contra vicia carnis habemus hac medicamenta, videlicet*   590
arta ieiunia, nocturnas vigilias, et plurimos labores. De tribus dictis hostibus ait scriptura: "Premit caro, fremit mundus, insidiatur diabolus."

De quarta specie orandi

Quartus modus deprecandi deum fit positis genibus in terra. Unde Marcus ait: "Venit ad Iesum leprosus, deprecans eum, et genuflexo dixit: 'Si vis, potes me mundare.'" Item Lucas refert de Christo: "Et positis genibus, orabat, dicens: 'Pater, si vis, transfer calicem istum a me.'" Item Ieronimus refert in vita beati Pauli heremite, quod sic invenit Antonius corpus beatissimi iamdicti Pauli, etiam post egressum et divisionem sancti
600 spiritus et felicis anime in celo triumphantis, cuius corpus talem gestum deprecantis representabat, quod est, mirabile dictu, aliquod exanime cadaver sine spiraculo vite sic posse subsistere. De quo prelibatus Ieronimus ait: "Nec introgressus speluncam, Antonius vidit genibus complicatis, erecta cervice, extensisque in altum manibus, corpus exanime. In primis et ipse vivere illum credens, pariter orabat," etc.

Genua esse flectenda

In memoratis utique, karissime, habes validum argumentum contra desidiam torporem et eorum negligentiam qui sunt impinguati, ingrassati, et dilatati de patrimonio crucifixi. Tales in labore hominum
610 non sunt, et cum eis non flagellantur. Isti sane miseri dedignantur flectere genua sua coram deo, quod etiam sola caro premortui viri agebat, representando post mortem quod gessit in vita. Erat profecto summum studium et omnis intentio sanctorum, maxime prefati Pauli et beati Antonii, orare veluti supra dictum est. Eapropter quidam illorum pernotabant in orationibus, decantando totum psalterium positis genibus. Alii vero illum dicebant erectis brachiis, ut preostensum est. Tertii autem expansis, quarti denique in terra prosternebantur, quinti porro incurvati orabant. *Rursus apostolus in epistola ad Ephesios testatur: "Huius rei gratia flecto genua mea ad patrem domini nostri Jesu Christi," etc.*

620 *De eodem*

Item in Actibus apostolorum docet Lucas de Stephano hoc: "Positis autem genibus, clamavit voce magna dicens: 'Domine ne statuas illis hoc peccatum.'" Sic orabat Iacobus apostolus, frater domini, de quo legitur quod centies in die et centies in nocte exorabat pro peccatis populorum dominum, positis genibus in terra. Unde genua eius ita calluerant et indurata erant ex frequentia genuum, ut essent partes ille que ponebantur in terra, dure utpote pedes camelorum. Quod autem est dictum, qualiter illud fiat imago presens ostendit.

DOMINE, SI VIS, POTES

De quinta specie orandi

Quintus modus nempe obsecrandi est iste, videlicet quando homo prohicit se   630
planum in terra super faciem suam, dicendo: "Deus propitius esto mihi pecca-
tori." Et: "Ego sum qui peccavi, ego inique egi" in omnem iustitiam tuam. Et
ideo non sum dignus videre altitudinem celi pre multitudine iniquitatum mearum.
De illo oratore ait propheta in psalmo: "Deus auribus nostris audivimus," etc. Ibi
habetur: "Quoniam humiliata est in pulvere anima nostra, adhesit in terra venter
noster." Item idem ait in psalmo alio, scilicet Beati immaculati, in quo legitur:
"Adhesit pavimento anima mea, vivifica me secundum verbum tuum." Et ponitur
ibi anima pro corpore, et est sensus, quia scio me esse pulverem et cinerem, ideo
corpus meum terre copulo et coniungo, flendo peccata mea. Item Matheus ait
de domino: "Et progressus pusillum procidit in faciem suam, orans et   640
dicens: 'Pater mi, si possibile est, transeat a me calix iste,'" etc. Item
Marcus de Christo: "Et cum processisset paululum, procidit super terram, et orabat ut si fieri posset, transiret ab eo hora." Item Iohannes
in apocalipsi: "Et XXIIII seniores ceciderunt in facies suas, et adoraverunt viventem in secula seculorum." Item Lucas: "Unus autem ex
illis ut vidit, quia mundatus est, regressus est, cum magna voce magni-
ficans deum, et cecidit in faciem ante pedes eius, gratias agens."

De differentia que est inter casum malorum et bonorum

Nota quod boni cadunt ante, mali retro. Hinc Beda: "Cadit vero in
faciem qui ex malis que se perpetrasse meminit, erubescit; ibi cadit   650
homo ubi confunditur." At contra de malis legitur: "Abierunt retror-
sum et ceciderunt in terram." Omnis qui post se cadit ibi corruit |19ᵃ|
ubi non videt. Iniqui ergo, quoniam in istis transitoriis et terenis, ini-
quis appetendo, cadunt. Post se cadere dicuntur, quia sic corruunt ut
quid eos tunc sequatur modo videre non possunt. Iusti autem, quoniam in istis visibilibus semet ipsos sponte deiciunt, ut invisibilibus
erigantur, quasi in faciem cadunt, quia timore compuncti, penis malorum consideratis, humiliantur. *Preterea Samuel ait de Heliseo: "Ingressusque*
clausit hostium super se et super puerum, et orabat ad dominum, et ascendit et
incubuit super puerum, posuitque os suum super os eius, et oculos suos super   660
oculos eius, et manus eius super manus illius. Et incurvavit se super puerum,
et calefacta est caro pueri." Idem fecit mater eius, secundum quod ibidem legitur:
"Venit illa et incurruit ad pedes eius et adoravit super terram." Amplius Matheus
ait de magis: "Et intrantes domum, invenerunt puerum cum Maria matre eius,
et procidentes, adoraverunt eum," etc. Iterum propheta ait: "Venite adoremus, et
procidamus ante deum; ploremus coram domino qui fecit nos," etc.

Quod genua sint flectenda omni tempore

In auctoritate vero David habes validum argumentum contra eos qui dicunt genua non esse flectenda in diebus festis. Quibus sic obiicitur, 670 aut genua sunt incurvanda in festivis vel non. Si vero dicatur quod genue sunt faciende in dominicis diebus, habemus propositum. Si autem negetur, queratur quare dicitur in magnis festivitatibus ille versiculus: "Venite adoremus, et procidamus ante deum," si non debet fieri quod ibi docetur. Sane quoniam verba intelligenda sunt cum effectu, ideo dicendum est esse bonum et meritorium orare positis genibus in diebus festivis, et etiam omni tempore est utile et honestum illud agere. Tenetur enim unusquisque facere opus dei, prout melius potest. Secus autem non meretur premium, sed supplicium. Non enim est credendum illis qui bono odore moriuntur, de quibus beatus Si- 680 meon in evangelio Luce: "Ecce hic positus est in ruinam, et in resurrectione multorum in Israel." Christus autem fuit malis odor mortis in mortem, et econverso cum bonis odor vite in vitam. Christus porro est signum et petra scandali, cui contradicunt heretici et omnes mali. *Amplius apostolus in epistola quam scribit Corinthiis ait: "Intret autem quis infidelis vel idiota, et convincitur ab omnibus: diiudicatur ab omnibus. Occulta cordis eius manifesta sunt, et ita cadens in faciem, adorat deum, pronuntians,"* *etc. Sed quia, ut ait Oratius: "Segnius irritant animum dimissa per auras, quamque sunt oculis subiecta fidelibus," idcirco species ista depingitur que orantem habet significare iacentem in terra super pectus suum, et facie sua osculando ter-* 690 *ram, timentem oculos ad celum levare. Est autem gestus sic prostrati et iacentis hominis significatio, et cum iactura humilitate, compuncte, contrite, devote, atque intente ad deum mentis.*

ADHESIT PAVIMENTO

De cautela operis dei

Item tunc orationes, petitiones vel execrationes sive gratiarum actiones erunt ut ait propheta: "Holocausta medulata offeram tibi," etc. Si fiant cum omni ilaritate et tota sinceritate tam humilitate corporis quam devote mentis et omni intentione cordis, potest esse medula cuiuslibet orationis pius affectus animi et plenus ac perfectus intellectus, cum recordatione omnium dictionum orationis. Item sa- 700 piens: "Omnibus his horis eadem vox cordis et oris. Vox est grata chori, quando cor concinit ori." Item dominus ait: "Si duo ex vobis convenerint, super terram de omni re, quamcumque petieritis, continget vobis," etc. Ostendi ibi non multitudini sed unanimitati depre-

cantium plurimum distribui. Concordiam mentis et unitatem contemplationis et pacem cordis deus exaudit. *Ille vero preces sunt holo-
caustomata saginata et deo plurimum accepta, quando omnis virtus rationis,
memorie et intelligentie in ingressu et progressu ac consumatione secuntur antecedunt et comitantur vocem orationis. Si vero non sequatur prolatione cunctarum
partium orationis intellectus orantis, non est talis oratio pinguis et medullata, sed
macilenta et sicca, hoc est, inutilis et vana.*   710

De fraude oratoris

*Nota quod quelibet oratio est frivola et macra que fit vaga mente et cum omissione
aliquarum partium illius. Ergo si pretermittas versum aliquem qui sit de integritate orationis vel dictionem aut sillabam seu litteram,* que sit de substantia
execrationis, *perperam et prave orasti. Itaque ut holocausta medullata* |19ʳᵇ|
*offeras, primo declina muscam vanitatis, que inquietat et maculat sacrificium
humilitati cordis; secundo devita muscam curiositatis, que inficit et vitiat sacrificium orationis; tertio fuge muscam voluptatis, que fedat et corrumpit sacrificium
mortificate carnis.*

De sexto modo orandi   720

*Insuper sciendum est quod preter modos iamdictos orandi est alius qui sic habet
fieri: cum orans, stans etiam erectus, toto corpore inclinat caput suum ante
sacrum et sanctum altare. Item debent viri catholici et fideles semper facere quando dicitur "Gloria patri et filio et spiritui sancto," et cum sit transubstantiatio
panis in carnem et vini in sanguinem in misse celebratione. Galli vero, apud quos
viget religio, ubi floret studium, qui habent scolas artium et virtutum, quorum
fides adhuc fervet aliquantulum, quoniam refrigescit caritas multorum, illi autem
viri dei et timorati non solum flectunt caput et renes, immo, remotis capuceis et
pilleis omnibus a capitibus, prosternunt se et cadunt in faciem suam in confectione et perceptione carnis et sanguinis Christi, taliter secum orantes: "Confectio,*   730

Hec orationes sunt *tractatio, susceptio carnis et sanguinis tui domine Jesu*
dicende in missa *Christe non proveniat mihi et cunctis fidelibus tuis tam
vivis quam defunctis in iudicium et condempnationem, sed
ex tua pietate sit nobis tuta mentium, animarum, et corporum, et prosit nobis ad
veram salutem atque premia eterne recipienda. Qui vivis et regnas cum domino
patre et filio."*

Orationes

"Corpus domini nostri Jesus Christi custodiat et conservet animas vestras in vitam eternam, amen."

740   Oratio

"Qui odore sumitur, mente capiatur, et de munere spera, fiat nobis premium eternum, amen."

                                   Alia oratio

"Purificent nos quesumus domine deus tua sancta misteria et patientia ut tui corporis sacramentum non sit nobis reatus ad penam, sed sit intercessio salutaris ad veniam, sit ablutio scelerum, sit fortitudo fragilium, sit contra mundi pericula firmamentum, sit quoque tam vivorum omnium quam cunctorum defunctorum remissio universorum delictorum penarum."

750   De laude predictarum orationum

Prefate vero orationes sunt valde efficaces et admodum utiles ad dei benivolentiam captandam, et ideo sunt sepe et sepius dicende cuilibet fideli anime, et precipue in qualibet missa, summa cum devocione et maxima diligentia. *Isto sexto modo deprecandi orabat propheta, dicens: "Incurvatus sum usquequaque rugiebam a gemitu cordis mei." Hoc enim exemplum invenitur in secundo: "Domine, ne in ira tua arguas me neque in furore tuo corripias me." Sic inclinati et humiliati tenemur orare in omni loco ubi est imago vel crux Christi aut figura alicuius sancti, sicut docet hec ymago. Possent longe plures valide auctoritates et vive orationes atque testes, omni exceptione*
760 *maiores, adduci de novo et veteri testamento ad probationem predictorum sex modorum, que sunt omittende. Nam sapiens paucis multa comprehendit, econtrario idiota multis pauca intelligit. Ideo ait Tullius: "Ab arte principium cetera diligens exercitatio comparabit."*

INCURVATUS SUM USQUEQUAQUE

De septimo modo orandi

Item nota Gregorius papa docet difficilem modum orandi, et alium a predictis sex, in expositione parabole illius: "Simile factum est regnum celorum homini regi," etc., ubi ait de quadam sorore patris sui hoc: "Cumque corpus eius de more mortuorum ad lavandum esset nudatum, longe orationis usu in cubitis eius et genibus,
770 *camelorum more, inventa est cutis obdurata excrevisse, et quod vivens eius spiritus semper gesserit vel egerit, caro mortua testabatur." Et ita habes septem utiles modos intercedendi pro peccatis tuis et omnium popullorum. Hec figura septima quam habes antea hic preoculis docet enucleatus quod dictum est a Gregorio superius* |19va|.

DOMINE EXAUDE

De octavo modo orandi

In iamdictis vero modis orandi continetur theorica, id est, ars que docet qualiter debeamus orare meritorie. Verumtamen scire legem parum prodest, nisi fiat quod est in lege. Nam factores legis iustificantur, non doctores tantum aut solummodo auditores. Idcirco recurrendum est ad practicam, hoc est ad exercitium et ad opera 780 *ipsius artis, que sunt causa quare quelibet ars est addiscenda et docenda. Quid enim valet scire physicam, id est, theoricam medicine, si careas pratica, id est, non agas secundum artis precepta, scilicet consulendo infirmis quibus possint uti et quibus non, et si non occuras morbo venienti ope et auxilio, etc., immo, quod est gravius, permittis egrotum mori quem potuisti tuo artificio liberare a morte saltem corporis. Item quid confert totam sacram paginam scire et prave vivere, etc.? Immo magne obest, secundum quod dicit auctoritas: "Ubi maius donum scientie, ibi transgressor maiori subiacet culpe." Si peritiam habes theologie et nosti omnes regulas iuris, et "predicas non furandum, furaris," etc., que in apostolo plenius leguntur, quid ad rubendum, factus es velut cimbalum tiniens et sicut* 790 *ficulnus, inutile lignum.*

De eodem

Item, cur non impendat miser homo divino amori quod tribuit humano timori? Si enim dominus tuus terrenus seu aliquis homo alius egeret tua opera sive tibi esset opus consilio aut benefitio alicuius, pro modico dampno vitando vel etiam ut parvam rem acquireres, longe tempore ei fideliter servires et diligenter, nec recusares ferre pondus die, et estus die noctuque fortiter laborando ut hominis morituri captares benivolentiam. Multo magis ergo debes totis viribus tuis et pro posse tuo conari ut placeas deo in eternum victuro. Itaque cum prosternas te ante pedes alicuius tiranni pro modica pena fugienda, potius teneris te proicere ante deum 800 *et coram altare eius et sancta cruce illius, pro vita eterna recipienda et pro morte vitanda perpetua.*

⟨De eodem

Quocumque modo oraveris, conare ut habeas cor ad id quod dicis imitare, itaque alium virum sanctum de quo legitur in historia Machabearum, hic est, qui multum orat pro populo et universa sancta civitate Ierusalem.⟩

Quare sit orandum tantum aliquo dictorum modorum

Sane si materiale et corporale bellum numquam bono fine concluditur a residentibus et otio et quieti vacantibus, quod est valde levius spirituali, longe minus 810 *mentalis et spiritualis pugna competenter et meritorie fiet sedendo et quiescendo a pigris et negligentibus. Non enim desidiosis sed laborantibus iura subveniunt. Item si omnis Christi actio nostra est instructio, et si eius membra sumus, debemus sequi caput nostrum. Turpis enim est pars que suo capiti non convenit. Saltem in quibusdam imitemur eum, licet non possimus in omnibus eum sequi. Ergo sicut oravit, et nos debemus orare, de quo ait Gregorius: "Qui expansis in cruce manibus traxisti omnia ad te secula." Sic orabant plures sancti qui pernoctabant in oratione, decantantes quandoque quinquaginta psalmos, expansis brachiis et manibus ad instar et modum crucis. Plerumque vero dicebant alios quinquaginta prostrati et plani ac resupini corpus, pectus, et os, copulantes terre superficiei, flendo et gemendo pro omnium delictis. Interdum autem viri sancti dicunt totum psalterium positis genibus. Hinc accidit quod talis alternitas sive diversitas orandi confert et prodest oranti, nempe quando fatigatus est aliquis orare manibus et brachiis erectis supra capite, ipse oret alio modo, ulnis depositis aut inclinando caput et renes versus orientem, vel stet erectus, toto corpore super pedes suos, manibus iunctis ante os, ut superius dictum est.*

820

Quod spirituale bellum sit maius corporali

Ideo spirituale bellum maius est corporali lucta, quoniam in pugna spirituali habemus hostes invisibiles et sapientissimos. Porro demones, licet perdiderint caritatem, non tamen ammisserunt sagacitatem, immo sunt sapientiores omnibus, et magis callidi, providi, et astuti, qui non cessant querere quem devorent et separent a dilectione que est in Christo Ihesu domino nostro. Unde quia non videntur neque palpantur, sunt ministri Sathane magis timendi quam si essent visu perceptibiles. Econtrario in pugna corporis videtur hostis cum quo congredimur, luctamus, |19ᵛᵇ| et pugnamus. Hinc est quod levius possumus eum subplantare vel repellere aut expugnare.

830

De verecundia duplici

Fortasse autem dicit aliquis cervicosus insolens et superbus: "Verecundor orare manibus extensis supra capite vel ulnis extensis sive in terra prostratus." Tali est sic respondendum, quod docuit reges: "Cur mihi turpe putem?" Item ipse dominus ait: "Qui me erubuerit coram hominibus, erubescam eum coram patre meo." Stolida et pessima est illa verecundia que retrahit hominem a bono opere. Illa siquidem verecundia est sana et utilis et approbanda, pro qua homo timet peccare. Eapropter dixit quidam legis peritus: "Cum quid turpe facit, qui, me spectante, ruberet, cur, spectante deo, non magis ipse rubet?" Hinc est quod si nolles comittere adulterium in presentia vilissimi hominis, neque aliud peccatum, timens ne te accuset, longe magis ergo debes cessare a peccato amore dei, ne te condempnet in conspectu cuius peccas, qui omnia videt, hic est, scrutans corda et renes. Ipse idem potest animam et corpus perdere in Gehennam.

840

De forma orandi   850

Circa formam orandi, hec sunt consideranda: orat enim quis corde, ore, opere, et corpore. Corde tripliciter. Primo ut circa id quod orat, afficiatur per dilectionem. Unde legitur: "Venit ora et nunc est, quando veri adoratores adorant patrem in spiritu et veritate," id est, vera et spirituali cordis affectione. Secundo ut circa id quod orat, cor tenetur per compunctionem, ad modum illius sanctissime mulieris de qua in libro primo circa principium regum legitur: Anna autem cum esset sterilis "oravit ad dominum, animo amaro, flens largiter." Super hunc locum dicit Augustinus, rectissima orandi forma est, ut non multiloquio sed compunctione cordis et lacrimarum effusione oremus, quia 860 sacrificium deo specie contribulatus, ut nulli quantumlibet honeste cause, preterquam ad id quod orat intendat, ne maledictionem illam incurrat, de qua legitur: "Maledictus qui fecit negligenter opus dei."

Quod est orandum ore

Ore etiam est orandum, sed triplici de causa. Prima est ut oris obsequium sicut et ceterorum membrorum domino impendimus iuxta illud: "Benedicam dominum in omni tempore semper laus eius in ore meo." Secunda causa ut ipso vocis sono affectum et nostram devotionem ostendamus secundum illud: "Ad ipsum ore meo clamavi; et exultavi sub lingua mea." Tertia est ut proximos instruamus. Unde in evangelio 870 sic legitur: "Luceant opera vestra bona coram hominibus, ut videntes opera vestra bona, gaudetur pater vester qui in celis est." Orandum est opere, quia scriptum est: "Qui declinat aurem suam, ne audiat legem, oratio eius erit execrabilis."

Qualiter est orandum corpore

Orandum est corpore, sed dupliciter, scilicet, capitis revelatione, de qua apostolus ait: "Omnis vir orans, velato capite, deturpat caput suum," hoc est, indevote orat et iniuriam facit Christo, qui est caput hominis. Hinc apostolus: "Caput enim viri est Christus; caput vero mulieris est vir." Ex verbis denique apostoli prelibatis emanavit satis 880 dura traditio Claravallensium monacorum, qui omni tempore, etiam in maximo frigore, debent orare detecto capite, deposito velamine universo. Et hoc siquidem omnibus est agendum qui ad hoc sufficiunt, et devota corporis positione, quod fit tripliciter: stando, et flexis genibus, et toto corpore ad terram prostrato. De primo legitur: "Stetit autem Salomon ante dominum et oravit ad dominum, dicens: 'Domine deus, audi ymnum et orationem.'" De secundo autem dicitur: "Positis autem genibus, Stephanus orabat, dicens: 'Domine, ne statuas illis hoc peccatum.'" De tertio in evangelio habetur: "Progressus pusillum, dominus procidit in faciem suam super terram."

De ordinata oratione

Item in directo ordine orandi est, animadvertendum quod orat: primo quis pro se, secundo pro fratribus, tertio pro inimicis debet orare. Quem ordinem dominus imminente passione orans docuit, dicens primo pro se: "Pater clarifica me, apud temetipsum, claritate, quam habui, prius quam mundus fieret." Pro fratribus secundo dicens: "Pater sancte, serva eos in nomine tuo quos dedisti michi, ut sint unum, sicut et nos." Tertio pro inimicis, cum ait in evangelio Luce: "Pater, ignosce illis, non enim sciunt quid faciunt."

Qualiter oratio fiat versus orientem

Item nota quod propter tres causas ad orientem nos vertimus. Una est quia in oriente est patria nostra, scilicet, paradisus. Unde et plurimum dolentes orando contra paradisum nos vertimus, quia reditum illuc petimus. Secunda causa est quod ad orientem nos vertimus quia Christum, qui est oriens et lux vera, nos adorare significamus, cui debemus esse celi, ut eius lux velit in nobis oriri. Tertia est quia sol oritur in oriente, per quem Christus sol iustitie exprimitur, ad cuius promissum etiam nos in resurrectione ut sol fulgebimus. In oratione ergo contra ortum solis nos vertimus ut solem angelorum nos adorare intelligamus et quod ad memoriam et gloriam nostre resurrectionis revocamus. Cum solem quem in oriente mori conspeximus magna gloria in oriente resurgere videbimus.

De consuetudine mala clericorum

Nolo inter cetera prudentia vestra latere, o lector pie recordationis, esse quosdam clericos et etiam claustrales nomine, sed non religiosos, qui statim cum intrant ecclesiam, incipiunt sedere, et precipue cum dicunt canticum graduum et vigilias mortuorum |20ra|, quorum minus docta sapientia est ammiranda plurimum, imo, salva eorum pace, reprehensione digna est. Nonne maxima desidia est et negligentia cuiuslibet et potissimum persone religiose, que est holocaustum deo, non orare solertissime? Quis non succenseat et obstupescat pro tanto defectu operis dei? Qua enim temeritate homo qui pausavit dormiendo usque ad noctis medietatem, si est sanus, cum primo intrat oratorium, presumat

sedere, qui tunc debet fortiter orationi insistere, cum multis genuflexionibus et habundantia lacrimarum suspirando et gemendo pro peccatis tuis et totius orbis? Allegant enim false claustrales predicti, pro
se talem esse domus sue consuetudinem non stare erectos toto corpore,
neque genua flectere in decantione cantici gradus et officii defunctorum.
Contra tales ait Ciprianus in VIII distinctione decretorum: "Si solus
Christus audiendus est, non debemus attendere, quid aliquis ante nos   930
faciendum putaverit, sed quid, qui ante omnes est Christus, prior
fecerit. Neque hominis consuetudinem sequi oportet, sed dei veritatem."

De eodem

Consuetudo autem sine veritate vetustas est erroris, propter quod, re-
licto errore, sequamur veritatem, scientes itaque quod veritas valet et
invalescit in eternum et vivit et optinet in secula seculorum. Item
Gregorius in eodem: "Si consuetudinem fortasse opponas, advertendum
est quod dominus ait: 'Ego sum veritas.' Non ait: 'Ego sum consuetudo,' sed 'veritas.'" Item Augustinus ibidem: nemo consuetudinem
rationi et veritati preponat, "nam consuetudinem ratio et veritas semper   940
excludit." Vere autem Christiani et omnes religiose persone, cum
intrant oratorium, tenentur dicere Pater Noster cum tribus genuflexionibus ad minus coram cruce. Similiter est agendum ante unumquod-
que altare.

Qualiter sit orandum ante altare

Idem postquam ita oraverint coram singulis altaribus ecclesie, invocato
nomine individue trinitatis, saltem tertio positis in terra, cantantes
dominicam orationem, incipient deinde vigilias defunctorum, quas debent devote dicere, non sedentes neque alicui rei inherentes, sed erunt
sursum toto corpore erecti usque ad finem illius cantici *Benedictus do-*   950
minus deus Israel, etc. Et hinc proicient se in terram ubi multas canent
orationes proprias mortuorum. Postea vero surgent et cantabant psalmos graduales, stando cum tribus ad minus genuflexionibus. Multum
valent namque ad impetrationem venie tam die quam in nocte sepe
et sepius genua flectere, fronte terram concutere et faciem lacrimis
rigare, cum anime amaritudine et tota mentis intentione, atque omni
animi devotione. Item qualis eorum conditio est qui in claustris non
caste, iuste, ac pie vivunt, dicitur: "Autem claustrum non castum." A
castitate enim videtur esse sumptum. Unde accidit quod tales qui
regulam non custodiunt inutiles ibi morantur. Quoniam ut ait aposto-   960
lus: "Circumcisio et preputium nichil sunt, sed observatio mandatorum

dei." Contra tale genus hominum ait sapiens: "Quid facis in claustro?
Quinta rota, quod addita plaustro!"

Quod idem dicendum est corde et corpore

Item Iacobus apostolus: "Fides sine operibus mortua est." Itaque,
venerabilis lector, ut obtineas rem et meritum tanti nominis, elabora
et conare pro posse quatenus quod ore cantas corde credas, et quod
mente intendis, factis compleas, et quod sermo sonat affectus sentiat.
Nam ut ait Augustinus: "Noveris non esse vocem ad aures dei, sed
970 animi affectum." Nec tantum exigit deus elationem seu altitudinem et
fractiones sonore vocis quantum requirit intentionem devote et caste
mentis. Nemo in veritate alterius et dulcius canit quam ille quem deus
audit.

Contra vanos cantores

Item Gregorius in distinctione XCII decreti: "In sancta romana ecclesia dudum consuetudo est valde reprehensibilis exorta, unde quidam
ad sacri altaris ministerium cantores eligantur, et in diaconatus ordine
constituti, vocis modulationi inserviant, quos ad predicationis offitium,
et elemosinarum studium vacare congruebat. Unde fit plerumque ut
980 in sacro ministerio, dum blanda vox queritur, congrua vita negligatur,
et cantor minister deum moribus stimulat, cum populum vocibus delec-
tat." Item Ieronimus: "Deo non in voce sed corde cantandum est. Nec
in tragediarum modum guttur et fauces medicamine liniende sunt, ut
in ecclesia theatrales moduli et cantica audiantur." Hec autem materia,
deo dante, diligentius et liberius decimabitur et tractabitur.

De vitiis orationis

*Verumtamen quoniam non vitatur malum nisi sit cognitum, idcirco post predicta
agendum est de vitiis que impediunt orationis effectum. Augustinus equidem ponit
duos modos quibus oratio impeditur in libro De Vita Christiana: "Si autem quis-*
990 *que ad huc mala committit vel cum delinquentibus sibi debita non dimittit, talis
quoniam a preceptis dei avertitur, quod in oratione postulat non meretur, nec impetrat ab illo quod poscit, cuius legi non obedit. Si enim quod precipit facimus,
quod petimus sine dubio obtinebimus. Multum enim apud deum utraque sibi
necessario comendatur, ut oratione operatio et opere oratio fulciatur." Item Iere-
mias ait:|20rb| "Levemus corda nostra ad deum cum manibus." Cor et manus*
⟨De eodem⟩ *ad deum levant qui bona agunt et devote orant. Hic habes
argumentum vehemens contra vocales clericos qui credunt sibi
sufficere orationem solam sine opere misericordie, quod falsum est. Tenentur*

autem omnes homines non solum ad piam et sanctam orationem, sed ad fidem rec-
tam et operationem perfectam — sine quibus non est salus —, ne igitur negligentia   1000
reprehendamur, dum salutem nostram vel sola oratione aut tantum operatione ob-
tinere contendimus. Postquam vero bonum opus agimus, lacrime in oratione fun-
dantur, ut meritum actionis humilitas impetret precis.

Quare non cito exaudiuntur boni

Amplius notandum est quod orationes electorum in pressuris differuntur, ut im-
piorum perversitas augeatur. Verum dum iusti temporaliter exaudiuntur, pro eorum
sit salute qui eos affligunt, ut dum illis temporali remedio subvenitur, pravorum
oculi ad conversionem aperiantur. Ideo ignis trium puerorum eos non offendit,
ut Nabuchodonosor deum cognosceret et unum et verum. Rursus ait Augustinus:
"Proinde tardius exaudiuntur quorumdam orationes ut, dum differuntur fortius   1010
⟨De eodem⟩ *excitate maioribus premiis, cumulentur exemplo messium, in*
quibus, quanto tardius sata semina exeunt, tanto ad frugem
cumulatius crescunt." Item: "Gratior est fructus quem spes productior
edit. Ultra obiectorum vilius est precium, magis illa vitiant que pluris
emuntur." *Preterea interdum, sancta desideria dilata crescunt. Nam quod per-*
severantes non cito exaudiuntur, utilitatis potius est quam adversitatis.

De eodem

Item Gregorius: "Adversitas que bonis votis obicitur, probatio est virtutis, et non est iudicium reprobationis." Item Augustinus: "Et quod
deus differt dare, hoc ideo fit ut amplius desideres delatum, ne vilescat   1020
cito datum." Et si differtur, non aufertur. Oratio frequens diaboli sub-
movet iacula. *Sepe autem multos deus non exaudit ad voluntatem ut eos exaudiat*
ad salutem. Multi utique orando non exaudiuntur, providente illis deo meliora
quam petant, sicut contingere solet parvulis, qui ne vapulent deum exorant, sed
non datur illis postulationis effectus, quia impediret talis exauditio ad profectum.
Nec aliter contingit quibusdam electis qui, deprecantes deum pro nonnullis huius
vite commodis obtinendis vel adversis fugiendis, providentia enim domini tempora-
liter eorum desiderio minime consulit, quoniam meliora illis in eternum permittit.
Oratio privatis locis oportunius funditur, magisque atque velocius suum impetrat
desiderium, cum tantum deo teste depromitur.   1030

De primo vitio

Sunt autem plura que impediunt orationem. *Unum sive primum est peccatum,*
quod maxime obest oranti. De quo ait Ieremias propheta in Trenis: "Opposuisti
nubem, ne transeat oratio." Quasi dicat Ieremias: "Ideo oratio tua non potest
pervenire ad aures domini, neque est ei grata, propter scelera que sunt in te." Item

David: "Peccatori autem dixit deus: 'Quare tu enarras iusticias meas,'" etc. Idem est ac si dicat propheta: "Quoniam malus et nequam es, et quia non vis deserere peccata tua, immo apponis iniquitatem super iniquitatem, idcirco non exaudiet deus preces tuas." Unde habes argumentum quod prius derelinquenda sunt peccata et
1040 *postea meritorie possumus ei sacrificare, laudare, atque psallere. Hinc propheta: "Dirupisti vincula mea: tibi sacrificabo hostiam laudis." Est autem sensus, quoniam per gratiam tuam delicta quibus ligatus eram confregisti, id est, me penitendo dimittere fecisti, placebit tibi oratio mea. Et postmodum dum talis oratio impetrabit anime et corporis salutem. Nam ut ait Iacobus apostolus: "Multum valet deprecatio iusti assidua." Quoniam qui bene penituit de omnibus peccatis suis, fere iustus est. Nota quod non dixit Iacobus apostolus: "Multum valet lectio," sed "oratio," sane lectio frequenter plus continet vanitatis quam caritatis aut utilitatis, verbi gratia, utpote est illorum qui ad hoc student ut ditentur, promoveantur et videantur. Contra tales ait sapiens: "Immoritur studiis et amore*
1050 *senescit habendi." O quanto est tutius et melius anime exire de carcere corporis orando et ieiunando, elemosinas largiendo atque in ecclesia deo serviendo, quam sit a scolasticis disputationibus recedendo.*

De secundo peccato oratoris

Secundum malum est celeritas nimia que aufert orationi suum effectum. Nullus potest cursim bene legere vel orare seu contemplationi vacare. Quis unquam possit meritorie et utiliter deo deservire in strepitu et fuga, linguam instringendo nimia velocitate? Illi vero miseri qui verius sunt tempestas domus et baratrum macelli et notissima fossa chinedum et appellerandi quam boni oratores. De quibus ait sapiens: "Quilibet et
1060 in quem vis opprobria fingere sevus, pernicies et tempestas, baratrumque macelli. Quicquid quesierat, ventri donarat avaro." Illi vero qui perperam orant non recolunt neque vigilanti oculo rationis contemplantur quod ait Gregorius de orantibus et psallentibus: |20va| "Devote, vox inquit psalmodie cum per intentionem cordis agitur. Per hanc omnipotenti deo ad cor ita paratur ut intente menti vel prophetie misteria seu gratia compunctionis infundatur." Idem: "Dum per psalmodiam compunctio infunditur, via nobis in corde fit, per quam ad Iesum in fine pervenitur." Prefato enim bono perfunctorie et male orantes privantur. Itaque, karissime, ut eternum premium adipiscas,
1070 insiste orationi morose, scrutabiliter, et non transitorie. *Cum enim aliquis orator currendo relinquit litteram vel sillabam aut dictionem seu orationem de horis quas debet dicere, perperam et male oravit.*

De tribus unguentis quibus est corpus Christi unguendum

Similiter illi non bene orant qui tantum pro terrenis deum adorant quemadmodum faciunt, qui pro vana gloria psalmos et orationes multiplicant ut ab hominibus videantur et dicantur sancti. Tales sunt magis diligentes gloriam hominum quam dei. Item Ysidorus: "Oratio cordis est et non labiorum, neque verba deprecantis deus intendit, sed orantis cor respicit." *Nec non musca moriens et unguento adherens perdiderit suavitatem unguenti. Sunt autem tria quibus tenemur ungere corpus Christi cum Maria Magdalena. Primum unguentum quo* 1080 *debemus ungere caput Christi dei est oratio, que illi reddit odorem suavissimum. Prave autem cogitationes que dicuntur musce morientes non sinunt nos assequi commodum et provectum orationis, quo unguentum oritur ab amore dei.* Ut ⟨Exemplum⟩ autem prelibatas muscas a se, quidam homo dei, magne fame et maioris religionis et sanctitatis, omnino repelleret, assuevit dicere ante ingressum oratorii: "Estote hic, moramini foris hostium ecclesie manu tangendo, nullum tamen videndo vel audiendo." Requisitus vero quare semper cum iret oratum, percuterit portam domus domini, preferendo stare hic, tale dedit responsum: "Omnis utique homo qui vult digne et meritorie orare et con- 1090 templationi vacare, tenetur penitus a corde suo excludere curam et sollicitudinem negotiorum seculorum, atque debet viriliter resistere desideriis carnis, que militant adversus animam." Prefatus enim dei miles tantam gratiam a deo fuerat consecutus, ut nichil alium tempore orationis quam de solo deo cogitaret, quod pro paucis solet contingere. Hinc est quod plurium orationes frivole et vane sunt. *A dilectione vero proximi procedit elemosinarum largitio, quod dicitur unguentum secundum. A caritate sane sui emanat carnis maceratio, quod potest dici tertium unguentum,* a quo inchoandum est.

⟨Unde in evangelio: "Qui odit animam suam, in vitam eternam custo- 1100 dit eam." Hoc autem ungentum ex variis spiritibus conficitur, aliis pertinentibus ad substantiam orandorum, aliis ad modum orantium. Ad substantiam orandorum pertinent septem spiritus quos continet dominica oratio, quibus duo principaliter expetuntur, bonorum adeptio et malorum remotio. Bonorum autem quedam sunt eternalia, quedam spiritualia, quedam temporalia. Eternalia petuntur in premium, spiritualia in meritum, temporalia in sustentaculum. De eternalibus dicitur: "Adveniat regnum tuum"; de spiritualibus dicitur: "Fiat voluntas tua sicut in coelo et in terra"; de temporalibus dicitur: "Panem nostrum cottidie da nobis hodie." Malorum aut alia sunt presentia, alia 1110 preterita, alia futura. Preterita sunt delenda, presentia vincenda, futura cavenda. De preteritis dicitur: "Dimitte vobis debita nostra"; de futura additur: "Et ne nos inducas in tentationem"; de presentibus subditur: "Libera nos a malo." Hec sunt illa que debemus orare, sed omnia propter beatitudinem, dicente domino: "Petite et accipietis, ut gaudium vestrum plenum sit." Unde his septem spiritus admiscende sunt alie septem beatitudines, quas enumerat Christe in evangelio: "Beati pauperes spiritu," etc. Omnes he species pistillo discretionis tunduntur in mortariolo memorie, ne durum conficiatur ungentum, id est, ne fiat

1120   oratio in peccatum. Sunt enim qui aliud orant quam debeant, et sunt qui aliter orant quam debeant. Aliud quam debebat orabat mater filiorum Rebedei, que ad suggestionem filiorum accedens ad Jesum, oravit et petiit: "Domine, dic ut sedeant hi duo filii mei, unus ad dextram et alter ad sinistram tuam in regno tuo." Propterea respondit illi dominus: "Nescitis quid petatis." Aliter quam debebat orabat Phariseus qui ascendens in templum ut oraret, hec apud se ait: "Deus, gratias tibi ago, quia non sum sicut ceteri homines: raptores, iniusti, adulteri," etc. Propter hoc dominus intulit: "Omnis qui se exaltat, humiliabitur," etc. Ad modum orationum pertinent he septem virtutes: fides, spes,

1130   caritas, justicia, fortitudo, prudentia, temperantia. His etiam admiscende sunt alie septem spiritus. He sunt dona septiformis spiritus que Ysaias enumerat, dicens: "Requiescit super eum spiritus domini: spiritus sapientie et intellectus, spiritus consilii ac fortitudinis, spiritus scientie et pietatis, et spiritus timoris domini." He spiritus omnes balsamo sancti spiritus in vasculo sapientie, que est odor suavissimus domino, per quem incensum dignum offertur domino in odorem suavitatis. Sunt enim multi qui multum orant sed negligenter et indevote, quod dominus prohibet cum inquit: "Vos autem cum oratis, nolite multum loqui sicut ethnici." Putant enim se in multiloquio exaudiri.

1140   Tales cum orant aliud locuntur ore, aliud meditantur in corde. De quibus convenienter accipitur quod dominus ait: "Populus hic labiis me honorat," etc. De talibus legitur in ore suo: "Benedicebant, et in corde suo maledicebant," quia meditantur in animo vanitates. Aliter oraverunt Moyses et Susanna, qui clamaverunt ad dominum quia de necessitatibus eorum liberavit eos. Clamaverunt non tam vocis intentione, quam cordis devotione, dicente propheta: "Delectare in domino et dabit tibi petitiones cordis tui." Expedit tamen ut cordis devotione oris pronunciatio commitetur. Nam quod facit flatus carboni, facit pronunciatio devotioni. Audi prophetam: "Ad ipsum ore meo clama-

1150   vi; et exaltavi sub lingua mea." Hoc ungentum conficiendum est in quodam secreto cubili, id est, in secreto conscientie, iuxta quod domi-

nus ait: "Tu autem cum oraveris, intra in cubiculum, et clauso ostio,
ora patrem tuum." Claudendum est ostium ne musce morientes sub-
intrent, que perdant suavitatem ungenti. Nam mors ingreditur per
fenestras. Si sic oraverimus, optinebimus quod dominus ait: "Quecumque petieritis in nomine meo, credentes, accipietis," vel iterum:
"Quidquid petieritis patrem in nomine meo, dabit vobis." Cum ergo
ieiunas, unque caput tuum ungento orationis et lava faciem tuam aqua
miserationis. Per aquam enim elemosina signatur secundum illud: sicut aqua extinguit ignem, ita elemosina extinguit peccatum. Unde   1160
elemosina non solum ab "elimino" dicitur, sed ab "hely," quod est deus,
et "moys," quod est aqua. Unde elemosina quasi "elymosina," id est,
aqua dei, quia per elemosinam macule peccatorum abluuntur a deo.
Hec aqua dividitur in tres fontes, quorum primus manat ex corde,
secundus ex ore, tertius ex opere. Elemosina quippe tripliciter erogatur:
ex corde per compassionem, ex ore per correctionem, ex opere per
largitionem. De compassione cordis dicit apostolus: "Quis infirmatur,
et ego non infirmor? Quis scandalizatur et ego non uror?" Proximorum
peccata frixoria sunt iustorum. De correctione oris dicit dominus in
evangelio: "Si peccaverit in te frater tuus, corripe eum inter te, et   1170
ipsum solum." De largitione operis dicit propheta: "Frange esurienti
panem tuum," etc. Singuli vero fontes in duos rivulos dividuntur,
quorum primus decurrit ad nos, secundus ad proximos. Elemosina
quidem danda est, et ordinate primo nobis, secundo proximis. Crudelis
enim est et fatuus qui aliis compatitur et sibi non miseretur qui alium
castigat, et se ipsum non emendat, qui alii subvenit et se ipsum
despicit. Econtra scriptum est: "Miserere anime tue, placens deo."
Item: "Eice primum ypocrita trabem de oculo tuo, et tunc videbis,"
etc. Item: "Cum videris nudum, operi eum, et carnem tuam ne de-
spexeris." Si sic dederimus elemosinam, tunc merebimus quod dominus   1180
ait: "Date elemosinam, et omnia munda sunt vobis." Elemosina quidem
magnam fiduciam prestat apud altissimum. Cum ergo, carissimi,
ieiunamus, unguamus caput nostrum oleo devote orationis, et lavemus
faciem nostram aqua pie miserationis. Illo misericorditer concedente,
cuius verba sunt ungentis fragrantia, qui est fons aque salientis in
vitam eternam.⟩

De tertio vitio orationis

Tertium impedimentum quare deus non exaudit orantes est hoc, videlicet, cum
petitur quod non pertinet ad salutem. Unde legitur: "Petitis et non accipitis eo
quod non recte petatis." Hinc est quod plura petuntur que numquam accipiuntur.   1190

Multotiens autem exiguntur a deo divitie et filii et ville et dignitates et alia multa
que numquam conferuntur. Quoniam potius impedirent quam prodessent. Ergo
ut hac auctoritas sit vera: "Quicquid petieritis patrem in nomine meo, fiet vobis."
Illi sane postulant in nomine salvatoris qui petunt ea que pertinent ad veram
salutem, utpote sunt ea que sequentibus verbis significantur.

Que sunt petenda pure a deo

"Erue a framea, deus, animam meam, et de manu canis unicam meam." Et: "Deus
meus, respice in me." Et: "Libera me ab ore leonis et a cornibus unicornium
humilitatem meam." Similiter et hoc aliud, quod est in hoc psalmo Iudica me
1200 *quoniam ego: "Ne perdas cum impiis, deus, animam meam et cum viris san-*
guinum vitam meam." Et hoc Salvum me fac, deus, quoniam: "Non me demergat
tempestas aque, neque absorbeat me profundum, neque urgeat super me puteus os
suum." "Doce me facere voluntatem tuam, quia deus meus es tu." "Participem me
fac, deus, omnium timentium te," etc. "Manus tua non occurrat mihi princeps
tenebrarum, et manus extranea non contingat me, sed aperi mihi pulsanti ianuam
vite." Et: "Deduc me ad convivium epularum tuarum, ubi gaudent et exultant
omnes amici tui et electi." Predicta siquidem omni tempore et ubique sunt petenda
a deo incessanter et absolute, pure et absque pendulo pie conditionis.

De iactura male orantis

1210 Item nota quod tripliciter dampnificatur negligens orator. Una iactura
qua patitur prave orans hec est, nam in tempore perfunctorie orationis
posset acquirere sibi aliquod terrenum quod ammitit. Secundum in-
commodum quod incurrit male orans est tale: denique premio eterno
privabitur perperam orans, quod potest obtineri et impetrari diligenti
oratione. Insuper scire debes, karissime, quod non eximitur ab onere
orandi aliquis quocumque modo et perverse orando, sed tantum ille
est liberatus ab orationis obligatione qui fideliter et diligenter orat. Et
solummodo talis orator a deo exaudietur.

De quarto vitio eiusdem

1220 *Quartum obstaculum quod non sinit orationem habere effectum suum provenit ex*
eo, quod oramus pro indignis et gratiam dei repellentibus. Unde hec auctoritas
sic est exponenda: "Petite et accipietis, querite et invenietis, pulsate et aperietur
vobis." "Petite" pro vobis, supple, et non pro aliis, pie et perseveranter, et ad
salutem, id est, in nomine meo, hoc est Jesu qui salvator dicitur. Sic ergo pe-
tentis utpote est dictum "Accipietis," id est, orantis desiderium impetrabitis. Nec
aliter potest quis pie orationis effectum obtinere nisi esset fideliter et diligenter.
Item |20vb| Iohannes Os Aurei: "Vidisti aliquem euntem ad furtum

deum orare ut bene prosperetur in furto, aut qui vadit fornicando,
numquid signum crucis imprimit fronti ut non comprehendatur in
crimine. Quod si fecerit, non solum non adiuvatur sed adhuc amplius   1230
traditur. Quoniam nescit iustitia dei patrocinium dare criminibus.
Colonus enim diaboli amminiculum indigne requiret divinum."

Quod sit fideliter orare

Tunc denique fideliter oramus, quando non relinquimus de substantia orationis. De substantia orationis sunt omnes littere, sillabe, dictiones perfecte et imperfecte orationes que sunt de integritate psalmi
vel alterius orationis, verbi gratia, ut est dominica oratio, scilicet, Pater
Noster, qui es in coelo, vel Gloria in excelsis deo, qui est imnus angelorum valde efficax ad dei gratiam promerendam, aut simbolum apostolorum Credo in deum patrem omnipotentem, sive ymnum trium   1240
puerorum, Benedicite omnia opera domini domino, in quo invitamus
ad laudandum deum pro omnibus creaturis, quid, si cottidie devote
dicatur per eius decantationes, liberat nos deus ab imminentibus peccatorum periculis.

De sancte orationis efficacia

Quantus equidem sit effectus sive utilitas bone orationis patet ex eo
quod legitur in vita beati Egidii, in qua docetur hoc: "Proxima namque
dominica die, dum vir sanctus missam de more celebrans, pro iamdic-
to rege dominum in canone deprecaretur. Apparuit ei angelus domini,
super altare cedulam ponens, in qua erat ordine descriptum regis   1250
pecatum. Et Egidii precibus illi esse dimissum si penitens tantum
desisteret ab eo." Maximus siquidem fuit illius orationis profectus,
videlicet, ut turpe facinus quod Charolus rex nolebat confiteri, ab
angelo significaretur sancto dei Egidio. *Porro ideo sic est intelligenda pre-*
libata auctoritas Petite, etc. Quoniam licet multi boni orarent pro malo qui nollet
converti, tamen non possent eum a doloribus inferni eripere.

Nichil est cogitandum in missa nisi de deo

Consequenter notandum est quod ait Ciprianus in tractatu de consecratione:
"Quando stamus ad orationem, fratres karissimi, et invigilare et incumbere ad
preces toto corpore debemus. Cogitatio hominis carnalis et secularis quelibet ab-   1260
scedat, nec ad quicquam aliud tunc animus quam ad id solum quod cogitet va-
getur. Ideo sacerdos ante orationem, prefatione premissa, parat fratrum mentes
dicendo: 'Sursum corda', ut dum respondet plebs 'Habemus ad dominum,' ammo-
neantur, nichil aliud se quam de deo cogitare debent. Claudatur contra adver-

sarium pectus et soli deo pateat, nec ad se hostem dei tempore orationis venire patiatur." Itaque si in missa aliud cogitas quam de deo, promissionem tuam infregisti et a fidelitate recessisti, neque aliquid promeruisti. Quid ergo erit illis qui in confectione eucharistie secularia et vana referendo, non solum non orant, immo, quod est gravius, alios orantes impediunt.

1270   Contra illos qui nocent bene agentibus

Isti sunt pessimi emulatores Sathane qui gloriam quam meruit ammittere hominem noluit diutius possidere. Similiter tales sunt pravi imitatores Phariseorum qui nec intrare volunt ad patriam neque, quod peius est, intrandi facultatem aliis habere permittunt. Quibus ait Salomon in persona filii: "Noli impedire quemquam bene facere, sed si tu ipse potes, bene fac." Bona enim quibus forte caremus, in aliis diligere et fovere tenemur. *Huiusmodi irridet Horatius, cum ait: "Amphora cepit institui, currente rota cur urceus exitur?"—ac si dicat auctor satiricus quod instar agamus: "Ob hoc congregati estis, ut missam devote celebretis, et audiatis quare carnalia et temporalia tractatis, et cum ad celestia et eterna anhe-*
1280 *lare debetis, amplexati estis stercora pro croceis, et lutum potius quam aurum obrizum desideratis."* ⟨Iterum exemplum familiare et quasi vulgare et domesticum hortatur, omnes homines pie, intente, atque devote missam audire et celebrare. Immo, quod est fortius et gravius, gementes, dolentes, ac flentes, admonet eos confectioni eucharistie adsistere. Si enim vulgus et quilibet popularis in septima seu in tredecima vel in centeminia, die obitus cari sui amare flet, doletque graviter, quoniam tunc refricatur et ad memoriam reducitur mors amici sui, multo magis ergo cunctis christianis est fortiter plorandum et plurimum dolendum quando recensetur et celebratur memoria passionis et
1290 etiam mortis domini nostri Jesu Christi, quod in missarum sollempniis agitur. Quotiens autem sacramentum altaris sive missa celebratur, mors Christi recolitur et eius passio representatur. Hinc est quod legitur in canone misse: "Hec quotienscumque feceritis, in mei memoriam facietis," id est, in replicatione et recordatione mortis et passionis mee. Unde apostolus ait in epistola ad Corinthios: "Quotienscumque enim manducabitis panem hunc, et calicem bibetis, mortem domini annunciabitis donec veniat," hoc est, eius mortem representabitis et ad vestri memoriam revocabitis, et in ea infigetis ei compatiendo, quia qui non compatitur, non conregnabit. Ut ait apostolus: "Qui
1300 non fuerat particeps tribulationis, non erit in portione consolationis." Et alibi legitur: "Post tempestatem, tranquillum facit: et post lacrimationem et flectum, exultationem et letitiam infundit." Ex prelibatis patet quod tam cantantes quam audientes missam teneantur interesse

confectioni eucharistie iuste et sancte, cum reverentia maxima et plurima devocione. Sicut non est magnum, ut ait sapiens, fuisse vel esse
Ierosolimis. Sed hoc est valde expediens vivere, ut est vivendum ibi
et etiam ubique, scilicet, honeste, iuste, et pie. Ita non est utile sacramentum altaris indigne et sine timore et compunctione tractare vel re-
cipere aut eius confectioni assistere. Verumtamen illud maximum et
meritorium est, et valde comodum, cum benignitate et humilitate et   1310
tremore missam celebrare, et devote et cum silentio atque mentis hilaritate et tota hominis cogitationis et cordis integritate illam audire.
Nichil fere prodest orare sine mentis intentione et interioris hominis
cogitatione. Eapropter ait propheta: "Quia cogitatio hominis confite-
bitur tibi, et reliquie cogitationis diem festum agent tibi." Quasi dicat
David: "Homo debet adorare et laudare te, ac servire tibi, o deus, tota
sui cogitatione, corde et contrito et spiritu humiliato, tantum celestia
cogitando, et ad ea tota anima et cunctis viribus aspirando." Tenemur
autem cogitatione et opere laudare deum. Ideo subiungit propheta "et
reliquie cogitationis," etc., id est, exibitio boni operis diem festum   1320
agent tibi. In dei laude primum est cogitatio, id est, voti conceptio.
Secundum sive reliquie illius sunt voti reditio, scilicet, post sanctam
cogitationem et honestum votum, debet sequi perfecta oratio. Vovere
autem est voluntatis, reddere vero est necessitas. . . .⟩

De malo oratore

Item ille qui orando facit afferesim sive sincopam seu apocopam vel etiam bar-
barismum aut solocismum, infideliter et prave orat. Quilibet itaque orator qui
aliquam vel aliquas partes orationis aliquo modo dimittit, infidelis est orator,
cum non reddat deo cunctas horas vocales totaliter et integre, immo furatur ac
subripit plures particulas illarum horarum. Similiter cum facit sistole vel dias-   1330
tole: fur est et latro reddendo vitiatum verbum dei, hoc est, male proferendo.
Peccavit enim graviter qui legit aut orat, si coripiat producendam et producat
corripiendam, nec non gravius errat qui pretermittit aliquam portiunculam de
mattutinis aut de aliis horis. Gravissime autem delinquunt qui non surgunt ad
orationes matutinas et qui occupatione vel occasione secularis negotii omittunt
canonicas et regulares horas. Nulla enim ratione opus dei, quod est oratio, est
relinquenda pro aliquo servili et mundano opere. Sunt autem orationes et alia
verba dei et ieiunia et elemosine cibus anime. Unde deus: "Non in
solo pane vivit homo," id est, anima, "sed in omni verbo, quod procedit de ore dei."   1340

Quod elemosina spiritualis fit melior corporali

Item Gregorius: "Et fortasse panem ut indigenti elemosinam porrigat non habet. Plus est autem verbi pabulo victuram in perpetuo mentem reficere quam ventrem moriture carnis terreno pane satiare." *Nam quantum est anima melior corpore, tantum oratio est dignior quolibet mechanico opere. Denique non est directa et propria collatio sive comparatio inter orationem* |21ra| *et opus materiale. Hinc est quod illi qui deserunt horas nocturnas vel diurnas pro aliqua temporali re et transitoria, aurum obrizum dimittunt pro stercore, et etiam amplexantur stercora pro croceis. Inde est quod illi qui circa memorata vitia laborant, infideles et pravi oratores sunt. Fideles dicitur a fide, qui totum quod debet reddere persolvit. Unde qui predicta mala incurrunt, non sunt absoluti a divina obligatione, cum horas quas cantare videntur, imperfecte et male dicant, et etiam, quod gravius est, multas insolidum et omnino pretermittant.*

Quod sit diligenter orare

Formam enim orandi atque legendi ponit Hesdra, ubi ait: "Et legererunt in libro legis dei distincte, et aperte ad intelligendum." Neque aliter bene legit vel orat aliquis nisi distincte, id est, divise proferat unam dictionem ab alia. Tenetur enim quilibet orator qui meritorie vult orare, prius unum nomen aut aliam partem orationis totam integre dicere antequam aliud incipiat enuntiare. Nempe quia multi cum debent orare, ante incipiunt secundam partem orationis quam dixerint primam. Ideo privantur orationis effectu. Aperte itaque orat qui auditur ab illis qui sunt cum eo. Itaque si tu conaris loqui distincte et aperte et etiam coram iudice forensi, ut eius captes benivolentiam, cur non idem facis creatori tuo, ut invenias eius indulgentiam? Omnis ergo qui cupit diligenter orare tenetur pro posse suo cuncta supradicta vitare.

⟨De eodem

Timeas sane quod legitur: qui enim orat sine cordis devotione, carebit sua peticione. Potius autem requirit deus intentionem mentis quam altitudinem vocis. Ideo dicitur quod Moyses tacens clamabat, loquebatur corde, silebat ore. Sic clamabant sancti et iusti. Unde propheta: "Clamaverunt iusti, et dominus exaudivit eos."⟩

Quod sit orare bonum et bene

Idem nota quod ait propheta: "Fiat oratio eius in peccatum." Illa enim oratio est cum peccato que non est cum Christo, quem non vult sequi. Sed quomodo potest dominica oratio aut quelibet alia fieri in peccatum? Ideo est sciendum quod oratio dicitur fieri in peccatum, id est, absorbere in peccato, videlicet, cum facit peccatum, ut illa oratio non sit utilis peccanti. Et secundum hoc, cuiuslibet oratio existentis in peccato mortali erit illi in peccatum, id est, non est illi utilis ad salutem. 1380 Dicitur autem oratio fieri in peccato, id est, de peccato, scilicet, quando aliquis orat facere malum, hoc est, impune peccare. Unde legitur: "Qui indevote orat, iudicium sibi postulat," id est, quod prava et contraria devotioni petit. Item nota quod illa oratio fit per Christum qua oratur bonum et bene. Plerumque autem oratur bonum et non bene, ut ab illis qui sunt in mortali peccato. Quandoque vero oratur bene sed non bonum, ut cum aliquis bonus petit aliquid quod sibi expedit, ut fecit Paulus orans pro stimuli remotione. Interdum enim oratur neque bonum nec bene, ut quando aliquis de peccato consumando orat, sicut egit Iudas. Sola utique illa oratio fit per Christum qua postulatur 1390 bonum et bene, et hec tantum est meritoria.

De pravo oratore

Negligenter orat quilibet sedens vel appodiatus, si sanus est. Similiter male orat qui, cum debet flectere genua vel prosternere se in terra seu incurvare, et ipse stat erectus. Gestus vero corporis est argumentum et probatio mentalis devotionis. Status autem exterioris hominis instruit nos de humilitate et affectu interioris. Orat quoque negligenter omnis qui aliud quam de ore proferat, cogitat. Unde accidit quod illi qui debent orare vel legere inutiliter laborant nisi sint intenti circa orationem et omnem particulam eius ut nullam pretermittant et nisi recordentur et sciant se dixisse cunctas partes totius orationis corde quas ore protulere. 1400

De eodem

Contra illos qui non laudant deum corde sed ore, ait dominus per Ysaiam: "Populus hic labiis me honorat, cor autem eorum longe est a me." "Sine causa colunt me." Quasi dicat: "Quia tantum ore et non corde clamant, et invocant nomen meum, ideo non prodest eis eorum oratio, nec mihi est accepta." Item Beda: "In ecclesia stantes, mente foris vagantes, omni fructu orationis privantur." Denique si quis vult orando deo placere, conetur et elaboret cor suum retinere, ne vagetur et relinquat orationem. Sane ut ait Gregorius: "Nichil fugatius corde." Et idcirco ut non deserat te, hoc frenis, hoc tu compesce catenis, quatenus valeas tecum habitare. 1410

De difficultate orandi devote

Item ut fiat qualiscumque comparatio inter spirituale et carnale, celeste et terrenum, quam difficile ac grave corpori est pati compedes ferreas

vel aliquo modo ligari, ut non valeat pergere quo est opus, tam durum est et honerosum, immo fere magis, menti seu cordi orationi, lectioni, et contemplationi omnino ardenter atque vehementer intendere. Tunc namque spiritus humanus est quasi compeditus et vinculis mancipatus, quando sancta quadam violentia cogitur divino operi totaliter et penitus adesse, cum sit velut proprie proprium nostri intellectus sive sensus,
1420 vagari, discutere huc et illuc, atque deserere, vacantes honestis et spiritualibus rebus. Item sanctus Benedictus: "Si cum hominibus po-
⟨De eodem⟩ tentibus volumus aliqua suggerere, non presumimus nisi cum humilitate atque reverentia, quanto magis domino deo universo cum omni humilitate et puritatis devotione est supplicandum." Item si cerdones, pelliparii, agricole, vinitores et omnes alii homines cuiuscumque sint professionis, elaborant fideliter et diligenter ea que acturi sunt |21rb| perficere, multo itaque fortius clerici et omnes religiosi debent niti summopere, ut meritorie agant opus dei, ad quod tenentur contemplatione officii et beneficii. Nec
1430 non quod inter cuncta hominum genera, nullum est quod deterius et minus bene opus suum exerceat quam persone ecclesiarum officium suum agunt. Imbecilis quoque sexus mulierum, varium ac mobile et debile genus feminarum procurat agere telas suas diligenter et omnia que eis convenit facere, nec non studet commode atque optime consumare. Econtra clerici quando tenentur orare, conantur potius ad finem orationis perperam et male pervenire quam bene eam inchoaverint.

Quid sit habitare vel esse secum

Secum namque habitare est ut ait Gregorius de Benedicto: "Hic in sua custodia
1440 *semper circumspectus ante oculos conditoris se semper aspiciens, se semper examinans, non divulgavit se extra oculum sue mentis." Item idem Gregorius: "Nam quotiens per cogitationis motum nimie extra nos ducimur et nos sumus et nobiscum non sumus, quia nosmetipsos minime videntes, pervagamur." Amplius idem Gregorius in vita sancti Benedicti docet: "Duobus modis extra nos ducimur, Petre. Quoniam aut per cogitationis lapsum sub nosmetipsos recidimus, utpote fecit prodigus ille filius qui porcos pavit vagatione mentis et immunditie sub semetipso cecidit, vel per contemplationis gratiam super nosmetipsos levamur, verbi gratia, sicut fecit Petrus apostolus, quem angelus solvit, eiusque mentem extasi rapuit. Hic beatus princeps apostolorum non extra se quidem, sed super semetipsum fuit.*
1450 *Uterque ergo ad se rediit quando et ille ab errore operis se collegit ad cor qui in longinquam regionem abiit, ubi portionem quam acceperat consumpsit, et altera a contemplatione culmine ad hoc rediit, quod ad intellectum prius fuit communi.*

Habitat itaque secum sive est secum, qui inter cogitationis claustra se custodit.
Nam quotienscumque aliquem cognitionis ardor in altum rapit, se procul dubio
sub se reliquit."

Quod nichil sit gravius quam bene orare

Heremita vero quidam prudens et discretus est protestatus atque confessus, dif-
ficile esse sine impedimento orare, ac difficilius esse absque offendiculo psallere.
Insuper in veritate debemus dicere quod nichil magis arduum aut asperum quam
diu confiteri et laudare deum toto corde. Citius enim invenirentur centum boni   1460
et strenui milites et urbium expugnatores quam decem meritorie orantes. Item cum
oramus gemere et flere debemus, reminiscentes quam gravia sint scelera que com-
misimus et quam dura sunt inferni supplicia que timemus. Mens sane qualem
se in oratione offert, talem se in ea conservet. Nam nichil proficit oratio si denuo
committitur unde venia postulatur, ille utique precum effectum percipit qui,
quod orando ablui postulat, delinquendo non iterat. Mens nostra celestis est que,
tunc deprecans, bene deum contemplatur quando nullis terrenis curis aut erroribus
impeditur.

De diligentia oratoris

Ad hoc itaque ut utiliter, prudenter, diligenter ores, necesse est tibi cogitare tan-   1470
tum de oratione usque ad finem eius, et de alia nulla re. Si autem qui debet dicere
Pater Noster, proferendo hoc, id est, dominicam orationem, cogitet de Miserere
Mei Deus, vel de alia oratione, minus bene et incaute oravit. Qualis ergo est il-
lorum oratio qui, cum debent orare ruminando psalmos, cogitant illicita et in-
honesta et turpia, talium deprecatio, quorum intentio vertitur circa meretricem aut
erga questum vel vanam gloriam, potius et verius est dicenda exsecratio et pec-
catum quam oratio. Unde propheta David: "Cum iudicatur, exeat con-
dempnatus; et oratio fiat in peccatum." *Si autem vis deo tua utique oratione*
placere, oportet te id solum tantum habere in corde quod pronuntias ore, et ut
recorderis, expleta prolatione totius orationis, te dixisse universas partes illius.   1480
Sicut enim sumendo cibum corporis gustu, comprehendis de qualibet parte eius
utrum sit dulcis vel amara, ita debes diligenter animadvertere et considerare de
cunctis partibus orationis an bene vel male illas protuleris. Porro si ita fueris
sollicitus atque intentus dum oras, erga orationem et eius partes, ut numquam
mens tua vagetur, recedendo a te, aliud cogitando, immo habitabis semper tecum,
non relinquendo te in tempore orationis, poteris vere dicere cum propheta: "Con-
fitebor tibi domine in toto corde meo," etc. Item idem ait propheta in alio psalmo:
"In toto corde meo exquisivi te, ne repellas me a mandatis," etc. Et in eodem
psalmo addidit: "Deprecatus sum faciem tuam in toto corde meo, mentis mei se-
cundum eloquium tuum." Item in eodem psalmo ait: "Clamavi in toto corde meo;   1490
exaudi me, domine," etc.

De muscis morientibus

Ergo ut auferas impedimenta orationis, abige aves et importunitatem muscarum, et excute multrale pectoris tui, ut exeant inde musce morientes, id est, cogitationes prave, vane, ac diverse atque inutiles et nocive, que suavitatem unguenti perdunt, hoc est, impediunt orationis effectum et utilitatem. Hec autem musce significant aves que fedabant sacrificium Habrahe, propter quas ipse fecit flagellum de resti- culis cum quo ipse repellebat eas a sacrificio. Tu quoque fac tibi flagellum |21va| ad instar Habrahe, videlicet, de compunctione, devotione, discretione, gemitu ac

1500 *flectu. Ut autem sapiens docet: "Numquam est orandum cum gaudio et letitia, sed semper cum planctu et dolore." Flere autem tenentur homines de peregrinatione vie et pro dilatione patrie. Unde: "Heu mihi quia incolatus meus prolungatus est." Si vero vitabis pessima que subruunt mente vagas, poteris cogitationes noci- vas, que separant te ab oratione, superare.*

Quomodo vincantur oratoris impedimenta

Item Gregorius: "Quanto graviori tumultu cogitationum carnalium premimur, tanto insistere ardentius orationi debemus. Nam plerum- que peccatorum nostrorum phantasmata orando patimur sed nimirum necesse est, ut vox cordis vestri, quo durius repellitur, valentius in-

1510 sistere nitatur, interpellando medullis cordis, clamitando vocibus mentis, quatenus illicite cogitationis tumultum superet, atque ad pias aures dei nimietatis sue importunitate erumpat et ascendat. Circa se autem que dicuntur, quisque potest recognoscere si ea vult oculo ra- tionis intueri. Nam quando ab hoc mundo animum ad deum mittimus et dum ad orationis opus convertimur, ipsa que prius delectabiliter gessimus importuna, post gravia in nostra oratione tolleramus. Vix sane illorum cogitatio manu sancti desiderii ab oculis abicitur et dif- ficulter eorum illusiones per penitentie lamenta superantur." ⟨Ob iam- dicta mala vitanda, docet Petrus apostolus in prima epistola: "Vigilate

1520 in orationibus." Ibi ait Beda: "Cum ad orandum stamus, est vitandum ne animus aliud cogitet preter id solum quod precatur. Omnis enim carnalis cogitatio recedat, intentione cordis sincera deum non sono vocis, sed sensu animi oret."⟩

De repetitione orationis

Item potest queri quid sit faciendum sacerdoti cum cor eius in canone sive in se- creta misse vagatur ad aliud, et precipue cum non recordatur se dixisse illa verba domini ad que, et propter prolationem quorum, fit transsubstantiatio panis et in carnem Christi, verbi gratia: "Accipite et manducate ex eo omnes. Hoc est enim corpus meum." Similiter ad prolationem horum verborum: "Accipite et bibite ex

hoc omnes. Hoc est enim calix sanguinis mei novi et eterni testamenti, misterium   1530
fidei," etc. Sic autem sit transsubstantiatio vini in sanguinem, in quibus et circa
que verba consistat tota virtus sacrificii et sacramenti altaris, atque confectio
eucharistie et illius efficacia. Solutio seu responsio memorate questionis est hec.
Dicimus autem precise et in veritate, omnem oratorem talem qui vagatur mente
quando debet orare, ad aliquid alium cogitando quam de oratione, et qui non est
secum tunc, nec recordatur neque scit se dixisse totam orationem, male et prave
orasse, nec est exemptus ab honere et debito orationis.

Quod agendum sit utiliter orantibus

Exortamur itaque universos omnes et singulos, ac maxime sacerdotes, cum non
habitant secum, corde fugiente ab eis in misse celebratione, ad iterationem sive   1540
repetitionem omnium illarum partium cuiuslibet orationis quas non recolunt se
dixisse, nec occurrit eorum menti protulisse. Fortasse autem obiciet aliquis dicen-
do, presbiterum scandalizare populum, prorogando missam, nec aliter posset ali-
quis secretam bis dicere, quin missa videatur populo nimis prolixa. Ita posito
sacerdotem primo recessisse a se, et dubitantem an protulerit totam secretam nec
ne, ea propter tenetur secundo dicere que ignorat se dixisse. Qualiter enim potest
eucharistiam conficere in vagatione et peregrinatione mentis, corpore existente in
oratorio et corde vagante in foro, videtur ergo quod illi non possint excusari a
mortali peccato qui, orando, non invocant deum toto corde suo. Dissimulant enim
et fingunt se orare ad instar ipocritarum, quatenus videantur ab hominibus sancti   1550
et boni, licet sint pravi et mali. Omnis ergo orator meritorie orat qui de nulla
re alia cogitat. Non potest utique cor sive pectus humanum in eodem instanti de
diversis cogitare. Unde sapiens ait: "Que peccatorum ingredienti terram
                              duabus viis. *Pectora nostra duas non admitentia curas."* Item:

Contra fugam   "Mens divisa non impetret. Deus enim noster non in-
      cordis   trat in sissuris." Item: "Pallium meum est breve,

utrumque operire non potest." Item dominus in Matheo: "Nemo autem potest duobus dominis servire." "Non enim potestis deo servire et
mammone." *Item conandum est summopere sacerdoti, saltem cum assistit al-*
tari, ut retineat secum cor suum. Nec transeat ad cogitandum de alia re quam   1560
de missa. Similiter omnis orator vel lector debet cogere cor suum quatenus in tem-
pore contemplationis non meditetur aliud. Sunt autem lectio et oratio species con-
templationis, quamobrem nullus potest bene et utiliter legere vel orare nisi coartet
mentem suam, tamdiu esse secum nusquam vagari, quousque totam expleverit ora-
tionem aut lectionem.

Quod sit melius orare in nocte quam in die

Rursum inter cetera est notandum, quod licet omni tempore scriptura clamat, teneamur deum benedicere, laudare, et adorare, nicholominus tamen commodius et oportunius et longe melius est in nocte orare quam de die, et precipue in crepusculo diurno, hoc est, valde mane in aurora. Tunc enim misera et fetida caro nostra magis movetur ad luxuriam quam alio tempore. Hinc est quod viri sancti et vere religiosi ac deo dicati statuerunt, ut nullus debeat ire dormitum, cantatis matutinis, quantumcumque expleantur ante auroram, ne accidat pollui eos vel sponte aut in|21vb|vite, nocturnis vel diurnis pollutionibus.

De eodem

Item eapropter plurimum expedit omnibus fidelibus de nocte vacare orationi vel lectioni et contemplationi, que levius etiam et magis meritorie fiunt circa medium noctis, quando forenses cause cessant et humane actiones conquiescunt, nec non et murmura fratrum sopita sunt. Nam illa siquidem hora libere, fideliter, atque devote habes copiam orandi, invocandi, et clamandi ad deum in toto corde tuo, quod non contingit tibi de facili aliqua ratione in plena die, ob secularia negotia, que retrahent imperfectum, si fieri potest, a contemplatione et laude divina. Idcirco si vis tota mente tua et cunctis viribus tuis deo orando placere, dic cum propheta vere, id est, opere: "Memor fui nocte nominis tui, domine," etc. Item: "Media nocte surgebam, ad confitendum tibi," etc.

De eodem

Item Ieremias propheta ait: "Consurge, lauda in nocte, in principio vigiliarum; effunde sicut aqua cor tuum ante conspectum domini," etc. Similiter si cupis carnis temptationes, turpesque motus fornicationis superare, et pro peccatis tuis et aliorum veniam impetrare, sit tibi, karissime, summum studium, maximaque cura orationibus, vigiliis, lectionibus matutinalibus summopere insistere. Item sancti pastores, de quibus ait beatus Lucas: "Pastores loquebantur ad invicem," etc., quoniam vigilabant et custodiebant gregem suum a lupis et ab omni malo, meruerunt ut docet Gregorius: "Non solum angelum domini cum clara luce videret, immo etiam in multitudine celestium audierunt agminum, que gloriam deo caneret, pacemque hominibus bone voluntatis predicaret." Iamdicti pastores gregum mistice significant, quosque rectores et doctores fidelium animarum, qui licet omni tempore teneantur vigilare et orare pro populo dei, tamen oportet eos

in nocte vigiliis insistere, ut superent carnis immunditiam et fugiant
diaboli insidias, atque ut vincant mundi pericula. Ergo, lector dilec-
tissime, ut non sis surdus auditor dictorum, animadverte quid dicat
Iohannes in Apocalisi: "Ego diligentes me diligo, et qui mane vigila-
verint ad me, invenient me." Item Isaia propheta: "Honus Duma ad
te clamat ex Seyr: custos, quid de nocte. Dixit custos: 'Venit mane et
nox; si queritis, querite; convertimini et venite.'"   1610

De eodem

Nota quod non dixit custos quid de die, sed de nocte, quia magis im-
pugnamur tunc quam in die. Item propheta in quinto psalmo: "Quoniam ad te orabo, domine, mane. Exaudies vocem meam. Mane
astabo tibi et videbo," etc. Item in psalmo LXIII: "Si memor fui tui
super stratum meum, in matutinis meditabor in te, quia fuisti adiu-
tor," etc. Item in psalmo LXXXVI: "Et ego ad te, domine, clamavi,
et mane oratio mea preveniet te." Idem in psalmo C: "In mattutinis
interficiebam omnes peccatores terre, ut disperderem de civitate domini omnes operantes iniquitatem." Peccatores terre vocantur primi   1620
motus, cum homo habet voluntatem peccandi carnaliter. Item nota
quod votum frangentes sunt adulteris peiores, quoniam peccant in
deum directe. Adulteri vero directe delinquunt in hominem, indirecte
in deum. Nam "quanto id quod iuratur magis est sanctum, tanto plus
est penale periurium," ut ait Augustinus in causa XXII, questione I,
Movet te.

Quod gravius peccent religiosi in eodem genere peccati quam alii

Sunt autem peccata carnis multa, ut stuprum, quod fit in violatione
virginis, incestum, quod fit quando persona religiosa corrumpitur, id
est, sanctimonialis vel conversa sive heremita. Similiter committitur   1630
idem crimen quotiens persone alique ad invicem carnaliter commiscen-
tur, inter quas est consanguinitas sive affinitas seu proximitas spiritualis, que est inter fratres et filios spirituales et compatres et comma-
tres. Prefati vero omnes in carnali copula gravius peccant adulteris,
incestum committendo et spirituale vinculum infringendo.

Qualiter sunt puniendi incestuosi

Pena sive penitentia qua prelibati simul peccantes debeant puniri,
habes in XXX causa, questione IIII: "Si pater et filius aut duo fratres
cum una muliere, aut si cum matre et filia, vel cum duabus sororibus,
sive cum duabus commatribus aliquis concubuerit, secundum anti-   1640

quam humaniorem diffinitionem, VIII annis peniteat." Sunt etiam
alia peccata carnis, adulterium et fornicatio corporalis, que variis
penis afficiuntur. Diversa enim peccata non currunt equis passibus,
immo varias exigunt medicinas. Unde Ieronimus in XXIIII causa,
questione I: "Non afferamus stateras dolosas, ubi appendamus, quod
volumus, pro arbitrio nostro, dicentes, hoc est grave, illud leve, sed
afferamus divinam stateram de scripturis sanctis, tamquam de the-
sauris dominicis, et in illa quid sit gravius, appendamus. Tempore
quo dominus priora delicta recedentibus penarum exemplis cavenda
1650 demonstravit, et ydolum fabricatum atque adoratum est, et propheti-
cus liber ira contemptoris regis incensus, et scissma temptatum. Ydo-
latria gladio est punita, exustio libri bellica cede, et peregrina captivi-
tate, scissma hiatu terre, sepultis auctoribus vivis, et ceteris celesti
igne consumptis. Quis dubitat sceleratius esse commissum, |22ra|
quod est gravius vindicatum?"

Non esse negligendam orationem nocturnam pro diurna

Iamdicta ideo premisimus quia plurimum impediunt orationem, que
vincuntur vigiliis, orationibus, elemosinis et ieiuniis. Nam sine Cerere
et Bacho friget Venus, que sunt valde fugienda. Vinum et mulier fa-
1660 ciunt sapientem apostatare. Iterum sciendum est, quod sicut stolidus
et erroneus viator est ille qui debet ire Romam vel Ierosolimam, et
in Galliam pergeret. Ita minus cautus et improvidus est orator qui,
pro diurna oratione, negligit nocturnam orationem, que tanto est
maior ac dignior diurna quanto aurum est carius et melius argento.
Non enim potest homo contemplari perfecte celestia, cum videt et
audit ac meditatur terrena. Ideo dominus, ut doceret nos verbo et exemplo orare, pernoctabat in orationibus continue et sine intermissi-
one orando. *In orationibus vero privatis et solitariis, melius et levius potest
homo habitare secum, nichil aliud quam de oratione meditando, quam in pub-*
1670 *licis, in quibus multi ac diversi conveniunt. Nam in multitudine fere non deerit
peccatum, sane ut ait sapiens: "Fuge turbam," quoniam turba faciet tibi turbationem.* Orationes sane private pertinent ad contemplativos.

De vita contemplativa

Est autem vita contemplativa, ut ait sapiens, cum longo quis bone actionis exercitio doctus, diutine orationis dulcedine instructus, crebra
lacrimarum compuntione adsuefactus, a cunctis mundi negotiis vacare et in sola dilectione dei conatur oculos mentis intendere, gaudium quoque perpetue beatitudinis quod in eterna recepturus est vita.

Nunc etiam inchoatus ardenti desiderio pregustare, et aliquando deni- 1680
que, prout mortalibus fas est, in excessu mentis raptus celestia videtur
attingere. Hec utique paucorum est, que non per mortem finienda
est, ut activa, sed post mortem perfectius domino veniente complenda.

De activa vita

Activa vero est Christi famulum informare, iustis laboribus intendere
et prius quidem se ipsum ab hoc seculo immaculatum custodire, linguam, mentem, manum ac corporis cetera membra, ab omni in-
quinamento culpe temptantis continere, atque divinis ea perpetuo
subiugare obsequiis. Deinde tenentur cuilibet iuxta vires in necessitatibus succurrere, esurienti cibum, potum sitienti, algenti vestimen-
tum prebere, egenos, vagosque in domum tuam colligere, infirmos   1690
visitare, mortuos sepelire, oppresos et inopes a diripientibus liberare,
nec non erranti viam veritatis ostendere, et alii se fraterne dilectionis
obsequio mancipare, insuper etiam usque ad mortem pro iustitia cer-
tare. Active namque labor cum morte deficit, premium post mortem
accepturus eternum.

Utrum sit melior contemplativa quam activa

Solet denique dubitari de iamdictis que alteri preferatur. Potest dici
ad hec quod habeant se ut excedentia et excessa. Plures autem sunt
contemplativi qui sunt meliores aliquibus activis, et econverso. Id est,
multi activi sunt qui excedunt quosdam contemplativos, et sunt eis   1700
utiliores. Activa sane vita cum partibus suis pertinet ad reales horas,
de quibus, deo dante, dicetur inferius. Contemplativa denique cum
suis speciebus convenit cum canonicis et vocalibus horis, quarum utique usus et exercitium a paucis meritorie consumatur et perficitur.
Nichil autem est difficilius in rebus humanis quam celestia omni nisu
et conamine contemplari, et deo mentaliter et toto corde inherere.
Item nota quod omnis homo tenetur aliquando esse activus et interdum contemplativus. Debet autem homo in primis querere regnum
dei et iustitiam eius, et deinde oportet ut agat opera misericordie.
Sunt autem connexe et coniuncte hec due vite, et ideo transeundum   1710
est ab una ad reliquam, hoc est, ab operibus contemplative ad opera
active, et econverso.

Quod meliores sint orationes private quam communes

In communibus vero orationibus tot sunt tibi occasiones vagandi quot ostacula
visui tuo se offerunt. Nempe oculo corporis videt cor extrinseca, qui est nuntius

et instrumentum quo homo interior scit exteriora. Cor enim sequitur oculum.
Unde contingit quod ad tot transfertur cor quot videt oculus, et totiens recedit
mens hominis ab eo, quotiens res vise variantur radiis visualibus transeuntibus
ad varia et diversa obstacula. Ideo dixit propheta: "Oculus meus depredatus est
1720 *animam meam." Quamobrem viri sancti fugiebant multitudinem populorum,*
commorantes in locis solitariis et privatis, ubi orabant cum gemitu et fletu.
Plorabant equidem et dolebant, effundentes se coram domino pro peccatis omnium
populorum, neque pre propere neque pre postero ordine, hoc est, inordinate et nimia cum festinatione verbo orationis proferentes, licet autem dicatur a philosopho, quod verba transposita idem significant.
Nichilominus tamen ordo est observandus in oratione verborum.

⟨De eodem

Neque conciliat sibi deum multiplex orantis sermo, sed pura et sincera deprecantis intentio. Nam non in multiloquio sed in compuncti-
1730 one cordis et effusione lacrimarum consistit virtus orationis. Illa denique oratio deum placat, que cum dilectione proximi emanat. Oratio
in privatis locis commodius geritur, que tantum deo teste deprimitur.
Nemo graviter et prudenter aliquid agit, qui quod operatur non intelligit.⟩

De furtivis orationibus

|22ʳᵇ| *Eapropter illorum orationes erant grate et accepte deo, sicut sunt omnes*
private et furtive orationes, que non procedunt tantum ex sumitate labiorum, sed
ex intimis cordium. Hinc est, quod tales orationes quia fiunt toto corde, non
sedendo nec pausando seu iacendo, neque dormitando, plurimum prosunt. Nam
1740 *ut ait Gregorius: "Intenta supplicatio dormire cor mundum vetat. Ideo sic orantes*
assecuntur pie petitionis effectum." Econtrario communes quedam orationes sunt
frustratorie et vane et fere inutiles, quoniam non fiunt aliquo modo prout debent
fieri. Speciales vel singulares seu furtive orationes aut private, si vaga mente
fiant, quod deus avertat, sunt repetende, et totiens sunt dicende quousque orans
sciat se dixisse omnia que dicere debuit, quod autem bene dicere potest sine scan-
dalo populi. Ibi vero non potest se excusare orator, quod verecundetur se erigere
brachia super caput vel orare ulnis extensis ad modum crucis, aut aliquo aliorum
modorum septem.

Quod non sit curandum qualiter deo serviatur

1750 *Obiciet fortassis aliquis de eo quod legitur: "Quacumque intentione, quocumque*
modo colatur, laudetur, glorificetur deus; gaudeo, et gaudebo." Solutio: vera sunt
que dicuntur, verumtamen plurimum interest, et maxima differentia est inter fi-

delem et sapientem oratorem, et inter desidem et negligentem. Omnis enim qui aliquo septem dictorum modorum orat meritorie et prudenter orat, si nichil quam de oratione cogitat. Qui vero secus agit, inutiliter et prave orat. Ad hoc siquidem est valde utile prelibatis modis orare, quia cum est fatigatus aliquis orare uno modo, oret alio modo. Nam illa varietas sive distinctio orandi est quedam recreatio seu pausatio et resumptio virium.

Quare mulier est fugienda

Item ut mentaliter deo inhereas, fuge copiam mulierum et frequentiam illarum, 1760
ne disiungant et separent cor tuum a deo. Ideo ait Ieronimus: "Hospitiolum tuum aut raro vel numquam mulierum pedes terant. Nam non potest cum deo toto corde habitare qui accessibus copulatur feminarum. Mulier enim conscientiam esurit secum pariter habitantis. Numquam igitur disputes de formis mulierum, femine nomen tuum nesciant. Feminam, quam bene videris conversantem, mente dilige, non corporali frequentia. Si bonum est mulierem non tangere, malum est ergo ipsam palpare." Itaque si vis a deo exaudiri orando, sive in privatis seu in publicis orationibus, noli respicere muliebrem formam, quoniam ut ait Augustius in XXXII causa, questione V: "Nec solo tactu et affectu, sed aspectu quoque appetitur. Et appetit concupiscentiam mulierum." 1770

De eodem

Porro si sis constitutus in presentia muliercularum, facile est te diligere et diligi ab eis. Sit ergo tibi cum illis rara accessio et omnino brevis collocutio. *Igitur si appeteris, malum est, et si appetis illam, peius est. Similiter quoque si concupiscis mulierem ad habendum eam, et ipsa hoc ipsum desiderat, pessimum est. Denique ut prefata mala evadas, fac ut ait apostolus: "Fuge fornicationem," id est, feminam, que est occasio fornicandi et materia adulterii et stupri atque incestus. Fuge dico voluntatem, fuge cogitando de muliere, fuge videndo, fuge etiam audiendo, fuge magis loquendo, ne blandis verbis illius capiaris. Vox enim blanda et nequam digitos habet, id est, aculeos. Vulnerat autem cor hominis* 1780
verbum luxurie. Fuge omnino et penitus numquam tangendo. Si vero iamdicta perfecte et diligenter egeris, toto corde et utiliter poteris deum invocare.

De eodem

Item nota quod sunt tria genera eunuchorum. Primi sunt gratie, secundi nature, tertii sunt violentie. Hinc sapiens: "Alios homines eunuchos natura facit, quosdam vis hominum." Michi autem illi soli eunuchi placent quos castravit non necessitas sed voluntas et gratia. De quibus ait dominus in Luca: "Beate steriles et ventres qui non genuerunt et hubera que non lactaverunt." Primi autem dicuntur castrati,

1790 quasi caste nati. *Miror minus doctam scientiam tuam non advertentem nichil aliud esse muliercularum habere copiam ac earum uti confabulationibus, et, quod est gravius, ab illis tangi vel eas tangere, quam addere oleum camino, et deferre ligna in nemus, et deviare ad mare aquas atque irritare voluntates admodum irritatas, et plurimum in carnali delectatione intensas et valde inflammatas in opere veneris. Quecumque dicta sunt tibi, lectori, domino sancto, meritisque beato, ita dico si facis que discis legendo. Nam si male vivis operando fere nichil proficis legendo, et eris opprobrium hominum et abiectio plebi, totum enim irritas, prave agendo quod commode et bene infers vel doces predicando. Quid enim prodest legem habere in ore et in codice, et eam excludere a corde, et pedibus conculcare?*
1800 *Omnia vero illa memorata que prefata sunt de fuga mulierum viris, intelligant femine sibi dici de fuga virorum. Quemadmodum mulier est viro arma diaboli, ut ait Iohannes Os Aureum |22va|, ita homo femine est occasio cuiuslibet iniquitatis. Fuge ergo tu, mulier, quecumque es, que vis caste et pie vivere in Christo, omnem virum quemadmodum agna lupum. Sane mulier que est frequens in foro et raro in domo, vix aut numquam erit pudica et honesta.*

De temporibus in quibus omnes tenentur continere

Est autem coniectura luxurie et malitie atque argumentum incontinentie et libidinis satis probabile, feminam non fugere consortia virorum, immo appetere cum affectu opere visum, auditum, colloquium, et tactum hominum. Fugiat coniugata
1810 *virum suum ad tempus, ut vacent orationi. Tenentur autem caste vivere sponsus et sponsa, saltem in toto adventu domini et in diebus festivis et in tota quadragesima. Ideo legitur in principio maioris quadragesime "egrediatur sponsus de cubili suo, et sponsa de thalamo suo," etc. Fugiat omnis alia mulier que caret viro omnem hominem, et precipue iuvenem. Nam ut ait sapiens: "A iuvene et cupido credatur reddita virgo." Fugiat etiam senem, ne peccet in eo. Ideo ait quidam dei senex: "Et decrepitus, femine venienti ad se, tolle paleas, adhuc vivit igniculus." "Est in canitie ridiculosa Venus, quedam cum prima resecantur crimina barba." Ne mireris, karissime lector, si longum diximus sermonem. Solent enim prefata multum officere penitenti oratori vel per se sive secum*
1820 *oranti aut cum aliis.*

De peccato carnis

Est autem tale delictum peccatum carnis et adeo generale, quod sine eo pauci reperiuntur. Ideo ait Gregorius in L distinctione decretorum: "Quid enim est gravius, aut carnale delictum committere, sine quo pauci inveniuntur, aut dei filium iureiurando negare"?, etc. Eapropter est necesse ut quicumque vult dei misericordiam invenire, conetur in primis caste vivere. Igitur quoniam pauci sunt sine delicto carnis, ut testatur supra Gregorius, elaboret unusquisque esse de paucitate

honeste viventium, superando inquinamenta luxurie, refrenando fluxum et illici-
tum appetitum carnis. Nullus enim potest venire ad maxima premia, nec valet
aliquis contingere supremos honores, neque ullus conscendet regna celestia absque   1830
magno labore. ⟨Absque labore gravi non possunt magna parari.⟩

Quare sit difficile salvari

Rursus plurimum niti convenit, ut sis de sancta paucitate electorum, de qua ait
apostolus Matheus: "Multi sunt vocati, pauci vero electi." Sane ut ait Iulius papa
in II causa, questione VII: "Quia rarum est et difficile omne quod est magnum."
Firmiter ergo tene et nullatenus dubites quod vana spe decipieris, si putas gaudere
cum mundo et regnare cum Christo, si caput tuum, ut ait propheta: "De torrente
in via bibit; propterea exaltavit caput." Et si omnes sancti "multa passi sunt tor-
menta," ut securi venirent ad palmam. Tu quoque fac simile. Sedisti enim ad
mensam divitis, qualia tibi apposita sunt. Talia oportet te ei apponere. ⟨In   1840
primis ergo, si vis esse quod diceris, est necesse te relinquere omnia
peccata tua, et recedere ab omni malo, et demum teneris insistere
bonis operibus, scilicet, elemosinis, ieiuniis, vigilibus, et privatis orationibus.⟩ Item Ambrosius: Consistentes autem in
⟨De eodem⟩   Ninive, cum non haberent aliud presidium nisi ut,
abiectis copiosis epulis, ieiunia continuata suciperent et, divitiarum
ambitione seposita, humilitatem et paupertatem induerunt, videlicet,
ut exinde remedium contraherent. Unde eis perditio contingebat, id
est, ut indignationem divinitatis quam luxuriando provocaverant, ab-
stinendo linirent et, ut offensam quam in eos superbia induxerat,   1850
benignitas mitigaret.

Quid sit agendum in tribulatione constitutis

Legitur autem in prophetis, cum ingrueret seu immineret tempus
destruendi Niniveh, iuxta dei sententiam, tunc ipse rex in adversitate
illa, deposita imperiali purpura et regali ambitione summota, membra sua precinxit cilicio, atque se in sacco sex diebus ac noctibus
volutavit. Iamdictus vero rex hostes virtute superabat, deum penitentia et dolore invocabat. Sapiens plane rex, qui intelligebat quibus ar-
mis uterentur pro temporis qualitate. Cum enim insidiantur ei homines, apprehendit arma bellica. Quando autem irascitur illi deus, cor-   1860
ripit arma iustitie. Deponit itaque diadema et cilicio vestitur et sacco
ieiuniis perseverat, orationibus quoque immoratur. Mira quidem rex,
dum se regem hominum esse non meminit, rex incipit esse sanctitatis.
Religiosus itaque princeps non perdidit imperium, sed mutavit. Ne-

cesse quippe fuerat, ut qui erat cunctis potentior, fieret universis devotior.

Qualiter dei gratia inveniatur

Exemplo suo igitur precessit pietatis exercitum non armis sed sola devotione munitum. Auxilium enim non aliunde petiverunt exorando, sed de suis visceribus exigerunt, ieiunando atque orando. Imperiti sane hominis est ab altero deposcere, quod intra se potest invenire. Nulla denique nocebit adversitas si nulla dominetur iniquitas, et si eris immunis a culpa, liberaberis a pena. Ex supradictis patet quanta sit utilitas devote orantium et vere penitentium. Idem legitur in Iacobo apostolo, qui ait: "Helias homo erat similis nobis passibilis, et oravit ut non plueret super terram, et non pluit annos tres et menses VI |22vb|. Et rursus oravit, et celum dedit pluviam, et terra dedit fructum suum." In iamdictis liquet et evidens est quod maxima est commoditas et efficacia et virtus pie sancteque orationis, que celum claudit et aperit.

De fletu et luctu orantis

Preterea tenetur orator flere et abstinere. Hinc Gregorius: "Iesum sciamus vocibus flentes, precantes sobrie." Item propheta: "Venite, adoremus, et procidamus ante deum," etc. Item dominus ait: "Plorabitis et flebitis vos, mundus autem gaudebit," etc. Nota quod non dicitur scriptura sedebitis ante deum, nec etiam ridebitis aut ludebitis coram domino, vel vacabitis otio et quieti dediti ventri et lateri, sed ait procidamus, et ploremus. Quasi dicat scriptura sacra, oportet vos humiliari et laborare, cum debetis agere opus dei, quod est oratio, que indiget maiori cautela, sollicitudine et studio quolibet opere servili. Et hoc satis animavertit caritas vestra. Videtis siquidem qualiter mens humana sive cor totum et totaliter sit in omni opere servili, et etiam, quod peius est, in aliquo ludo perditionis, scilicet, alee vel scaccorum. Ita dico quod numquam aliud cogitabit nisi de pessimo et nocivo ludo alee fati, quod vero non contingit in oratione. Erga quam vix habetur aut violenter retinetur cor humanum vel mens circa unum psalmum, quin vagetur et fugiat ab homine, aliud meditando quam de oratione, quod videtur accidere ex diabolica procuratione, qui insidiatur nobis die ac nocte et invidet humanis provectibus.

Quomodo deo est serviendum in humilitate

Ergo ut superbie resistatis, humiliamini sub potenti manu dei, ut vos exaltet in tempore tribulationis. Ipse autem deponit potentes et exaltat humiles, non desides et pigros, otio marcidos, sed laborantes, bonis et honestis rebus vacantes. Unde ipse dominus ait: "Venite ad me omnes qui laboratis, et honerati estis," etc. Ita quod adhuc ut flendo et orando placeas deo, teneris orare sicut propheta, qui ait: "Et erunt ut complaceant eloquia oris mei, et meditatio cordis mei in conspectu tuo semper." Idem ac si dicat propheta: "Tunc vero oratio mea erit tibi grata et accepta, cum cor meum tantum cogitat de oratione tua et de nulla re alia."

⟨Ut Leo papa ait, duo sunt abstinentie et crucis genera. Unum est corporale et aliud spirituale. Primum est a potu atque epulis temperare, appetitum glorie, eumque a delectionibus et mollibus suavitatibus cohercere, ab his que tactum et gustum visumque decipiunt, sensum viriliter revocare et violenter abstrahere. Secundum vero abstinentie ac crucis genus est pretiosius et sublimius, videlicet motus anime quasi bestiales et nocivos, cohibere seu regere, et perturbationes illius modestie tranquillitate placare, atque ire et superbie sue vitiis non consentire, immo fortiter eis repugnare et increpare se quadam censoria austeritate virtutis, et rixam quodam modo cum homine interiori conserere. Pretiosa in conspectu domini et gloriosa crux, cogitationes malas in potestatem redigere, potentias proprias abnegare, easque intrinseco examine discutere ac regentis imperio subiugare et a sermone atque opere, quo anima leditur tamquam a cibis noxiis abstinere et sensum ab hiis que contraria sunt spirituali temperantie sobrium custodire. Hec qui facit prerupto passionis muro, violenter ad celorum regna conscendit, vim sibi tenetur anima facere, ut palmam laborum quam sibi subtrahi multis inimicis adversantibus sentit, viribus contendat eripere. Ideo ait evangelista: "Regnum celorum vim patitur," etc. Nam mens humana in diversis huius mundi illecebris et concupiscentiis devicta, familiariter expetit voluntatem et vix abducitur, ut consuetudinem a se vite prioris excludat. Verumtamen conceperit excogitare ultimi diei aversitatem et futuri iudicii pondus, incitata vel spe premii aut timore supplitii, voluntarium bellum indicit passionibus, violentiam infert pristinis desideriis, et violenter se vincere ipsa contendit. Non enim sine violentia fieri potest ut de habundantia et delitiis ad famem transeat et sitim et ad abstinentiam et crucem, ut sompno prius amicam carnem atque otio contritione vigiliisque conficiat. Item nec absque magna vi valet unusquisque iracundiam patientia, superbiam humilitate superare, amore paupertatis ac sufficientie affluentiam commutare, atque violentiam sobrietate, luxuriam castitate condempnare, quatenus homo subito in virum transformetur perfectum, et quodam modo alter reddatur ex altero. Necesse est ergo cum summo labore de hoc mundo rapere palmam salutis et velut cir-

1910

1920

1930

1940

cumiectis hostibus obsessos fructus pervigili intentione decerpere, atque predicta ad thesaurum, vite quasi de medio arreptam, seculi huius incendio reportare.⟩

De negligentia et vitio oratoris

Preterea sciendum est quod omnis homo negligenter orat qui se ipsum non audit, et qui ignorat se dicere quod profert. Unde colligitur illum stultum esse opera-torem qui nescit se agere quod facit. Igitur qui a se ipso non auditur qualiter ex-audietur a deo? Hinc est quod multorum orationes sunt vane et inutiles, quia non fiunt cum meditatione cordis, sed tantum ex summitate labiorum procedunt. Si-
1950 *militer et inutiliter orat quilibet qui non pie et perseveranter et pro se, et qui non ea que pertinent ad salutem petit. Nec non prave orat unusquisque qui non profert cunctas dictiones orationis distincte et aperte et secundum quod bene et ordinate sunt scripte, hoc est, sine soleocismo et barbarismo et absque aliis figuris.* ⟨Item Gregorius: "Virtus enim vere orationis est celsitudo caritatis. Et tunc vere quod quisque petit adipiscitur cum eius animus in petitione nec inimici odio fuscatur, et voces orantis emittuntur confessione pecca-torum."⟩

Quod nichil est dimittendum de oratione

Eapropter illi graviter peccant qui negligentia relinquunt vel litteram aut sillabam
1960 *seu dictionem sive orationem cum orant. Si vero aliquid relinquas de capite, erit ibi afferesis. Unde ait sapiens: "Afferesim dicunt de vertice quando recidunt." Cum autem pretermittis de medio, est ibi figura que dicitur sincopa. Inde ait gramaticus: "De mediastina fit sincopa, parte recisa." Quando enim demis ali-quid de fine, facis apocopam. Hinc idem: "Fineque subtracta, dicetur apocopa facta."* ⟨Contra negligentiam orantium ait Salomon: "Maledictus omnis qui facit opus dei negligenter et fraudulenter."⟩ *Item: "Qui orat indevote, iudicium sibi postulat." Amplius: "Minus malum opus dei fere omnino preter-mittere atque deserere, quam perperam et prave agere."*

Quod melius sit pauca bene proferre

1970 *Nota quod deus magis gaudet de frequentia cordium in canonicis horis quam de concursu populorum. Ideo ait Ieronimus: "Numquid verborum flecti multitudine potest deus ut homo? Non enim verbis tantum, sed corde deus est orandus." Quapropter "melius est V psalmorum decantatio cum cordis puritate ac serenitate et spirituali hilaritate, quam psalterii totius modulatio, cum anxietate cordis atque tristitia." Iterum Ieronimus ait: "Numquam de manu tua aut oculis tuis liber psalterii discedat. Ad verbum oratio dicatur," id est, iuxta verbum. Hoc est ut mens et intentio ad id quod dicitur dirigantur et non ad aliud evagentur quam ore profertur vel ad verbum quasi, non transcurrendo nec transiliendo verba, sed tractim singula dicenda* sunt et universa.

Quomodo vitia orationis vincantur   1980

Item Ieronimus ait: "Sine intermissione inviliget sensus, nec vagis cogitationibus sit patens corpus sed pariter cum anima tradatur ad deum." "Nec vacet mens tua variis perturbationibus que, si tuo pectori insederint, damnabuntur tui et te deducent ad delictum maximum. Facito ergo aliquid continue operis, ut semper diabolus inveniat te occupatum." Nam plurimum damnatur ociosis et nocet pigris. Item apostolus in epistula prima quam misit |23ra| a Corinthiis docet:

⟨De eodem⟩   *"Volo quinque verba loqui meo sensu, ut alios instruam, quam decem milia verborum lingua tantum," hoc est, sine mentis*

intentione. In illa apostoli auctoritate habes argumentum contra vanum predicatorem et adversus malum lectorem et pravum oratorem. Est autem sensus auctori-   1990
tatis, melius est et utilius pauca cum corde et devotione proferre, quam multa solummodo labiis, lingua, et ore, sine commoditate et utilitate dicentis et audientis. Itaque, ut hoc evites, dic cum apostolo, qui ait in eadem epistola: "Orabo spiritu, orabo et mente: psallam spiritu, psallam et mente."

Obiectio

Fortasse dicet emulus noster, qui non est secum quando orat, et ideo negligenter orat; Augustinus docet: "Nam plerumque precis vitium superat precantis affectus." Si vero dicat adversarius quod sic debet intelligi auctoritas Augustini, intentio oratoris vincit corruptionem orationis, nichil sibi prodest, cum ille qui vagatur mente in tempore orandi, cogitet prorsus aliud quam de oratione. Itaque non   2000
excusatur vitium orationis per intentionem sive affectum orantis, cum non meditetur de oratione, recedendo a se, illicita cogitando. Igitur quia non cogitat de oratione, nichil de ea intendit, ergo nullum habet affectum circa illam orans. Et ita habes quod affectus talis non purgat vitium precis. Quomodo posset intentio sive affectus alicuius excusare illud de quo non cogitatur? Ex supradictis potest constare, quod tota virtus et omni efficacia orationis vocalis pendet et habet provenire ex toto clamore cordis atque compunctione et devotione et intentione mentis. Unde evidens est illam orationem esse penitus inutilem que fit tantum sono oris et non contritione cordis, mente ab ea recedente et corde fugiente, et aliud quam de ea cogitante.   2010

De tribus hominum diversitatibus

Dicant ergo illi qui debent et tenentur orare pro peccatis suis et alienis, in quo vel unde credant salvari, cum prave ac pessime orent, mali quidem oratores, in

quo hominum genere computabuntur. Sunt porro tria genera hominum salvando-
rum.

⟨De eodem⟩.

Ieronimus tamen non ponit nisi duo in XII causa decreti, questione
I, ubi ait: "Duo sunt genera Christianorum. Est autem unum genus
quod est mancipatum divino officio et deditum contemplationi et ora-
2020   tioni, cui ab omni strepitu temporalium convenit cessare: ut sunt omnes
clerici et deo dicati, videlicet conversi. 'Cleros' enim grece, latine sors,
id est, in sorte dei electi," etc. "Aliud autem est genus Christianorum,
ut sunt laici. 'Laos' grece, latine dicitur populus," qui comprehendit
milites et alios.

De primo genere

Primum autem est oratorum, utpote sunt persone ecclesie, et omnes deo devote,
videlicet, hospitalarii, templarii, et clerici omnes, tam monachi quam seculares,
et regulares, *canonici, presbiteri, et conversi, predicti quia comedunt peccata*
populi, quibus committitur patrimonium Christi et bona pauperum, quorum sunt
2030   *dispensatores, que sunt tantum pauperibus reddenda et non divitibus tribuenda.*
Sunt utique pauperes domini omnium rerum ecclesiarum. Unde Ieronimus:
"Quoniam quicquid habent clerici pauperum est, et domus eorum omnibus debent esse communes, susceptioni peregrinorum et hospitum
debent invigilare." *Et ideo peccant mortaliter qui eorum bona in alios usus*
consumunt.

De prolatione verborum orationis et lectionis

Idem quam dabunt commutationem pro animabus suis, illi qui sunt obligati deo
orare die ac nocte pro peccatis totius mundi, perfecte ac studiose? Itaque ad ver-
bum oratio dicatur, hoc est, prius debet dictio precedens tota dici, quam sequens
2040   *inchoetur, et antea est dicendum quicquid precedit, quam proferatur aliquid de*
consequenti. Nulla vero ratione potest confidere de salute persona religiosa que
negligenter orat, cum eius sit officium diligenter, fideliter, et pie ac perseveranter
orare. Nec aliter valent portare peccata pugnantium et terram colentium ecclesi-
astice persone, nisi viriliter et fortiter insistant orationi. Est proprie proprium ac
speciale officium clericorum ferre, id est, delere peccata sua, et bellatoris et opera-
toris suis orationibus. Itaque si peccaverit sacerdos, quis orabit pro eo? Quid ergo
faciendum est, cum non sit iam videns nec intelligens aut requirens deum, quan-
doquidem in hac fece temporum, ⟨hoc est, in hac ultima etate,⟩ *inveniatur*
sacerdos peior populo? ⟨Cum esset valde absonum et abusio magna anti-
2050   quitus, si non fuisset sacerdos melior populo.⟩

De secundo genere

Secundum genus hominum est bellatorum, hoc est, militum qui debent expugnare inimicos ecclesie, scilicet, Saracenos, ethnicos et publicanos, et hereticos et falsos fratres, ut relinquant errorem suum, et serviant creatori celi et terre. Tales iam sunt facti predones et raptores, obliti precepto Iohanis Baptiste dicentis: "Neminem concutieritis; estote contenti stipendiis vestris."

De tertio genere hominum

Tertium genus est agricolarum et pauperum atque operariorum labore et sudore, quorum omnes degunt et vivunt. Isti sane sunt velut pedes et quasi rectores mundi, quoniam eorum opere |23ʳᵇ| ac studio homo exteriori reficitur, atque illorum usitato et materiali pane, corpora nostra sustentantur. Quos tam oratores quam pugnatores tenentur protegere ac defensare, atque pro eis intercedere et orare, et non iniquis exactionibus, violentis angariis et collectis gravare et expoliare. Si vero oratores essent quasi oculi, et bellatores ceu manus, et operarii velut pes, erit ut castrorum acies ordinata mater et ecclesia.   2060

Quid prius sit dicendum oranti, quid postea

Item fortuitu aliquis dubitavit post suprascripta, quibus orationibus sit utendum potius prius vel posterius. Talem vero questionem seu dubitationem non reprobamus, cum philosophus terrestris doceat hoc. De singulis autem dubitare non erit inutile. Est autem questio occasio sapientie, et precedit eam tamquam antecedens suum consequens. Hinc est quia vulgus preteriens dubitationem, caret scientia, que est fons et origo questionis. Ideo non est populus sequendus sed docendus. Ignorat nempe quid sit eligendum et fugiendum indoctum vulgus , licet enim questionum alie sint frivole et vulgares, et alie philosophice et utiles, et alie quedam questiones sunt que indigeant penitentia, alie sensu, ut ait prelibatus philosophus. Verumtamen quia hec questio est dubitabilis, que est digna sensu, scilicet, unde sit inchoandum oranti, et a quibus sit orationibus incipiendum, sic eam determinamus.   2070

De responsione

Videtur profecto nobis exordiendum et in primis esse dicendum Pater Noster, in qua oratione dominica continentur cuncta que necessaria sunt salvandis. Deinde potes dicere orationes sancte et individue trinitatis vel econverso, id est, postponere Pater Noster iamdictis orationibus. Non enim refert, nulla est differentia, seu antedicas Pater Noster sive prius invoces sanctam trinitatem. Postea debes decantare orationes incarnationis, nativitatis, apparitionis, passionis, et crucis resurrectionis et ascensionis domini nostri Iesu Christi. Quarto, oportet te honorare, invocare, et adorare spiritum sanctum suis orationibus utendo. Quinto, est necesse   2080

subsidia beate matris semper virginis totis viribus implorare, eius ymnum, sci-
licet "Magnificat anima mea dominum," etc., referendo, et alias plures orationes
2090 *speciales sancte Marie matris domini decantando,* et hanc maxime: "Maria
mater gratie, mater misericordie, tu nos ab hoste protege, et in hora
Oratio   mortis suscipe, per. . . ." Quam orationem qui cottidie septies saltem, et si non pluries, devote cantabit,
maximum premium comparabit. *Sexto, teneris angelicum imnum, videlicet:*
"Gloria in excelsis deo," etc., non pretermittere. Septimo, expedit tibi apostolo-
rum simbolum, hoc est: "Credo in deum," etc., minime deserere. Deinde autem
cunctis aliis orationibus quibus per universum orbem utitur catholica ecclesia con-
venit omnibus modis et toto conatu insistere, atque omni nisu mentis
et corporis incumbere.

2100   Qualiter varii modi et multe orationes sint

Item ad hoc plurimum valere potest iamdicta diversitas VII modorum orandi et
pluralitas orationum, ut auferat tedium et fastidium orantibus. Nam sicut mater
satietatis est identitas, ita quasi quedam quies et pausatio, alternitas et varietas
orandi et multitudo orationum. Que autem sunt prelibata seu supradicta, non
ideo diximus ut legem sapientibus prescriberemus, sed ut simplicibus formam
bene agendi ostenderemus. Magis enim videtur nobis expedire alieno intellectui
cedere quam contemptionibus deservire, ut sequamur Augustinum dicentem: "In
eo quippe numero sumus, ut non dedignemur etiam nobis dictum ab apostolo ac-
cipere, et si quid aliter sapitis, hoc vobis deus revelavit. Cum enim aliquid re-
2110 *velatur minori quam non maiori, sedeat maior."* Unde dixit sapiens: "Regnat
in exiguo magno pro corpore virtus."

                   Qualiter est orandum euntibus ad ecclesiam

Sic namque tenetur orare fidelis anima cum intrat ecclesiam, et hec
in primis sunt dicenda persone christiane atque religiose quando ingreditur aulam dei: "Introibo, domine, in domum tuam. Adorabo ad
templum sanctum tuum in timore tuo. Deduc me, domine, in tuam
iustitiam propter inimicos meos. Dirige in conspectu tuo viam meam.
Emitte lucem tuam et veritatem tuam. Ipse me deduxerunt quia ad-
duxerunt in montem sanctum tuum, et in tabernacula tua."

2120   De eodem

Deinde orans, se totum planum proiciat in templi pavimento in faciem suam, sive positis genibus in terra, hic secreto et submissa voce
cordis et oris, dicat ad honorem sancte et individue trinitatis: "Te in-

Quomodo est
adhoranda
sancta trinitas

vocamus, te adoramus, te laudamus, te benedicamus, o sancta et indivisa trinitas. Tibi onor, tibi gloria, tibi gratiarum actio, o benedicta trinitas. Te decet laus, tibi convenit ymnus, o veneranda trinitas et une deus, equalis divinitas et indivisa maiestas. Benedicamus patrem et filium cum spiritu sancto. Laudemus et superexaltemus eum |23va| in secula. Benedictus es, domine deus patrum nostrorum, in firmamento celi, et laudabilis sine fine."

2130

Oratio

"Presta, diligenda et timenda trinitas, concede simplex trinitas, ut fructuosa sint mihi et cunctis fidelibus tuis, tam vivis quam defunctis, ieiuniorum et orationum et elemosinarum munera."

Oratio

"Placeant tibi cogitatio, locutio, et operatio mea, o ineffabilis et tremenda trinitas. Suavis sit tibi laudatio mea, intret ad te gemitus cordis mei."

Oratio

2140

"Omnipotens sempiterne deus, qui dedisti famulis tuis in confessione vere fidei eterne trinitatis gloriam agnoscere, et in potentia magestatis adorare unitatem, quesumus, ut eiusdem fidei firmitate ab omnibus semper muniamur adversis, per. . . ."

De epilogo.

Post plurimas vero genuflexiones, multarumque lacrimarum effusionem, predictis peractis et expletis cum mentali devotione, summave diligentia et cordis intelligentia, seu scientia atque integritate, nil alteri cogitando quam de oratione, tunc poterit a solo surgere talis orator. Hic autem stans super pedes suos, non sedens neque appodiatus versus aliquam partem, sed erectus toto corpore, erigat brachia sua ad celum, elevando ea supra caput in quantum prevalet, sic orando

2150

Oratio

et deprecando deum, dicat: "Dirigatur, domine, ad te oratio mea, sicut incensum in conspectu tuo. Elevatio manuum mearum placeat tibi velut sacrificium vespertinum. Pone, domine, custodiam ori meo et hostium circumstantie labiis meis, ut non declinet cor meum in verbum malum." Ad excusandas excusationes in peccatis: "In manus tuas, domine, commendo animam meam et corpus meum. Christus vincit, Christus regnat, Christus imperat."

Quomodo est crux adoranda

2160

"Salve crux pretiosa, que de corpore Christi dedicata es, et ex membris eius tamquam margaritis ornata. Adoramus te Christe, et benedicimus tibi, quia per crucem tuam redimisti mundum. Omnis terra adoret te, et psallam tibi, et psalmum dicam nomini tuo domine." Nos autem gloriari oportet in cruce domini nostri Iesu Christi, in quo est salus mundi, vita et redemptio noster, per quem salvati et liberati sumus. "Deus misereatur mihi, et benedicat nos. Illuminet vultum suum super nos, et parcat nobis. Salva nos, Christe salvator mundi, per virtutem sancte crucis, qui salvasti Petrum in mari, miserere no-

2170 bis. Redemptor mundi, libera nos, qui per beatam passionem et sanctam mortem et gloriosam resurrectionem tuam redemisti nos, auxiliare nobis te, deprecamur deus noster."

Oratio

"Adesto nobis, domine deus noster, et quos sancte crucis letari fecisti honore, eius quoque perpetuis defende subsidiis."

Orationes

"Perpetua, quesumus, domine, nos tua pace custodi, quos per lignum beate crucis redimere dignatus es, per. . . ."

Oratio

2180

"Domine Iesu Christe, qui in hunc mundum venisti, et tuum sacrum sanguinem pro nobis in cruce fudisti, libera nos a cunctis insidiis diaboli, et ab universis operibus malis, quatenus te adiuvante, ad eternam valeamus pervenire felicitatem, per. . . ."

De modo orandi ad beatam Mariam

Demum et deinceps hoc modo erit orandum in honore beate Marie semper virginis: "Ave Maria, gratia plena, dominus tecum. Benedicta tu in mulieribus, et benedictus fructus ventris tui. Salve sancta parens, enixa puerpera regem, qui celum, terramque regit in secula seculorum. Virgo dei genitrix, quem totum non capit orbem, in tua se

2190 clausit viscera, factus homo. Gloria patri et filio et spiritui sancto," etc.

Oratio

"Sub tuum presidium confugimus, sancta dei genitrix Maria, nostras deprecationes, ne despicias in necessitatibus, sed a periculis libera nos, semper virgo benedicta dei gloriosa."

Oratio

"Beata dei genitrix Maria virgo, ante partum et postea et in perpetuo, templum dei, sacrarium spiritus sancti. Tu sola sine exemplo placuisti domino nostro Iesu Christo. Ora pro populo, interveni pro clero, intercede pro devoto femineo sexu. Sentiant omnes tuum iuvamen, quicumque agunt tui commemorationem, atque celebrant tuam sanctam venerationem."   2200

Orationes

"Sancta Maria semper virgo, dei genitrix, succurre nobis miseris. Iuva pusillanimes, refove debiles, suscipiant tuum auxilium omnes qui recolunt tuam beatitudinem."

Oratio

"Deus, qui salutis eterne beate Marie virginitate fecunda humano generi, premia prestitisti, quesumus, ut ipsam pro nobis intercedere sentiamus, per quam es dignatus conferre salvatorem mundi dominum   2210 nostrum Iesum Christum filium tuum, qui tecum vivit et regnat in unitate spiritus sancti deus, per omnia secula seculorum."

Oratio

"Concede nos famulos tuos, quesumus, domine deus noster, perpetua mentis et corporis sanitate gaudere, et gloriosa beate Marie semper virginis intercessione a presenti liberari tristitia et futura |23vb| perfrui letitia, per. . . ."

Oratio

"Presta, quesumus, omnipotens et misericors deus, ut intercessio nos sancte dei genitricis, semperque virginis Marie et cunctorum beatorum   2220 spirituum ordinum atque omnium aliorum sanctorum, sanctarumque tuarum patriarcharum, prophetarum, apostolorum, martirum, confessorum, virginum, et universorum electorum, electarumve tuarum, ubique letificet, quatenus dum eorum merita recolimus, pariter illorum patrocinia sentiamus, per. . . ."

Oratio

"Infirmitatem nostram, quesumus, domine, propitius respice, ut mala omnia que iuste meremur, beate Marie perpetue virginis, et omnium sanctorum atque sanctarum tuarum, orationibus a nobis avertas, per. . . ."   2230

De forma inveniendi gratiam dei

Illi vero qui ita oraverint, utpote est dictum in superioribus, videlicet genua flectenda, pectus manibus tundendo, deum gemitibus exortando, faciem cordis et oris lacrimis irrigando, orationis voces cum delictorum confessione proferendo et emittendo, tales in quantum poterunt suis obsecrationibus, petitionibusque mitigare ac pacificare iram dei. Et etiam quicquid pie et perseveranter pro se petierint, orantes obtinebunt.

De metafora

2240 Nimirum quod teneatur quilibet homo dum fit sive celebratur aut agitur opus dei, hoc est, in tempore orationis, non sedere neque iacere nec orare negligenter, patet et evidens esse potest ex corporis pugna, que numquam vincitur nec etiam prudenter et bene perficitur aut consumetur, nisi summa cum diligentia et fortiter athleta seu bellator dimicet et pugnet, non sedens neque iacens neque aliqua parte appodiatus, immo stans super pedes suos et sursum erectus, paratus viriliter ac fortiter impugnare hostem.

De eodem

Sane si materiale sive sensuale bellum quod fit gestu corporis minime
2250 potest fieri graviter et prudenter, nisi actor totis viribus dimicet contra reum, resistendo atque repellendo eum et renitendo, multo ergo minus spiritualis lucta seu pugna habet exerceri vel poterit fieri sapienter, meritorie atque utiliter et competenter atque maxima et habundanti cautela sine supremo et diligenti studio.

De spirituali bello

Est siquidem oratio pugna spiritualis, que tanto est difficilior ac maior corporali certamine, quanto anima est melior et dignior corpore. Quamobrem oportet et est necesse oratores eniti summopere, atque conari omni nisu debent, ne priventur et amittant perdantque eorum
2260 negligentia orationis fructum et utilitatem.

Contra malos oratores

Qualis namque est illorum deprecatio sive obsecratio vel oratio iudicanda et dicenda, que fit cum torpore, desidia, et accidia, et negligenter, puta ut sunt quidam qui, cum tenentur et debent orare, non sunt contenti duobus pedibus naturalibus, immo ad detrimentum et dedecus dampnumque sui, quod peius est, et execrabilis, utuntur

pedibus artificialibus, scilicet, ligneis aut lapidibus. Porro tales qui in
tempore et hora orandi appodiantur, substentantur, seu inherent baculo vel arche aut scamno sive muro, videntur contempnere atque
reprehendere deum, ac si dicant: "Non sufficiunt, o domine, nobis   2270
duo pedes quos dedisti, et cum quibus creasti et fecisti nos. Idcirco
opus tuum, id est, orationem tuam, non curamus prudenter ac diligenter et bene agere, quoniam impotentes et minus perfectos et imbecilles et infirmos nos condidisti et fecisti. Hinc est quod orando tertium aut quartum aut etiam plures nobis acquirimus, construimus, et
facimus artificiales pedes."

De negligentia orantium

Isti denique homines minus bene, perperam et prave orant, inherentes mendicatis suffragiis lignorum vel lapidum, nolentes stare super
pedes suos quando exercetur lucta sive bellum spirituale. Unde accidit   2280
quod tam orationes predictorum, qui habent pedes accidentales, hoc
est, faciendo sibi extrinseca amminicula ligni vel lapidis, quam seden-
tium aut suas voces et se non audientium, sunt frivole et vane et quasi
inutiles. Propterea a deo non exaudiuntur, nec etiam ab eo audiuntur.

De eodem

Nempe iniquum esset illorum petitiones, verba, et orationes deum
audire, que ipsimet qui fundunt non audiunt, porro preces orantium
negligenter nequeunt penetrare seu transcendere celos. Ob hoc autem
non contingunt neque perveniunt tales obsecrationes ad aures divinas.

Qualiter est orandum   2290

Igitur quicumque vult sapienter et utiliter legere aut orare vel canere,
conetur, laboret, et studeat se audire quod dicit ipse vel alius, et non
sedeat neque appodiet se aut inhereat |24ra| parietibus vel aliis rebus.
Insuper et colligat cor suum totum, ne ad aliud transeat et vagetur.
Nam si aliud cogitaverit et non tantum circa orationem seu lectionem
ferat omnem intellectum, sensum, atque meditationem, carebit, am-
mittet, et perdet earum fructum et utilitatem.

Oratio propria cuiuslibet ecclesie

"Omnes sancti et sancte dei, quorum reliquie in presenti venerantur
ecclesia, quorum memoria in hac domo dei habetur vel agitur, quo-   2300
rum patrocinio dego, atque cunctos alios exoro, qui assidue in conspectu dei assistunt, quos ego non honoram, et quibus neque servio,

ut debeo, orate et intercedite pro me, misero peccatore, ad dominum nostrum Iesum Christum, ut me liberet, et universos qui in eo confidunt, ab imminentibus peccatorum nostrorum periculis, et quatenus nunc et semper custodiat et conservet nos in suo sancto servitio, et necnon ut faciat nos fideliter vobis servire per eundem dominum Iesus Christum."

Explicit liber quintus

2310 *Incipit VI Liber, ubi tractatur de reali oratione atque partibus eius. Hactenus egimus de vocali oratione.* . . .

* * * * *

|12rb|*De genuflexionibus*

Sane quoniam potissima et principalis pars est penitentie exterioris genuflexio, ideo circa hanc materiam aliquantulum est inmorandum. Fit autem fraus genuflexioni sive peccatur in ea, quotiens genua imponuntur et apodiantur super aliquem lapidem vel aliquod lignum, ita quod sit magis remota a terra quam digiti pedum. Omnis ergo genuflexio falsa est cum genua minus distant a solo quam pedum extremitates. Illa enim et sola est vera genuum inflectio quando sunt in eadem equalitate digiti pedum et genua, ut non plus elongentur a pavimento genua
2320 *quam pedum summitates. Tunc precipue genuflexio est sincera et optima cum os et genua et digiti pedum pariter inherent terre. Est autem maxima utilitas in genuflexionibus. Quelibet autem temptatio potest ea superari.*

De utilitate genuflexionum

Scire utique debes in veritate, o lector bone memorie, quod nulla tibi tribulatio est tam intensa et aspera sive temptatio, que non recedat et mitigetur multitudine genuflexionum, si invoces deum toto corde tuo. Inter omnes autem modos orandi iste est quasi melior et fere utilior: iacere in solo, ita quod os et pectus et venter et brachia et genua nec non et crura atque digiti contingant terram. Cum enim sic es in pavimento ecclesie constitutus planus toto corpore, non videndo feminam
2330 *nec aliquid alium quod retrahat cor tuum ab oratione, leviter poteris in dei contemplatione perseverare. Cum tali ergo humilitate et reverentia, si mens concordet voci, quicquid pie et sancte, perseveranter, a deo postulaveris, poteris optinere. Nam ut ait Sanctus Benedictus: "Non in multiloquio sed in puritate et contritione et devotione cordis et effusione lacrimarum nos exaudiri sciamus."*

Quare genua flectentur

Item nota quod est duplex causa quare genua flectimus. Una est quod
ad memoriam reducimus quo modo in paradiso cum angelis stetimus;
nunc inter bruta animalia in terra iacemus et animam nostram corporali mole in terra deprimi ingessimus. Alia vero causa est, quia ille
qui stat erectus aliis omnibus coequatur. Qui in terra iacet, bestiis   2340
assimilatur, et nos dum in iustitia stetimus rationabilibus similes fui-
mus. Postquam vero in carnis desideria cecidimus; cum bestiis quasi
inrationabilibus in luto reperimus. Quia ergo aliis omnibus nos dis-
similes in factis cernimus, eis etiam ipso corporis statu equari erube-
scimus, et lapsum anime nostre in vitia penitendo clamamus dum corpore terre inheremus. *Item signum est penitentis et dolentis genuflexio. Hinc
Beda: "Pro certo genuum flexio penitentie ac luctus inditium est, quod multum
debeamus uti genuflexionibus cum ad opus divinum assistimus," id est, cum
oramus. Docent nos virtutes et miracula capitis nostri, id est, Christi, et omnium
sanctorum eius, qui orando, positis genibus proni in terra, multa signa et pro-*   2350
digia faciebant.

De causis quare penitentia non est differenda

*Prima causa quare penitentia est festinanda consuetudo peccandi est, a qua
|12va|quis difficile avelli potest.* . . .

|13rb|De genuis

*Item nota quod genuflexiones sunt potentissima pars exterioris penitentie et for-
tissimum ferramentum eius. Nam omnis temptatio potest vinci, dei gratia comitante et subsequente, genuflexionibus et orationibus. Nam sicut ieiunio caro at-
teritur et elemosinis peccata remituntur, ita orationibus dei gratia aquiritur.
Neque sine illis homines sani bene agunt penitentiam. Item si non vis agere pe-*   2360
*nitentiam extrinsecam, quod deus avertat, noli deserere intrinsecam saltem, scili-
cet, cor contritum et humiliatum et conpunctum confusionem atque verecundiam
peccati tui. Si autem et istam interiorem contempnis facere, apprehende tertiam
speciem penitentie, que est levissima et aliis duabus magis necessaria.* . . .

Apparatus of Variants

2. pr: no title in text, break from and space after previous text (hereafter: "break").
13. pr: no title, no break from or space after previous text (hereafter: "no break").
29. a: est peccare, omitting "non" (hereafter two such surrounding words indicate omission of a word or words in the printed edition).
32. pr: sepultus. Iamdicti.
35–38. ⟨Non . . . penarum⟩: a, pe.
40–41. pr: penarum. Noli.
41–42. a, pe: sane exemplum.
46. pr: no title, break.
48. pr: superficie habetur apertior videtur, tanto (hereafter such reformulations are framed by the surrounding first and last words in the printed edition).
50–51. a, pe: cibus prudentium.
56–77. pr: obscuris. Denique.
67–68. ⟨Hic . . . salus⟩: a, pe.
69. a, pe: que sunt observanda. Hic.
69–70. a, pe: sane docentur premia que sunt speranda; ibi.
105. pr: no title, no break.
108. a, pe, pr: constructione (hereafter thus indicates a significant variant of a word in the printed text).
124–25. ⟨fugitur . . . paupertas⟩: a, pe.
128. pr: no title, no break.
133. a, pe: "Felix.
137–38. pr: sic (hereafter thus indicates that pr includes the a and pe texts). ⟨viro . . . problemata⟩: a, pe.
142–43. pr: Christi. Nimia porro subtilius est trivii.
148–50. pr: title added in margin, no break.
159. a, pe: Oratius: "Verum operi longo fas est obrepere.
161. pr: apostolus Johannes: "Si.
162–63. pe: omnes." "Nec.
162–64. pr: omnes." Item.
166–74. pr: potest. Ista siquidem plena sunt ponita in civili iure a Iustiniano. Item.
183–84. a, pe: declarabitur.
186. k: XI.
193–95. ⟨Item de eodem⟩: a, pe.
201–2. pr: no title, no break. a, pe: DICENDORUM ASSERTIONE. Noli. (hereafter all the titles in the apparatus are given in upper case lettering).

211-14. ⟨Item . . . sententiarum⟩: a, pe.
211-16. pr: copiosa. Declina (no title, no break).
216. k: astro/lo/mie (hereafter slashes thus indicate inserts). z: astromie.
241. a, pe: sunt iamdicta. pr: sunt siquidem iamdicta.
243. pr: no title, no break.
249. k, z: greziti. a: hieritici. pe: ieritici. pr: gyezitui.
262-63. pr: docet Horatius, ut.
263-65. a, pe, pr, z: immo. INCIPIT.
265-66. a, v, pa: V [VIII] DE ORATIONE. k, z: PARIENSIS. v, pa: EIUS. o, m: ET EIUS DIGNITATE.
267-68. o, m: qui mihi et omnibus sit expediens.
268-69. pr: sapientibus debitor.
270. v, pa: prius est invocandum auxilium. o, m: illius primo imploro auxilium.
273. k: diximus.
274. pr: eius. Omnis meritorie.
281. o, m, v, pa, pr: no title, no break. z: title added in margin, no break.
282-83: o, m: facienda, sicut ferrum, quod.
283. a, pe, pr, v, pa: evidens in ferro. o, m: cultelli, lignum, quod.
288. o, m: et membra.
290. pr: colunt, utpote.
293. v, pa, o, m: no title, no break. pe, pr: no title, break. a: break and title, but extending into margin as if added.
297. o, m: sane quicumque caret predictorum alique reputet se quasi insufficientem.
298. o, m: consumandum. Predicta enim satis.
300. a, pe, pr: littere et similes dictiones.
302-3. o, m: orandus, et etiam laudandus. Ipsa admonet.
304. pa: diligendus, quatenus.
304-6. o, m: nos collocet. In primis, scis.
305. v, pa, pr: Potest tibi constare, lector karissime.
308. v, o: seu modos.
309. o, m: considerare quantum illud. o, m: advertere.
311. v, pa, o, m: no title, no break. pr, z: title added in margin, no break.
312-13. o, m: effluere et in.
313. v, pa: superhabundare.
314. o, m: incidentia omittamus.
314-24. v, pa: incidentia omittamus, et etiam [321] ne illud Horatii nobis obiciatur, scilicet: "Nec non . . . simulare, ad rem est properandum." DE.
317. a, pe: Hactenus.
319. pr: barbarissum gramatice.
323. v: DE ORATIONE, QUID SIT. o: DIFFINITIO ORATIONIS.
324-26. pr = v (captatio. Effectus).
327. o, m: nobis facere." Item.
335. pr: intus", id est, intrinsecus.
339. a, pe, pr, z: die", id est, ab.
340. o, m: inter omnia opera.
344-46. pr, v, pa, o, m: no title, no break. z: no break, title in margin.
345-47. o, m: orare. Quod patet.
346. v, pa: bonum est. Si non potest, melius orare quam legere, quoniam in lectione cognoscimus quod facere debemus, in oratione vero eadem accipimus que postulamus. Ideo melius. k: Ceterum non.

350–58. ⟨Immo . . . orat⟩: a, pe.

360. a, pe, pr: lectionibus.

363–83. pr = v (expedit." Plerumque).

367–68. a, pe: sapiens: "Iamdictus tertius.

372. k: title misplaced to 376, before "Secundum.

376. pe: illam." Item sapiens ait: "Carmina . . . [382–83] . . . querunt." Item secundum.

382–83. k: mei." "Carmina . . . querunt." Item sapiens: "Plerumque (Item sapiens misplaced). pe: mei." Plerumque (sentence moved forward, see above, 376).

383. k: multis. pe, pr, o, m: lectioni.

385. o, m: specificatur hoc nomen.

386. o, m: qui, ne pigritetur.

390–91. v, pa, o, m: fugabat.

391–92. ⟨qui . . . erat,⟩: a, pe.

391–95. o, m: fugabat. DE.

392–93. v: molliorem soluto.

395. v: no title, no break.

398–99. o, m: Quicumque enim tenetur predictas horas cantare, vel etiam vult privatas.

400–1. o, m: prosit, intenta supplicatio dormire cor mundum vetet, quia "non dormittabit neque dormiet qui custodit Israel." Sunt.

401. o, m: vii autentici. pr: modi autentici. v, pa: autem sex modi autentici.

402. o, m: orandi, qui commendantur auctoritate.

402–3. o, m: scripturarum. Nam "Quicquid.

404–5. o, m: facilitate reprobatur qua asseritur. DE.

410–15. pr, z = v (disceptatione." Similiter), but z: intervening text is at foot of folio.

410. pe: disceptatione." Item in eadem porro epistula quam scribit Thimotheo, docet idem apostolus sic esse.

418. v, pa, o, m, pe, pr: dominationis.

422–26. o, m = k, not v.

427. v, pa, o, m, pr, z: no title, no break, but z: title added in margin. pe: DE DIGNITATE ORATIONIS.

437. v, pa, o, m, pr: no title, no break.

439–41. o, m: extollo." Idem: "In noctibus.

442–43. v, pa, pr: hoc tertio psalmo:.

442–44. o, m: sancta", etc. Sic.

445–50. o, m: semper intentus", etc. Ad hoc.

446. v: relevabat.

451–56. pr: demonstrat. Secundus (break, no title).

454. Text on scroll, only k.

455. v: DE SECUNDO MODO. o, m: SECUNDUS MODUS.

457–58. o, m: Unde propheta: "Tota die ad te manus meas." Item alibi: "Expandi.

472. k, z: chinnabantur.

473. k, z: benificat.

477–93. pr = v (habitat. Verumtamen).

491. z: concordant—beatus quoque vir.

493. pe: demonstrativa.

493–94. pa: Verumtamen demonstratam est efficacior et levior quam intellectualis, ideo.

496. o, m: viri docti et.

497. pr, glosses at figure; in the left margin: "Ista figura debet esse in loco expansis manibus, et ista ibi ubi est expansis manibus, quia pictor transposuit"; to left of pic-

ture: "Stetit Finees et cessavit placatio"; to right of picture: "Non esse sedere cum oramus."

497-509. pr, z = v (aperte. DE), but z: intervening text is at foot of folio [therein, 506-7: libri sunt comunes omnium].

506-9. a, pe: conspiciuntur." DE.

508. Text on scroll, only k.

509-10. v: DE TERTIO. Tertius. pa: DE TERTIO MODO DEPRECANDI. Tertius. o, m: TERTIUS MODUS. Tertius.

510-11. o, m: stando, capite existente directo et corpore.

512. pr: in hoc modo tenetur.

513-14. o, m: iamdictis—habes ymaginibus manus.

516-17. pe: "Stetit Hesdra scriba.

518. pe, o, m: gradum ligneum et.

519-20. pe: maledicere, ut presens figura demonstrat. Nam. v, pa, o, m: demonstrat.

520. pr, gloss at figure: "ista ymago debet esse ante. Expandi ad te manus meas."

520-26. pr = v, but no title, no break (declarat. Quod).

524. Text on scroll, only k.

525-26. o, m: no title. v, pa: QUARE SIT STANDUM IN OMNI ORATIONE. Quod.

527. a, pe: iudicantium. Unde.

528-29. o, m: hominis a dextrio dei stantem, qui.

531-32. o, m: eum, agnovit nomen meum", etc. Item (o,m = k).

533. o: orabat, et factus est sudor eius sicut gutte sanguinis decurrentis in terram"; agonyia. (repeated below, 537-38). m: orabat, et factus est sudor eius sicut gutte sanguinis decurrentis in terram." Unde apostolus: "Omnis.

533-34. o: pugna. Nota.

540-41. o, m: laborantes. O quanto contrarium pigris oratoribus, qui.

541-42. o, m: orare, sedere vel appodiare se incipiunt, impatientes huc et illuc. Et tales.

544-76. o, m: deo in choro. Ille sane.

545. pr: no title, no break.

546. k: sancti, ex prelibatis canonicis.

568. pr: no title, no break. a, pe: ITEM QUOD OMNIA SINT AGENDA. Item.

582. o, m: fratribus. Ait enim quidam: "Impia.

582-83. a, pe, v, pa: parti.

582-84. a, pe: fratribus. NON ESSE PACEM CHRISTI AD BELIAL. "Impia. pr: NON ESSE OPEREM CHRISTI AD BELIAL.

583. pr: festa morum." Confortamini.

589. o, m: Hinc poeta Oratius:.

590-91. o, m: habemus remedia, arta.

591-93. a, pe: labores. DE.

593-94. pe: ORANDI AD DOMINUM. Quartus. v: IIII MODUS. Quartus. pa: DE QUARTO MODO. Quartus. o, m: QUARTUS MODUS ORANDI. Quartus.

597-616. o, m: me.' " Item apostolus.

620. v, pa, o, m: no title, no break.

621-22. o, m: Item Lucas in Actibus apostolorum: "Positis genibus, beatus Stefanus clamabat voce.

623. o, m: legitur quod calles in genibus orando fecerit. Simili modo Bartholomeus orabat, de quo legitur quod. Cf. DVV, 321c.

624-25. o, m: positis in terra genibus. Idem faciebat et supradictus Iacobus frater domini. Unde.

626. pa: ponebantur camelorum.

627. o, m: qualiter autem illud presens ymago declarat. pr, gloss at figure: "Sic orabat frater domini Jacobus." v, pa: ymago docet.

628. Text on scroll, only k.

629-30. pr: no break, but title in margin. v: QUINTUS MODUS. Nempe modus. pa: DE QUINTO MODO EXORANDI. Nempe modus. o, m: QUINTUS MODUS ORANDI. Quintus modus obsecrandi est. Also a, pe, z: Nempe modus.

633-35. o, m: multitudine. "Quoniam.

636-37. o, m: idem: "Adhesit.

638. v, pa: nescio.

639. o, m: peccata mea. Item Matheus (o, m = k).

642. k, z: paululum super.

642-43. k, z: terram orabat, ut fieri potes.

645-58. o, m: seculorum. Preterea.

647-49. pr: faciem suam ante. Nota (no title, no break).

657-58. pr: compunctivi dante humiliabantur.

659-62. o, m: puerum." Idem.

663. o, m: terram." Item Matheus. pr: terram." DE EADEM. Amplius Matheus.

666. o, m: ante dominum", etc.

666-84. pr = v (nos", etc. Rursus apostolus).

670. a, pe, z: in festivis diebus vel.

674-75. k: affectu.

682. a, pe: econverso est bonis.

684. v, pa, o, m, pr: Rursus, not Amplius.

685. o, m: omnibus: dum iudicatur et omnibus.

691. o, m: significatio, et coniecturata humilitate.

692. pr, written below figure, upside down: "Nota quod boni cadunt ante altare."

693. Text of scroll, only in k.

694-95. pr: no break, title in margin. v, pa, o, m: no title, no break; Nec secum, not Item tunc.

696. v: medulatur offerantur", etc.

698. o, m: medula orationis cuiuslibet sed pius. pa: affectus intellectus et.

699-705. pr: orationis. DE EODEM. Ille (pr = v).

707. pr: et processu ac.

708. o, m: comitantur et antecedunt vocem.

710-12. pr: vana. Quod omnis deprecatio est macra (no title, no break).

714-15. k, z, pr, a, o, m: litteram, perperam.

720. Only v is without title.

722-23. pr: ante sacrificium et altare sanctum. Item.

726. o, m: studium theologie, qui.

727. v, pa, o, m: refriguit.

729-30. o, m: confectione carnis.

730. pr: orantes. ORATIO. "Confectio.

730-54. o, m: orantes: "Benedictus qui venit in nomine domini.
                                  Osamna in excelsis.
                                    Ave principium nostre creationis.
                                    Ave precium nostre redemptionis.
                                    Ave viaticum nostre peregrinationis.
                                    Ave premium nostre remunerationis.
                                    Benedictus dominus deus Israel, quia visitavit.

Kyrie eleison.
Christe eleison."
Pater Noster.
Oratio: "Perficiant in nobis quas domine tua sancta quod continent, ut quod nunc spere gerimus, rerum veritate capiamus, per dominum", etc. In isto sexto modo orandi orabat.

731-32. pr, v, pa: tui non.
732. k, z: MISSE.
732-33. pr, v, pa: tuis in.
736. v, pa: patre et spiritu sancto."
736-38. pr: filio." HEC ORATIONES SUNT DICENDE IN MISSA. "Corpus. a: patre." ALIA ORATIO. "Corpus.
738-39. a, pr: animas nostras in.
739-41. v, pa: amen." "Qui (no title).
739-44. a: amen." "Purificent (no title).
742-44. pr: amen." ORATIO. "Purificent.
749-50. delictorum." DE.
749-51. pr: delictorum. Prefate (no title, no break).
755. a, v: sum et humiliatus sum usquequaque.
755-59. o, m: usquequaque. "Domine, vivificame secundum verbum tuum." Sic inclinata Maria Magdalena prospexit in monumentum et vidit duos angelos in albis. Sic et nos, ut mereamur visionem angelorum, inclinati et humiliati oremus in omni loco ubi ymaginem beate virginis respicimus, dicendo: "Ave Maria, gratia plena"; vel crucifixum, dicendo: "Tuam crucem adoramus, domine"; vel in introitu cuiuslibet ecclesie, orando: "Iniquitates meas aufer a nobis", etc. "Salvator mundi, salva nos omnes [m: omnipotens], sancta dei gratia", etc. [m: dei genitrix."]. SEPTIMUS MODUS. Possent longe.
756. pr: secundo: DE EODEM. DOMINE, ne.
757. pa: tenemur.
763. pr, gloss at figure: "Incurvatus sum et humiliatus sum nimis."
763-66. o, m: comparabit. Gregorius (title entered earlier, in apparatus, 755-59.
764. Text of scroll, only in k.
765. Only v is without title.
767. o, m: expositione illius evangelii: "Simile.
771. v, pa: semper egerit. o, m: gesserit, caro. k: gesserit vel caro.
772. pr, gloss at figure: "Sic orabat Maria soror Moysy." o, m: peccatis propriis et extraneis. In iamdictis . . . [follow text 777- 85] . . . morte, etc. Hec septima figura. v, pa: populorum. In iamdictis . . . [follow text 777-85] . . . morte, etc. Hec septima figura.
772-77. pr: populorum. In iamdictis (no title, no break; see below, at apparatus 786).
773. v, pa, o, m: habes preoculis. pr: ante ea preoculis. z: antea hic et preoculis.
773-77. Only k has title; z, a, pe: superius. In iamdictis.
773-86. v, pa, o, m: superius. Item quid (see intervening lines above, at apparatus 772).
775. Text of scroll, only in k.
779-80. o, m: iustificantur, et non doctores aut auditores.
783-84. k, z: infirmis, possint quibus et quibus non uti, et si. v, pa, o, m, pr: infirmis, quibus cibis possint uti et quibus non, etiam [pr: et] si.
786 pr: corporis. Hec vero figura quam habes preoculis docet enucleatus quod dictum est agendi superius [cf. 772-73]. Item quid.

787. a, pe: etc.? DE EODEM. Item immo.

791–93. v, pa, o, m, pr: no title, no break.

797. o, m: noctuque diligenter laborando.

799. k, z, v, pa: te ad pedes.

801–8. pr: recipienda. QUARE.

801–9. v: recipienda. Sane (no title, no break). pa: recipienda. EST SIC ORAN-
DORUM IAMDICTORUM VI MODORUM. Sane. o, m: recipienda. NE
FIDELES A CHRISTO CAPITE SUO DISSERERENT. Sane.

803–7. ⟨De . . . Ierusalem⟩: a, pe.

808. z: ORANDORUM TAMEN ALIQUO. a: ORANDORUM ALIQUO.

809. z: materiale numquam. o, m: materiale bellum.

809–10. o, m: resistentibus.

810–11. k, v: minus materialis et. z: spirituali, multoque ita minus. pr, pe, a: spirituali,
multo itaque minus.

811. o, m: competenter fiet.

812–13. pr: laborantibus, distinctio VII, *Adversus*, c. *Que contra mores*. Item.

813. z, pe: est doctrina, et. pr, o, m: est lectio, et.

814–15. z, pr, pe, a: non congruit. Saltem. o, m: est enim omnis pars . . . non congruit. Saltem.

815–16. z: quibusdam mutemus, cum licet non possimus in omnibus sequi. Ergo. pr:
initemur. pe, a: quibusdam imitetur eum, licet non. o: quibusdam imitemus eum,
cum licet non possimus in omnibus. Ipse enim tempore suo oravit. m: quibusdam
imitemur eum, cum licet non possimus in omnibus. Ipse enim Christus sua oravit.

817. pr: orabant omnes sancti.

818–19. o, m: brachiis ad modum crucis.

820. o, m: plani corpus.

821. pr: autem quidam viri.

822–23. o, m: talis diversitas sive alternitas confert.

823. pr: aliquis manibus.

824. o, m: capite, oret.

826. o: ut dictum est. m: ut predictum est.

827. pr: the title from line 808 is erroneously repeated here; it was then crossed out,
and the correct one was added at the top of the folio. a: BELLUM MAIUS EST
CORPORALI. pa: QUOD SIT SPIRITUALE BELLUM MAIUS CORPORALI.
o, m: QUOD SPIRITUALE PUGNA GRAVIOR EST CARNALI.

828. o, m: corporali, quoniam.

829. o, m: et astutos, scilicet demones, qui licet.

830–31. pe, a, v, pa: sapientiores hominibus, et. o, m: immo superant omnes homines
calliditate, prudentia, et astutia, quorum dolus non cessat querere.

831–32. o: quem devoret et separet a delectione dei et proximi. Unde.

833. o: palpantur magis sunt timendi. m: palpantur magis timendi sunt quam.

834–35. o, m: congredimur. Unde levius.

836–38. pr, v, pa: no title, no break. o, m: repellere. Fortasse dicit.

838. v: insolens: "Verecundor. pa: cervicosus: "Verecundor.

839. pr, o, m: ulnis expansis sive. pe, v, pa: supra caputi. a: supra caputi vel ulnis
expansis sive.

840. k, v, pa, o, m: decuit.

841–42. o, m: erubuerit", et in eos sermones, etc. Pessima est enim illa.

842. v, pa: est verecundia.

843. pr, pe, a: est utilis. v, pa, o, m: est bona et approbanda.

843–44. o, m: peccare. Unde quidam legis peritus dixit: "Cum.

845–48. o, m: ribet?" In presentia enim villisimi hominis timere commitere adulterium vel aliud peccatum, quia fortasse proderet te, longe magis cessare debes a peccato amore dei et amore illius quem nil latet ac omne cor patet, qui non tantum prodit, sed etiam in perpetuum punit, quia potest.

847. pr, v, pa: dei, in.

848–49. z, pr, v, pa, o, m: potest perdere animam et corpus in.

849–914. pr: Gehennam. DE CONSUETUDINE. Nolo.

849–987. v: Gehennam. Verumtamen quia non. pa: Gehennam. DE VITIIS. Verumtamen quia non. o, m: Gehennam, etc. QUOD VITIA IMPEDIANT ET EXAGITENT ORATIONEM. Verumtamen non.

852. k: ore. Corde.

857. a: libro regum.

863–65. pe: opus domini. QUALITER ORE ORANDUM EST CORPORE. Ore. a: opus domini. QUALITER ORANDUM EST CORPORE. Ore (both titles confused with line 875).

865. k: ut omnis obsequium.

866. z, pe, a: impendamus.

874–76. a: execrabilis. QUOD SIT ORE ORANDUM. Orandum.

901. pe, a: vertimus. Prima est.

915. pe, a: non religione, qui.

932–34. pr: veritatem." Consuetudo sine.

945–46. z: ALTARE. Deum postquam. pr: ALTARE. Deinde postquam.

947. z, pr, pe, a: positis genibus in.

953–54. z, pr, a: Multum namque valent ad.

955. z, pe, a: figere, fronte.

958. z, pr, a: claustrum quasi castum.

960. pe, a: inutiliter.

962. pr: dei." "Quid.

962–63. pe, a: claustro? Rota quinta, quod.

964–65. pr: ET ORE. Item.

970–71. pe, a: altitudinem sonore.

971. pr: inquirit.

973. z, a: exaudit.

975. k: Gregorius, tertio distinctione, XII decreti: "In. z, pr, pe, a: XII.

985. z: liberius infra declinabitur et. pr: liberius infra decimabitur. pe: declarabitur. a: liberius infra declarabitur et.

987. pr: Verumtamen non. o, m: nisi cognitum.

988. v, pa, o, m: Augustinus ponit.

990–91. pr: dimittet, qui a. v, pa: dimittet, quid a. o, m: dimittet, vel quia.

993. pr, v, pa, o, m: obtinebimus omnia. Nam scriptum est: "Qui avertet aurem suam ne audiat legem, oratio eius est execrabilis." Multum.

994–95. o: Iremias propheta ait.

996. pe, a: agunt, hic est, reales horas, et.

996–97. o: Hinc habes argumentum contra. m: Hinc habemus exemplum contra. ⟨De eodem⟩: a, pe.

998. pr, o, m: oratione sine.

999. k: ad penitentiam et.

1000. pr, o, m: ne negligentia. v, pa: ne de negligentia.

1001. v, pa: nostram obtinere vel.

1001-2. v, pa: operatione contendimus.
1003. o, m: impetret orationis.
1003-5. pr, a: precis. QUARE BONI NON CITO EXAUDIUNTUR. Amplius. o, m: orationis. QUOD ELECTI ALIQUANDO NON EXAUDIUNTUR. Amplius.
1005. v, pa, o, m: notandum quod.
1009. v, pa, o, m: cognosceret verum.
1011. o, m: excitate merites maioribus.
1011-12. ⟨De eodem⟩: a, pe.
1013-15. pr, v, pa, o, m: crescunt." Preterea.
1015. pr: desideria crescunt. o, m: interdum quod.
1015-16. v, pa: interdum, perseverantes[pa:-ter] orantes, non. pe, a: perseverantes, dum non.
1016-18. pr: adversitas. Item.
1019. pr: indicium.
1022. o, m: Sepe enim deus omnipotens exaudire differt ad voluntatem.
1025. v, pa: datur postulationis affectum illis, quia impeditur talis.
1026. v: electis qui deprecantur enim deum. pa, o, m: electis, deprecantur enim deum.
1027. pr, v, pa, o, m: commodis vel adversis, providentia.
1028. pr: promittitur. pe, a, pa: promittit.
1029. o, m: funditur, atque.
1029-30. o, m: suum obtinebit desiderium.
1030-32. v, pa: desiderium. Sunt. o, m: deprimitur. QUOD PLURA SUNT OBSTACULA ORATIONIS. Sunt.
1032. v, pa: plura. Unum.
1034. v, pa: nubem", id est, peccatum, "ne.
1040. o, m: sacrificare vel laudare. Hinc.
1042. o, m: tuam vincula quibus.
1044-45. o, m: salutem. "Multum enim valet. v, pa: Jacobus: "Multum.
1045-46. o, m: assidua." Nota.
1047. v, pa: lectio", etc., sane.
1046-47. o, m: quod dixit "oratio", non "lectio", sane.
1048. z, pr, v, pa: student legendo ut.
1049. pr: videantur et promoveantur. DE EODEM. Contra. o: promoveantur. Contra.
1051. o, m: ieiunando, deo.
1053-54. pa: DE SECUNDO VICIO ORATIONIS. Secundum. o, m: DE ALIUD PECCATO.
1054. v: affectum.
1055-70. o: vacare. Cum. m: orare. Cum.
1059-61. pr: oratores qui.
1066-67. pr: infundatur. "Via.
1071-72. k: dictionem de.
1072. pe, a, pa, o, m: et prave orant.
1072-74. pr, v, pa, o, m: oravit. Similiter.
1072. v, pa, o, m: sancti magis.
1077-79. o, m: dei. Omni enim oratori summopere cavendum est, ne musca morientes perdant suavitatem.
1079-80. o, m: quibus debemus ungere.
1081. v, pa, o, m: que reddit.
1083. o: unguentum procedit a dilectione dei.
1083-96. pr, v, pa: dei. A.

1083–1100. o, m: dei. Secundum vero unguentum procedit a dilectione proximi, scilicet elemosinarum largitio. Tertium vero unguentum procedit ab odio seu prope deum, scilicet carnis maceratio. Unde.

1084–85. ⟨Exemplum⟩: a, pe.

1088. pe, a: vero vir iamdictus quare.

1096. z, pe, a: frivole sunt et vane. A.

1100–86. ⟨Unde . . . eternam⟩: o, m.

1162. m: "elymona",.

1167. m: compassione dicit.

1185. o, m: fraglantia.

1187–88. pa: VITIO ORATORIS. Tertium. o, m: DE TERTIO IMPEDIMENTO. Tertium.

1189–90. o: Unde ne scitis quid petatis, hinc est.

1190. v: petuntur quod non accipiuntur. pa: petuntur quod numquam.

1190–92. o, m: que non impetrantur, quia non petuntur in nomine filii sed in nomine seculi, sicut sunt divitie, fortuna, questuum et multa que non conferentur quia potius.

1192–97. o, m: prodessent. Orationes vero effuse in nomine salvatoris sunt hec: "Erue.

1195–97. v: sunt hec orationes: "Erue. pa: sunt hec orationes. QUE SUNT PETEN-DA A DEO ABSOLUTE. "Erue.

1197–1203. o, m: animam meam", etc. "Libera me de ore leonis." "Participem.

1197–98. v, pa: uricam meam." Et hoc: "Libera.

1199–1200. v, pa: aliud: "Ne.

1201. pe, a: quoniam intraverunt aque", etc.: "Non.

1203. v, pa: suum." Et etiam istud: "Duce.

1204. z, pr, v, pa: te, et custodientium mandata tua non. o, m: etc. "Non.

1205. m: non moveat vel contingat. o, m: mihi ianuam.

1207. pe, a: amici et electi tui." Predicta.

1207–8. o, m: omnes sancti et electi tui." Hec et his similia, devote petita, exaudiun-tur, et imo sunt petenda omni tempore incessanter, absolute, et absque pendulo conditionis.

1207–10. pr: amici et electi tui." Item.

1208. v, pa: absolute et absque.

1210. pr, a: dupliciter.

1213–14. pe, a: premio privabitur.

1214–15. z: quod . . . oratione, added in margin.

1219–20. a: VITIO ORANTIS. Quartum. pa: DE QUARTO VITIO. Quartum. o, m: DE QUARTO. Quartum.

1220. v: affectum.

1220–21. o, m: obstaculum est quare orationes non habent effectum, scilicet cum oramus.

1221. o, m: et repellentibus gratiam dei sicut Samuel cum oravit pro Saul, sibi dictum est a domino: "Usquequo tu luges Saul, cum ego obiecerim eum." Item in epistula Johannis: "Est peccatum ad mortem: non pro illo dico ut roget quis." Unde.

1222–25. m: et adacapietis", id. o, m: invenietis", etc., "Petite et accipietis, queritis", etc. Petite fideliter et accipietis, id.

1225–33. o, m: impetrabitis. Querite pie, id est, ut pietas non se subtrahat. Subtrahat enim se pietas cum sine spe eterne beatitudinis orans laborat. Pulsate, id est, perseveranter in bono opere usque in finem, salvus esse non poterit. Et ita petite per fidem, querite per spem, pulsate per caritatem. Sed quid sit fideliter orare dicamus. QUID SIT.

1226. pr: nisi oret fideliter. v, pa: affectum obtinere nisi oret fideliter.

1226-54. v, pa: diligenter, pie, perseveranter pro se et ad salutem. Porro.

1233-44. v, pa: these lines are located after "necessitas" on line 1324, but variants are given at this point, as follows.

1233-34. pa: QUOD SIT FIDELITER ORARE. Tunc. o, m: ORARE. Fideliter.

1234-35. v, pa: quando nichil relinquimus. o, m: quando de substantia orationis nichil relinquimus. De.

1237-38. o: oratio, Gloria.

1238. v: coelo, sive Gloria. pa: Noster, sive Gloria.

1239-40. o, m: simbolum Credo in unum deum sive.

1240. pa: in unum deum sive.

1241. pa: opera, in.

1242. z, pr, pe, a, v, pa: creaturis, qui inus, si.

1242-59. o, m: laudem creaturis, pro omnibus creaturis. Qui cum devotione dictus optinet nobis memoriam omnipotentis. Item Ciprianus: "Quando.

1244-46. pr: periculis. Quantus.

1253. pr: Charolus nolebat.

1254-55. v, pa: intelligenda dei. auctoritas prelibata, quoniam.

1256-58. pr: eripere. Consequenter.

1257-58. pe, a: DEO. Ciprianus.

1258. z: Ciprianus de deo in.

1260. m: toto corde debemus. m: carnalis quelibet. pa: secularis abscedat.

1261. pr: nec quicquam tunc animus cogitet quam id. v: nec quicquam tunc. o, m: nec quicquam animus tunc quam id.

1261-62. pr: solum aliud quod peccatur. Ideo. o, m: solum cogitet quod peccatur. Ideo. v: cogitet. Quod predicator ideo sacerdos. pa: solum cogitet. Quod predicator ideo sacerdos.

1262. o, m: ante prefationem in missa, parat.

1264. o, m: contra diabolum pectus.

1266-67. o, m: infregisti, nec aliquid meruisti.

1269-71. o, m: impedunt. TALES SUNT IMITATORES DYABOLI. Isti.

1271-72. o, m: gloriam amissam hominem possidere dissuasit. Similiter.

1272. v, pa: pravi sectatores Phariseorum.

1273-74. o, m: patriam, nec alios intrare permittunt. Isti abutuntur consulta Salamonis, qui ait filii:.

1275-76. o, m: fac." Bona . . . irridet poeta, cum.

1277. o, m: dicat satiricus.

1278-79. o, m: hoc ad missam venire debetis, ut devote celebretis, et intente audiatis.

1279. v, pa, o, m: tractatis, cum celestia.

1279-80. v, pa: eterna cogitare debetis. o, m: eterna cogitare debetis, amplexarunt stercora.

1280-81. pe, a: quam anime salutem seu aurum. o, m: aurum desideratis. EX-EMPLUM. Iterum.

1281. k, z: consideratis.

1281-82. o, m: familiare et domesticum.

1281-1324. ⟨Iterum . . . necessitas . . . . ⟩: v, pa, o, m.

1285. o, m: secularis.

1285-86. o, m: tredecima, die.

1286. o: obitus alicuius dilecti sui. m: obitus sui.

1287. o, m: reducitur dilectio et omnia bona sibi impensa ab eo, et quod mors hec omnia destruxit, multo.

1288. o: ergo christianis.
1288-89. o, m: plorandum, dolendum.
1289. o, m: quando celebratur.
1292. o, m: recolitur. Hinc.
1295. o, m: apostolus: "Quotienscumque.
1298-99. o: et cordi infigetis ei compaciendo, flendo, dolendo, bene agendo, quia. m: et infigetis ei compaciendo, flendo, dolendo, bene agendo, quia.
1299-1300. pa: compatitur, non erit.
1302-10. o, m: infundit." Valde enim magnum et meritorium.
1310. o, m: est missam celebrare cum.
1311. o, m: tremore cum. o, m: atque devota mentis.
1317. o, m: sui intentione, corde.
1318-21. o, m: aspirando." In dei.
1321-22. pa: cogitatio, sive. o, m: cogitatio et voti conceptio. Secundum est reliquie illius, scilicet sunt voti.
1322-23. o, m: sanctam conversationem et.
1323-24. o, m: perfecta operatio. Unde propheta: "Vovete et reddite." Vovere enim voluntatis, reddere necessitatis. . . .
1324/6. v, pa: there follow lines 1234-44; see the variants above. Then: periculis. Ergo ille.
1324-28. o, m: necessitas. CONTRA EOS QUI NEGLIGENTER PSALLUNT. Infidelis.
1325. pe, a: MALA ORATIONE.
1326. pa: sive sinon sincopam.
1327-28. z: qui aliquas.
1328-29. v, pa: infidelis potest dici, cum. o, m: infidelis et inanus est.
1328-34. o, m: orator, qui sane devotione cordis laborat labiis, qui aliquas partes orationis subtrahit, viciando verbum dei, syncopando vel apocopando. Gravissime.
1330-31. v, pa: sistole: fur.
1331. v, pa: est, verbum male.
1334-35. z, a, pa: ad omnes matutinas. o, m: delinquunt legitimis horis qui negligunt divina et.
1335. o, m: et occupatione seculari omittunt. v, pa: secularis omittunt.
1336. o, m: canonicas horas.
1337. o, m: servili opere.
1340-42. pr: dei. Item.
1345. o, m: quantum anima dignior est corpore, tantum anima dignior est quolibet.
1348. o: aliqua re temporali, aurum. pr: transitoria, obrizum. v, pa: obrizum derelinquunt pro.
1348-49. v, pa: pro luto, et.
1348-50. o, m: stercore, et qui transitoria nimis inhianter appetunt, infideles.
1350. o, m: pravi operatores sunt.
1351. o, m: quod reddere, laborat persolvere. Unde. o, m: qui negligenter et confuse dicunt horas canonicas, non.
1352-56. o, m: obligatione. Et heu multi, etiam patrimonio Christi luxuriantes, omnino per incuriam pretermittunt, non attendentes illud prophete: "Maledicti qui declinant a mandatis tuis, et vere maledicti qui in omnibus temptationibus succumbunt victi. DE FORMA LEGENDI. Formam.
1356. z, pr, pe, a: legendi diligenter ponit. pa: atque diligenter legendi ponit.
1357. pe, a, v, pa: neque aliter bene. o, m: neque enim bene.

1357–58. o, m: orat nisi distincte et divise.
1358–60. o, m: alia. Nempe.
1361. o, m: quam finiant primam.
1362. o, m: effectu. Itaque.
1363. o, m: aperte coram.
1364–65. o, m: ut eius consequeris indulgentiam.
1365–95. o, m: indulgentiam. Gestus.
1366–92. pr: vitare. DE.
1366–93. v, pa: vitare. Negligenter.
1367–72. ⟨De . . . eos.”⟩: a, pe.
1381. a: Dicitur etiam oratio.
1386–87. pe, a: Oratur nec bonum nec bene.
1387. pe, a: quod non sibi.
1388. pe, a: remotione. Similiter enim.
1391. a: hec est.
1395. o, m: est probatio.
1395–96. v, pa: Stratus autem et afflictio hominis exterioris instruit.
1397. pe, a: omnis orator qui. pr: quam ore. pe, a: aliud proferat quam cogitat. Unde.
   v, pa: aliud cogitat quam ore properat. Unde.
1397–1408. o, m: qui non recordatur se dixisse que forsan dixit. Isti tales motu labiorum
   laudant deum, et corde contradicent ei. Contra quos ait.
1402. o, m: Ysaiam prophetam:.
1404–5. v, pa: clamant, nec.
1406. pr: mente vagantes.
1406–8. o, m: Denique ut.
1409. k, z: catenis, qua valeas.
1410–12. pr: habitare. Item.
1415–16. pe, a: orationi et.
1422–23. ⟨De eodem⟩: a, pe.
1424. z, pe, a: puritatis dilectione est.
1427. pr: acturi perficere. pe, a: sunt, multo.
1429–30. z, pe, a: beneficii. Item nota quod. pr: beneficii. Item vero quod.
1432. pe, a: peragunt. k, z: ac molle et.
1433. pr: procurat telas et. pe, a: procurat telas.
1436. pr: orationis male.
1438–39. pr: QUID HABITARE. v: Secum habitare. pa: QUID . . . SECUM. Secum
   habitare. o, m: QUID SIT SECUM HABITARE. Tecum habitare.
1439. o, m: de sancto Benedicto.
1439–40. pr, pe, a, v, pa: sua semper custodia circumspectus.
1442. o, m: motum extra nos ducemur, nos.
1443. v, pa, o, m: per alia vagamur.
1444–45. z: ducimur. Quoniam. “Petre” added in margin. pr: duobus, Petre, extra nos
   ducimur. Quoniam. pe, a: duobus modis, Petre, extra nos ducimur. Quoniam. v,
   pa: Petre. Quia aut. o, m: duobus quibus extra nos ducimur. Quia aut.
1446–47. o, m: immunditie se subiecit, vel.
1448. pr, pe, a: angelus.
1449. o, m: extra, sed.
1452. pa, o, m: a contemplationis culmine.
1452–53. pe, a: intellectum communem, est reversus, quem prius habent. Habitat. v:
   intellectum communi, et prius fuit habitat. Itaque. pa: quod in intellectum com-

muni, et prius fuit habitat. Itaque. o, m: quod in intellectum prius communi fuit. Habitat.

1454. z, a: cogitationis. v: contemplationis.

1456. pa: QUOD . . . ORARE. o, m: QUOD DIFFICILE EST ATTENTE ORARE.

1457. v, pa: quidam sapiens et. o, m: quidam protestatus est, difficile.

1459. o, m: Insuper de experto possumus dicere. pe, a: arduum et difficile quam.

1460. o, m: corde. Facilius enim.

1461-64. o, m: quam duo devote orantes et meritorie confitentes. Expedit enim oranti gemere, flere, commissa in corde memorari eternam beatitudinem consortium angelorum et supplicium inferni corde imprimere et illud intendere. Qualem te invenero, talem te iudicio. Mens qualem in.

1464. pr, v, pa: in oratione conservet.

1468-78. o, m: impeditur. Si.

1470. v: utiliter et diligenter.

1476. pe, a: est execratio.

1476-77. v, pa: execratio quam.

1478. v, pa, o, m: Sane vis deo tua oratione.

1479. o, m: id habere.

1480. o, m: dixisse omnes partes.

1481. o, m: cibum corporalem gustu. v, pa: gustu, deprehendis de.

1482. pr: debes adminus animadvertere. v, pa: debes adminus diligenter. o, m: debes adminus advertere.

1482-83. o, m: de partibus totalis orationis.

1487-88. o, m: etc. Et alibi: "In.

1488-89. o, m: etc. Et alibi: "Deprecatus.

1489-1501. o, m: meo." Semper enim est orandum cum fletu et gemitu. Flere tenetur quilibet de.

1492-93. pa: DE MUSCIS MORIENTIBUS. Ergo.

1493. pe, a: oratoris.

1494-95. v: cogitationes vane, varie, ac.

1496. pe: impediunt effectum.

1497-98. v, pa: flagellum cum.

1499. pr: devotione, gemitu.

1502-3. z: Unde . . . est: added in margin. pr, a, v, pa: patrie. Si.

1502-25. o, m: patrie pro peccatis propriis et alienis. QUID FACIAT PRESBYTER QUI ALIQUID OMITTIT DE CANONE. Item potest.

1503. v, pa: vero totis viribus tuis pessima. z, pe, a: mentes.

1504-6. pr: superare. Item.

1513-14. pr: oculo mentis intueri.

1518-23. ⟨Ob . . . oret⟩: a, pe.

1525-26. o, m: cor vel mens eius in missa vagatur.

1526-27. o, m: verba ad quorum prolationem fit.

1528. o, m: carnem et vini in sanguinem, videlicet: "Accipite.

1529-30. o, m: prolationem illorum verborum: "Hoc.

1530. k, z: et veteri testamenti.

1530-31. o, m: testamenti", fit transsubstantiatio.

1531. pr: fit. v, pa: etc., fit.

1532-34. o, m: vis sacramenti, atque efficacia confectionis eucharistie. Dicimus ad hoc precise.

1533. pr, v, pa: eucharistie efficacia.

1534-35. o, m: mente tempore orationis, aliud cogitando.
1536. o, m: recordatur tunc se.
1536-39. o, m: orationem. Hortamur universos orantes, ac.
1538. pa: QUID AGENDUM ... ORANTIBUS.
1539. z, pr, pe, a, v, pa: universos orantes et.
1541. pe, a: repetitionem illarum. o, m: iterationem omnium.
1541. o, m: recordantur.
1541-42. pr, v, pa: recolunt, nec.
1542. pr, v, pa, o, m: protulisse. Forte obiciet. pe, a: protulisse. Forte autem.
1542-43. o, m: aliquis, presbiterum.
1543-44. o, m: missam, quia propter prolixitatem misse iterari non posset canon. Ita.
1545. o, m: totum canonem nec.
1547-48. o, m: mentis, cum nesciat se protulisse illa verba virtutis, corpore exultante in oratorio.
1549-1668. o: suo. In orationibus. m: suo. DE SOLITUDINE ORATIONUM. In orationibus.
1553-54. pr, v, pa: ait: "Pectora.
1554-59. v, pa: curas." Ideo est conandum summopere.
1555-56. z, pe, a: non habitat in.
1557. pr: opere .... Item in.
1561. v: cogitare.
1565-1668. pa: lectionem. DE ORATIONIBUS PRIVATIS. In orationibus.
1567. pr, pe, a: tempore ut scriptura.
1571. pr: misera caro.
1573. pr: ac dicati.
1584. pr, pe, a: retrahent etiam perfectum.
1588-90. pr: etc. Item. pe: etc. Item: "Consurge. a: etc. Item Ieremias.
1603. pr, pe, a: tamen precipue oportet.
1606. pe, a: auditor, animadverte.
1610-12. pr: venite.'" Nota.
1621-28. pr: carnaliter. Sunt (the missing text is after "infringendo", line 1635).
1625-26. pe, a: I, capitulo *Movet*.
1630. pe, a: heremita assistera. Similiter.
1633-34. z: et matres. pe, a: compatres. Prefati.
1635-36. pr: infringendo. Ideo nota ... [lines 1621-26] ... *te*. Sane ibi propositum desevitur et religio violatur. QUALITER.
1639-40. pr: duabus commatribus.
1653. z: terre, auctoribus.
1655-57. pr: vindicatum?" Iamdicta.
1663-64. pr: est melior ac.
1667. pr: exemplo, pernoctabat.
1667-68. o, m: orationibus. DE ORATIONIBUS PRIVATIS. In.
1671. o, m: peccatum: "Fuga ergo turbam, quia turba.
1681-82. z: mortem, perfectius.
1685-86. z, pr, a: custodire, mentem, linguam, manuum.
1689. pr: esurienti, potum si algenti.
1695-97. pr: eternum. Solet.
1700. k, z: multi activi sunt eis.
1708. k, z: primis regnum.
1712-14. pr: econverso. In.

1714–15. pr, v, pa, o, m: quot visui.

1715. k: exteriora.

1718. v, pa, o, m: mens tua a te, quotiens. pe, a: variantur et offeruntur et impediuntur radiis.

1721–22. o, m: fletu, effundentes.

1723. k, z: populorum, non pre. pr: populorum, non propere. pe, a: populorum, neque pre postero.

1723–24. pr: neque preposcere, hoc inordinate.

1726–36. pr: verborum. Eapropter.

1727–34. ⟨De . . . intelligit⟩: a, pe.

1736. o, m: [22rb] Unde eorum orationes.

1736–44. o, m: orationes accepte erant coram deo. Ita et nunc multum acceptat deus deprecationes custorum assiduas. Et quidquid fiat de publicis orationibus private semper sunt repetende quousque.

1736–37. z: sunt private.

1739. k, z: dormitando. Nam.

1741. pr: Econtrario orationes quedam sunt.

1743. v, pa: vel furtive.

1745–51. o, m: que inchoans dicere proposuerat. Et in private potest orator omnis gestus orationis seu genuflexiones exercere. Quia omnis orator qui.

1745. v: bene potest. pa: bene facere potest.

1747–48. pr, v, pa: aliquo alio modorum.

1751. v, pa: modo ubicumque laudetur, colatur, glorificetur.

1754–55. z, pr, pe, a, v, pa, o, m: nichil aliud cogitat quam de oratione. Qui.

1756–57. o, m: quia si fatigatur uno modo, oret alio. Nam.

1757. v, pa: illa alternitas sive diversitas orandi est quasi quidam. o: illa alternitas orandi est quedam. m: illa alterternitas orandi est quasi quedam. pr, a: est quasi quedam.

1758–60. o, m: virium. Si vis meretorie orare, nitaris caste vivere. Igitur quoniam pauci sunt sine delicto carnis, ut testat beatus Gregorius: "Laboret unusquisque esse de paucitate bene viventium, superando inquinamenta luxurie, refrenando luxum et illicitum appetitum carnis. Fugiat copiam.

1760–61. o, m: mulierum. Nam ut ait.

1761–62. o, m: Ieronimus: "Non.

1763. o, m: accessus frequentat feminarum.

1764–69. o, m: secum habitantis. Ait enim Augustinus: "Nec.

1766. pr: non diligere, malum.

1769. k, z: questione VC.

1770–72. pr: concupiscentiam mulierum. Porro. v, pa: concupiscentia feminarum. Porro. o, m: concupiscentiam feminarum. Porro.

1774. o, m: est; si appetis, peius.

1776–90. o, m: est. Miror.

1777. pr: materia et stupri.

1781–84. pr: tangendo. Item.

1787–90. pr: gratia. Si vero iamdicta perfecta et diligenter egeris toto corde et utiliter, poteris deo invocare. DE EODEM. Miror.

1793. a, pa: derivare.

1794. o, m: delectatione universas et valde.

1795–1814. o, m: venereo. Sane.

1796. k, z: que didicis legendo. v, pa: que legis.

1799–1800. v, pa: corde, et conculcare opere? Omnia.

1807–8. o: coniectura incontinentie feminam.
1809. v, pa: effectu visum.
1809–13. o: opere. Fugiat. m: affectu. Fugiat.
1812. pr, v, pa: principio quadragesime.
1813–14. o, m: caret matrimonio virum, et precipue.
1814. o, m: ait poeta: "A.
1816–29. o, m: ad huc igniculus vivit. Nullus (for the missing text, see the apparatus, lines 1758–60, o).
1819. v, pa: officere oratori.
1820–22. pr: aliis. Est.
1822–23. v, pa: pauci sunt. Unde Gregorius ait in.
1825–26. v, pa: vult deo sua oratione placere, conetur.
1830. o, m: ullus pertinget regna.
1831. ⟨Absque . . . parari⟩: a, pe.
1831–33. o, m: magno labore. QUOD GAUDIUM MUNDI LUCTUS SEQUITUR. Rursus.
1833. pr: ut super de. v, pa: ut simus in sancta. o, m: ut simus de paucitate.
1833–34. o, m: qua dominus ait: "Multi.
1834–35. o, m: electi." "Quia.
1835. pe: in distinctione II, questione. o, m: est omne.
1837. o, m: tuum. "De.
1838. o: bibit. Et homines sancti. m: bibit. Et si omnes homines sancti.
1839. v, pa: securi pervenirent ad. o: quoque similiter.
1840. o, m: tibi sunt apponita. Considera quoniam talia.
1840–44. ⟨In . . . orationibus⟩: v, pa, o, m.
1840–1907. o: apponere. DE DIVERSIS BELLIS HOMINIS. m: apponere. DE DIVERSIS BELLIS HOMINIS CHRISTIANI. Ut.
1844–45. ⟨De eodem⟩: a, pe.
1851–53. pr: mitigaret." Legitur. pe, a: mitigaret." DE EODEM. Legitur.
1854–55. pr: in tribulatione illa.
1859. pe, a: qualitate. QUID . . . [line 1852] . . . CONSTITUTIS. Cum.
1865–67. pr: devotior. Exemplo.
1872. k, z: adversitas sine qua dominetur. pr: si non aliqua dominetur.
1873. pr: eris timens a.
1881. pa: DE . . . ORATORIS. Preterea.
1885. pr, pe, a, v, pa: dicit.
1888. k, z, pr, v, pa: laborare, qui debetis.
1890. pe, a: vestra. DE EODEM. Videtis.
1897–99. pr, v, pa: provectibus. Ergo.
1898–99. pe, a: SERVIENDUM. Ergo.
1902. pr: ipse ait:.
1905. pr, pe, a: dicat: "Tunc. v, pa: dicat propheta David: "Tunc.
1906–7. pr, pa: alia." DE ABSTINENTIA ET CRUCE PENITENTIS. Item Leo papa ait: "Quot sunt.
1907–43. ⟨Ut . . . reportare.⟩: v, pa, o, m, pr.
1908–11. o, m: est appetitum gule a cibo et potu temperare, animumque ab his a delectionibus que tactum, visumque et gustum odoratum decipiunt, utiliter revocare.
1909. pr: appetitum gule, cumque.
1911. pa: abstinere.
1912–13. m: anime bestiales.

1913. o, m: nocivos, coercere atque patienter regere.

1913-14. o, m: illius tranquilitate modestie se dare et vitiis.

1915. o, m: immo viriliter resistere et increpare.

1916. o, m: rixam cum.

1917. pr: Pretiosa est hoc in. o, m: conerere. Hec est pretiosa in conspectu et.

1919-20. o, m: et ab omnibus quibus anima.

1920. o, m: a toxicatis cibis abstinere.

1922. pr: custodire. DE CRUCE PENITENTIS.

1924-26. pr: adversitatibus . . . eripere. Nam.

1925. o, m: eripere. Nam ut ait Johannes evangelista.

1926-27. o, m: illecebris devicta.

1929. pr: futuri diei pondus.

1931. infert, QUALITER ETERNA VITA INVENIATUR, pristinis.

1932. pr: de humana habundantia.

1932-34. o, m: habundantia transeat ad famem, ut sompno.

1935. pr: conficiat. QUALITER. Item.

1935-38. o, m: conficiat, ut homo.

1940. pr: mundo diripere palmam.

1941-42. m: decerpere vel decipere atque.

1942-44. pr: vite reportare quasi de medio huius seculi incendio. DE.

1942-70. o, m: atque predam arreptam, de medio huius seculi ad thesaurum reportare. DE PURITATE ORATIONIS. Nota.

1944-45. pe, a: ORANTIS. pa: DE . . . ORANTIS. Preterea.

1949-50. pr, pe, a, v, pa: Similiter inutiliter.

1950. k, z: orat qui non pie.

1950-51. v, pa: se, et que.

1953. v: soleocismo et absque.

1953-57. ⟨Item . . . peccatorum."⟩: a, pe.

1953-59. pr: figuris. Eapropter.

1964. pr: apocopam. DE EODEM. Hinc.

1969-70. z, pr, pe, a, pa: PROFERRE QUAM MULTA MALE. Nota.

1970. o, m: magis exaudit de frequentia.

1971. pr: Ieronimus in distinction III, questione V, capitulo *Non mediocriter*, circa medium: "Numquid.

1973-74. pe, a: ac sinceritate et. o, m: puritate et.

1974-75. o, m: cum impatientia atque.

1976-77. o, m: est, ut.

1977-78. pr, pe, a: quam transcurrendo.

1978-81. o, m: profertur. Item idem: "Sine.

1979-80. pr: dicenda. QUOMODO.

1981. v, pa: Item idem ait:.

1984. pr: ergo tunc aliquid continue aliquis operis,. pe, a, v, pa: continue aliquis operis. o, m: ergo continue aliquid operis.

1985-2012. o, m: pigris. QUOD SOLI CONTINENTES, CONIUGATI, ET VIRGINES SALVENTUR. Dicant.

1987-88. ⟨De eodem⟩: a, pe.

1989. v, pa: apostoli autem habes.

1989-90. pa: predicatorem et pravum.

1991. pr: est utique et.

1992. v: labiis, et ore.

1992-93. pe, a: dicentis. Itaque.

1994-95. a: mente. DE EODEM. OBIECTIO.

1996. v, pa: Fortasse opponet emulus.

2004. pr, pe, a: Quomodo autem posset.

2007. pe, a: compunctione mentis.

2009. v: recedente, et aliud.

2010-12. pa: cogitante. DE . . . DIVERSITATIBUS. Dicant.

2012. o: debent orare pro propriis peccatis et.

2013. pe, a: vel non credant.

2013-29. o, m: orent, et peius vivant. Sunt enim tantum genera hominum salvandorum,
que previdit propheta, scilicet Job, Noe, et Daniel, per quos intelliguntur coniugati,
continentes, et virgines. Verumtamen tenentur hi omnes orare, sed maxime qui com-
medunt peccata populi, scilicet clerici, conversi, monachi, moniales, templarii,
hospitalarii, quibus.

2014-17. pr: salvandorum. Ieronimus.

2016. ⟨De eodem⟩: a, pe.

2017. pe: causa, questione.

2021. pr, pe, a: deo devoti, videlicet.

2024-26. pr: alios. Primum est.

2027-28. v, pa: quam canonici.

2029. pr, a, v, pa: Christi, id est, bona.

2029-37. o, m: Christe. Tales enim tantum sunt dispensatores rerum ecclesiarum. Et
mortaliter peccant qui convertunt eas in illicitos usus, putantes sibi ad hoc commissas
ut luxoriosius vivant, quam commutationem dabunt pro.

2035-37. pr, v, pa: consumunt. Idem.

2037-41. o, m: qui obligati sunt die ac nocte orare, pie et caste vivere, et ipsi in contrarium uttuntur. Nulla.

2038-39. v, pa: Ita quod ad verbum dicatur.

2041. k, z: vero potest. o, m: persona ecclesiastica que.

2042-43. o, m: orat, et male vivit, cum sit eius officium diligenter orare et bene vivere.
Nec.

2043. o, m: peccata sibi commissorum, scilicet pro fide pugnantium.

2043-44. o, m: colentium, nisi viriliter insistat.

2044. pe, a: viriliter insistant.

2044-46. o, m: orationi. Itaque.

2045. k, z: est, peccata.

2046-55. o, m: eo? Pro fide enim pugnare tenentur milites et ecclesiam defensare ab
inimicis et se opponere Saracenis et omnibus qui impugnant veritatem. Hec debent
esse eorum arma: et realis oratio adiunta vocali. Sed heu iam utuntur eis in contrarium. Contemptunt vocalem orationem et pervertunt realem, quia quamplures
sunt inimicis ecclesie, et pro defensione veritatis facti sunt detractores [m: vel destruc-
tores] religionis et amatores iniquitatis, predones.

2048. ⟨hoc . . . etate,⟩: a, pe.

2049-50. ⟨Cum . . . populo.⟩: v, pa, o, m.

2053. pa: ethnicos et falsos.

2055-56. o, m: Baptiste: "Neminem.

2056-58. pa: vestris." DE TERTIO. Tertium.

2056-82. o, m: vestris." Hi enim qui medii deberent sub alis suis obumbrare distinctos
servitio dei, et eos quorum labore omnes homines pascunt, scilicet agricolas, que
sunt pedes mundi, milites vero brachia, sacerdotes oculi, caput ipsi solus papa. Sic

est ecclesia unum corpus. Prevideant ergo oculi obstacula, unde pedes possint offendi. Brachia autem caveant et oculos a nocivis quibus possint ledi, et pedes, baculo antecedente et prohibente, morsus sapientiam. Sic erat mater ecclesia ut castrorum acies ordinata. Et quoniam ad orationem faciendam exortando laboravimus, ad incidentem questionem, scilicet quid sit orandum, respondebimus. Videtur enim nobis sic expediendum. QUID QUILIBET DEBEAT ORARE. In primis Pater Noster. Deinde oratio sancte trinitatis.

2059. pr: Isti sunt. v, pa: Isti sunt pedes.

2063. pr, v, pa: violentis collectis.

2064. pr, v, pa: bellatores manus. pr, v, pa: operarii pes.

2065. pe, a: et sancta ecclesia.

2068-69. pe, a: improbamus. v, pa: probamus.

2071-73. pr, v, pa: scientia, licet.

2075. pr, v, pa: questiones indigeant pena, alie.

2077-80. v, pa: incipiende, dicimus. Solutio. Videtur nobis.

2078-80. pr: determinamus. Solutio. Videtur nobis.

2082-85. o, m: trinitatis. Postea sequitur memoria incarnationis.

2083-84. pr, v, pa: refert. Postea.

2085-86. v, pa, o, m: passionis resurrectionis.

2086-89. o, m: Christi. Deinde invocatio spiritum sanctum: "Veni Sancte Spiritus", etc., huic consona. Post hoc necesse implorare subsidia beate virginis per multas preces speciales quas in honore eius recolit ecclesia, sicut est canticum illud: "Magnificat.

2088. z: beate Marie semper.

2089. v, pa: "Magnificat", etc.

2089-91. o, m: mea", "Ave Maria gratia plena", et versus ille: "Ave Maria, mater.

2090. pr: matris misericordie decantando, et hanc maxime que sunt subscripti: "Maria. v, pa: Marie inviolate decantando.

2092-94. o, m: suscipe, qui si cottidie septies iteratur per tot [m: (pro tot) genuflexionibus seu per tot] genuflexiones, nisi mortali peccato impediatur, ab ipsa in extremis non deseritur. Deinde angelicum.

2093. pr: septies devote.

2095-97. o, m: deo", et simbolum apostolorum, scilicet: "Credo in [m: unum] deum", vel: "Credo in unum." Demum omnibus aliis.

2096-97. pr: deserere. Et deinde autem omnibus aliis. v, pa: deserere. Et demum omnibus aliis.

2097-2105. o, m: universum mundum utitur sancta ecclesia convenit modis omnibus, et toto conatu insistere. Hec autem ideo non diximus.

2099-2101. pr: incumbere. Item. v, pa: incumbere et invigitare. Item.

2101. v, pa: valet iamdicta.

2106. o: ostenderimus. Videtur etiam magis nobis.

2110. z, pe, a, v, pa: minori quod non. v, pa: . . . maior." (= end of book).

2109-10. m: revelatur maiori vel minori quod non minori vel maiori, sedeat minor vel maior."

2110. o, m: maior." Negare non possum nec debeo sicut in ipsis maioribus, ita in multis opusculis meis, multa esse que possent iusto iudicii et multa temeritate culpari. "Regnet.

2111. pr, o, m: virtus." (= end of book).

2124-25. a: laudamus, o beata trinitas.

2131. a: laudabilis et gloriosus sine fine.

2133. pe, a: trinitas, ut.
2133. k, z: simplex unitas, ut.
2135-37. a: munera." "Placeat.
2139-41. a: mei." Item: "Omnipotens.
2144-46. a: adversis." Post.
2148. pe: diligentia seu.
2160. k, z: QUALITER EST.
2164. z: te, et psalmum dicam. pe, a: et psallum dicat nomini.
2166. pe, a: et resurrectio nostra, per.
2168. pe: et pateat nobis.
2168-70. pe, a: nobis. Redemptor.
2172-74. z: noster." "Adesto. a: noster." ALIA. "Adesto.
2175-77. pe: subsidiis." ALIA. "Perpetua. a: subsidiis, per . . . . " ITEM. "Perpetua.
2177-78. pe, a: lignum sancte crucis.
2178-80. k: es." ORATIO. z: per. . . ." "Domine. a: per . . . ." ITEM ALIA. "Domine.
2184-85. pe, a: AD SANCTAM MARIAM. Deinceps.
2191-93. a: etc. ALIA. "Sub.
2195-97. pe, a: nos, virgo benedicta mater dei gloriosa." "Beata.
2199. pe, a: domino Iesu.
2201-4. pe, a: commemorationem." "Sancta.
2204-5. z, pe, a: succurre miseris. Iuva pusillanimitas.
2205. k: pusillanimitas.
2209. z: prestitisti que sunt ipsam. a: prestitisti tribue, quesumus. pe, a: ipsam semper pro.
2211. a: nostrum Christum.
2211-14. a: tuum." "Concede.
2212-14. pe: seculorum." "Concede.
2217-19. pe: petitia." ALIA ORATIO. a: letitia." ITEM. "Presta.
2219-20. pe, a: intercessio sancte genitricis.
2220. pe: semperque virginis et. a: genitricis, Marie semper virginis et.
2221-22. a: sanctorum, patriarcharum.
2225-27. a: sentiamus." ITEM. "Infermitatem.
2234. k: rigando.
2251. z, pe, a: atque et renitendo, repellendo eum, multo.
2264. k, z: qui tenentur.
2270. pe, a: sufficiunt nobis.
2272. z, pe, a: orationem, non.
2284-86. z: audiuntur. Nempe.
2286. pe, a: petitiones deum.
2287-88. pe, a: preces negligentium nequeunt.
2289-91. pe, a: divinas. DE EODEM. Igitur.
2304. z, pe, a: ut liberet me.
2305. pe, a: peccatorum periculis.
2306-7. pe, a: custodiat nos fideliter.
2307. z: dominum nostrum Iesum.
2310. z, pr: INCIPIT VI. a: INCIPIT LIBER VI DE. o, m: LIBER VI[added: iiii]
[m: SEXTUS] DE REALI ORATIONE ET EIUS EFFECTU. Hactenus.
2312-64. pa: missing.
2312-13. o, m: QUAM UTILIS EST GENUFLEXIO. Sane.
2313. a: potissima pars.

2315. v: genua deponuntur et appodiantur super. o, m: genua flectentur, deponuntur et appodiantur super.

2319. v, o: qualitate.

2320. m: quam extremitates. Tunc.

2322–24. v, o, m, pr: superari. Scire (no title, no break).

2324. o, m: veritate, quod.

2325. v: aspera, que non remittatur et. o, m: aspera, que non remittatur multitudine.

2327–28. pe: pectus et brachia.

2328. v, pr: atque pedum digiti. o, m: crura et anteriores pedes extremitate contingant.

2329. z, pr, v, o, m: es constitutus in pavimento ecclesie. a, pe: eris constitutus in pavimento ecclesie.

2332. v: sancte a deo postulaveris. o, m: sancte postulatus a deo, poteris.

2333–34. v, o, m: puritate cordis.

2334. v, o, m: cordis et compunctione lacrimarum.

2334–36. pr: sciamus. Item nota (no title, no break).

2339. pr, a, pe: ingemiscimus.

2347. o, m: Beda: "Genuflexio pro certo penitentie.

2347–50. o, m: est. Quod ad impetrandam misericordiam divinam necessarie sint genuflexiones, docemus a Christo, a sanctis patribus in veteri testamento, et a sanctis apostolis, qui orando.

2350. k, z: eius orando, qui positis.

2352–53. v: DE CAUSIS QUARE PENITENTIA NON DEBET DEFFERI. Prima. o, m: PROPTER USUM PECCANDI, MATURANDA EST PENITENTIA.

2355–56. pr: DE EODEM. Item. a, pe: DE UTILITATE PENITENTIE EX-TERIORIS. Item.

2356–57. o, m: potentissima exterioris pars penitentie. Nam.

2357–58. pr, a, pe: gratia precedente et comitante. v, o, m: gratia precedente, comitante.

2358–60. v, o, m: genuflexionibus. Neque.

2361. o, m: avertat, numquam deseras intrinsecam.

2362–63. o, m: compunctam. Sit tibi semper confusio et verecundia peccatum et conscientia peccati. Si autem.

Apparatus of Authorities

11: Cf. Dt 32.5.
15-20: *Sermones* 67 and 77; PL, 38, 433-34; 485-86.
30-31: *Epistolae ad Galatas*; CSEL, 84, 124.
33-34: W, 14699.
35-39: *Sermo* 352; PL, 39, 1547.
82-93: C.12 q.2 c.70.
94-104: C.12 q.2 c.71.
123-24: W, 8902a.
124-26: Ovid, *Remedia Amoris*, 749-50.
126-27: cf. W, 33742.
131-32: DVV, 166b; W, 21633.
133-34: W, 4959.
148-52: cf. W, 2820a and p. xxxiii.
159-60: *Ars Poetica*, 359-60; W, 23576.
161-62: 1 Jn 1.8.
162: Ja 3.2.
163: Vergil, *Eclogues*, viii, 63.
163-64: W, 17421.
171-72: DVV, 25c.
174-75: Ps 138.16.
186-87: D.9 c.7.
189-92: C.3 q.9 c.17.
193-99: de cons. D.3 c.7.
199-200: 1 Co 5.6.
227-28: W, 13864.
232-35: 1 K 5.2,4-5.
237-40: 1 Ch 13.9.
268-69: Ro 1.14.
321-22: *Ars Poetica*, 19-20.
324-26: *Expositio in Psalterium* (39); PL, 70, 285.
328-29: Ps 55.12.
331: Ps 65.13.
334-35: Ps 44.14.
338-39: 1 Co 4.3.

340 (from "inter") -47 (to "orare"): Cf. DVV, 318ab.
347-48: Cf. DVV, 318b; Mt 17.20.
349: *Enarratio in Psalmum LXXXV*; PL, 37, 1086. Cf. DVV, 318b.
352-53: Ps 4.2.
356: Ps 21.21.
356-57: Ps 142.10.
358-59: *Enarratio in Psalmum LXXXV*; PL, 37, 1086. Cf. DVV, 318b.
374-75: Ps 45.11.
375-76: Ec 38.25.
377: Wis 1.4.
378: Ps 64.14.
379-80: Ja 1.21.
381-82: Pr 8.34.
382-83: W, 2380.
383 (from "item")-94: Cf. DVV, 318bc; Ps 108.4.
387-88: Ps 108.4.
409-10: 1 Ti 2.
410-14: 1 Ti 2.1.
418-19: Ps 102.22.
423-24: Is 1.15.
425-26: La 2.19.
438-39: Ps 27.2.
440: Ps 27.
441-42: Ps 133.2.
443-44: Ps 140.1-2.
445-46: Cf. DVV, 318cd.
457-59: Ps 87.10.
459-61: Ps 142.1.
461-62: Ps 142.6.
463: Lk 23.46.
465-67: 1 K 17.21.
471-72: Jl 2.17.

502: Dn 7.10.
503-4: Ph 4.3.
505-6: Ro 1.20.
515-16: Lk 4.16.
516-17: Ps 105.30.
517-18: 2 Es 8.4-6.
520-23: de cons. D.3 c. 27.
531-32: Ps 90.14.
532-33: Lk 22.43.
533-34: 1 Co 9.25.
537-38: Lk 22.44.
561-64: D.82 c.5.
589-90: W, 30146.
595-96: Mk 1.40.
596-97: Lk 22.42.
597 (from "Item")-605: Cf. DVV, 318d.
617: Eph 3.14.
621-22: Ac 7.59.
622-24: Cf. DVV, 321c, with Bartholomew correctly identified.
631-32: Lk 18.13.
632: 1 K 24.17.
635-36: Ps 43.25.
637: Ps 118.25.
640-41: Mt 26.39.
642-43: Mk 14.35.
644-45: Rev 19.4.
645-47: Lk 17.15.
651-52: Jn 18.6.
658-63: 2 K 4.33-4.
664-65: Mt 2.11.
665-66: Ps 94.6.
673: Mt 2.11.
680-81: Lk 2.34.
684-86: 1 Co 14.24-25.
687-88: W, 27865.
696: Ps 65.15.
700-1: W, 34176.
701-3: Mt 18.19.
754-55: Ps 37.7-9.
756-57: Ps 37.2.
768-71: PL, 76, 1291.
789: Ro 2.21.
790-91: 1 Co 13.
841: Mt 10.33.
853-54: Jn 4.23.
858: 1 S 1.10.
859-60: *De diversis quaestionibus ad Simplicium*; CCSL, 44, 86f.
867: Ps 33.2.

869-70: Ps 65.17.
871-72: Mt 5.16.
873-74: Pr 28.9.
877-78: 1 Co 11.4.
879-80: 1 Co 11.3.
885-87: 1 K 8.22,28.
887-88: Ac 7.59.
889-90: Mt 26.39.
895-96: Jn 17.5.
896-98: Jn 17.11.
898-99: Lk 23.34.
929-32: D.8 c.9.
937-39: D.8 c.5.
940-41: D.8 c.6.
961-62: 1 Co 7.19.
962-63: W, 25024.
965: Ja 2.20.
969-70: *De Catechizandis Rudibus*; CCSL, 46, 125.
975-82: D.92 c.2.
982-84: D.92 c.1.
988-94: Not found.
995: La 3.41.
1013-15: W, 10440.
1018-19: C.7 q.1 c.48.
1019-21: *Sermo* 105; PL, 38, 619.
1033-34: La 3.44.
1036: Ps 49.16.
1041: Ps 115.16.
1045: Ja 5.16.
1049-50: W, 11542c.
1064-66: *Homilia in Hiezechihelem Prophetam* (I,1); CCSL, 142, 12.
1084-93: Not found.
1100-1: Jn 12.25.
1108-10: Mt 6.10.
1112-14: Mt 6.13.
1123-25: Mt 20.21.
1126-27: Lk 18.11,14.
1132-34: Is 11.2.
1138-39: Mt 6.7.
1141-42: Mt 5.8.
1146-47: Ps 36.4.
1149-50: Ps 65.17.
1152-53: Mt 6.6.
1157: Jn 14.13.
1167-68: 2 Co 11.29.
1170-71: Mt 18.15.
1171-72: Is 58.7.
1177: Ec 30.24.

1178: Mt 7.5.
1179–80: Is 58.7.
1181: Lk 11.41.
1189–90: Ja 4.3.
1193: Jn 14.13.
1197: Ps 21.21.
1197–98: Ps 21.2.
1198–99: Ps 21.22.
1200–1: Ps 25.9.
1201–3: Ps 68.16.
1203: Ps 142.10.
1203–4: Ps 118.63.
1222–23: Mt 7.8.
1245–46: Cf. DVV, 318d.
1247–52: *Acta Sanctorum*, Sept., I (Antwerp, 1746), pp. 302–03.
1259–66: de cons. D.1 c.70.
1274–75: Pr 3.27.
1276–77: W, 1001a.
1280: Cf. La 4.5; Is 13.12.
1339–40: Mt 4.4.
1348–49: Cf. Is 13.12; La 4.5.
1356–57: Neh 8.8.
1372: Ps 33.18.
1374: Ps 108.7.
1403: Is 29.13.
1403–4: Mt 15.9.
1408: *Liber regulae pastoralis*; PL, 77, 72.
1421–25: *Regula*, ch. XX.
1439–55: *Vita Sancti Benedicti*; PL, 66, 136–38.
1477–78: Ps 108.7.
1486–87: Ps 9.2.
1488: Ps 118.10.
1489–90: Ps 118.58.
1490–91: Ps 118.45.
1492 ff. Cf. Ec 10.1.
1494–95: Cf. DVV, 321a.
1497–98: Cf. DVV, 321b.
1506–18: *Homilia in Evang.* (I,2,4); PL, 76, 1083cd.
1519–20: 1 P 4.7.
1528–29: 1 Co 11.24.
1529–31: Mt 26.27.
1554: W, 21103a.
1556–57: Is 28.20.
1557–58: Mt 6.24.
1586–87: Ps 118.55.
1587–88: Ps 118.62.
1590–91: La 2.19.

1596–97: Lk 2.15.
1607–8: Pr 8.17.
1608–10: Is 21.11–12.
1613–15: Ps 5.4–5.
1615–17: Ps 62.7–8.
1617–18: Ps 87.14.
1618–20: Ps 100.8.
1624–25: C.22 q.1 c.16.
1638–41: C. 30 q.4 c.2.
1645–55: C.24 q.1 c.21.
1658–59: Cf. DVV, 331d.
1671: W, 20656a.
1719–20: La 3.51.
1761–67: D.32 c.17.
1769–70: C.32 q.5 c.12.
1776–77: 1 Co 6.18.
1788–89: Lk 23.29.
1812–13: Jl 2.16.
1817: W, 7516a.
1823–25: D.50 c.16.
1834: Mt 20.16.
1835: C.2 q.7 c.4.
1837–38: Ps 109.7.
1838–39: Wis 3.4.
1844–51: *Epistola* 42 (chap. I); PL, 16, 1176.
1875–78: Ja 5.17.
1883–84: Ps 94.6.
1884–85: Jn 16.20.
1885–87: *Sententiae*; PL, 83, 671.
1902: Mt 11.28.
1904–5: Ps 18.15.
1907–8: *Canones Ancyritani Concilii*; PL, 56, 439.
1925–26: Mt 11.12.
1965–66: Jer 48.10.
1971–75: de cons. D.5 c.24.
1975–76: de cons. D.5 c.33.
1981–85: de cons. D.5 c.33.
1987–88: 1 Co 14.19.
1993–94: 1 Co 14.15.
1997–98: *De Baptismo contra Donatistas*; PL, 43, 213.
2018–23: C.12 q.1 c.7.
2032–34: C.16 q.1 c.68.
2055–56: Lk 3.14.
2069–78: Not found.
2110–11: Cf. W, 14220.
2118–19: Ps 42.3.
2153–58: Ps 140.2–4.

2158–59: Cf. Lk 23.46.
2167–68: Cf. Ps 66.2.
2333–34: Cf. Augustine, lines 859–60.

The Christian at Prayer introduces a little-known work attributed to Peter the Chanter (fl. 1170-1197). It will be received with excitement by those who are familiar with Peter's influence on the educational and theological attitudes of his time. This work collates the nine known manuscripts and presents from eight of them the illustrations of the seven prayer postures which the writer prescribed.

In his substantial introduction, Trexler analyzes the written texts and the illustrations to reach an understanding of the medieval view of prayer. The second half of the study provides a detailed analysis of the manuscript tradition of *De penitentia* as a whole and of the texts of its *De oratione*. The volume contains a table of incipits and explicits and a map of the manuscript locations, as aids to a graphic overview. Full notes to the study, apparatus of variants and of authorities used, genealogies of the manuscripts and the pictures, and chronologies of the texts and pictures are included.

Richard C. Trexler has held a number of fellowships, including ones from the Guggenheim Foundation, the Center for Advanced Study in the Visual Arts, and Villa I Tatti. Among his many publications are *The Spiritual Power, Republican Florence Under Interdict* (Leiden, 1974), *Public Life in Renaissance Florence* (New York, 1980), and *Church and Community, 1200–1600. Studies in the History of Florence and New Spain* (Rome, 1987); he edited *Persons in Groups: Social Behavior as Identity Formation in Medieval and Renaissance Europe* (Medieval & Renaissance Texts & Studies, 36; New York, 1985). He is currently Professor of History at the State University of New York at Binghamton.

mRts

medieval & Renaissance texts & studies
is the publishing program of the
Center for Medieval and Early Renaissance Studies
State University of New York at Binghamton.

mRts emphasizes books that are needed —
texts, translations, and major research tools.

mRts aims to publish the highest quality scholarship
in attractive and durable format at modest cost.